Salt.v16

Cover image by Judy Durey

Fy Mam Mair, Merthyres, shown at the Perth Institute of Contemporary Arts in 1996 as part of the *Art, Medicine and the Body* project, reframed the bureaucratic process of 'closed adoption', and engaged with the corporeal and the pre-verbal. This work included the images and collective writings from the postcards. The installation addressed loss, by offering a palpable sense of (dis)placement beside a 'visceral' (re)connection with the mother. Playing with the temporal collapse of (re)presenting historical documentation, official letters and imagery within a contemporary context, the piece was a collage of image, voice and sound, inviting memory within a sensory environment.

In recent work, *Translating Hiraeth* again references the postcards and extends *Fy Mam. Mair. Merthyres* by negotiating bodily issues of cultural '(im)placement' within the 'new' story. This work also includes reconnections with my father's 'line'. Working with Installation I explore the physical necessity of story, and the challenges of incorporating previously silenced, yet 'new' fundamental information about identity, into a felt sense of self. The work reveals unexpected cultural difference associated with family, history, heritage, language, sense of locality and place.

As a 'performative archaeology' *Translating Hiraeth* uses contemporary letters, perceptions and reflections to expose the tensions held within the past/present. Through the exploration of family and social silence this necessity of story draws on other narrative positions – other memories, to negotiate a 'text' which falls somewhere between transgression and empathy. Through 'writing' installation I attempt to conflate the idea of experiencing a particular physical space/place with metaphorically entering the space of a particular story – where the 'visitor', always in translation, remembers aspects of that narrative through the details of their own life.

JUDY DUREY

Salt.v16

AN INTERNATIONAL JOURNAL OF POETRY AND POETICS
EDITED BY TERRI-ANN WHITE

Memory Writing

PUBLISHED BY SALT PUBLISHING
PO Box 202, Applecross, Western Australia 6153
PO Box 937, Great Wilbraham, Cambridge PDO CB1 5JX United Kingdom

All rights reserved

Selection copyright © Terri-ann White 2002
Individual pieces copyright © individual contributors, 2002

This book is in copyright. Subject to statutory exception
and to provisions of relevant collective licensing agreements,
no reproduction of any part may take place without the written
permission of Salt Publishing.

First published 2002

Printed and bound in the United Kingdom by Lightning Source

Typeset in Swift 9.5 / 13

*This book is sold subject to the conditions that it shall not,
by way of trade or otherwise, be lent, re-sold, hired out,
or otherwise circulated without the publisher's prior consent
in any form of binding or cover other than that in which
it is published and without a similar condition including this
condition being imposed on the subsequent purchaser.*

This publication has no connection, nor intends to bear
resemblance, to the Australian Army Education Service
magazine SALT (September 1941–April 1946).

ISBN 1 876857 58 7 paperback

SP

1 3 5 7 9 8 6 4 2

Contents

Introduction ix

PAUL CARTER
Little Places *Loculi* 11
SUSAN MIDALIA
My Father's Story 16
BETH YAHP
Thursdays 26
ANGELA ROCKEL
Remember: A working definition of blessing 34
ROBYN FERRELL
The Kingdom of God 39
TONY BIRCH
Ashes 61
DANIEL BROWN
Norma Desmond as star-sign: Being and being seen in Billy Wilder's Sunset Boulevard 69
NANCY BERG
Memory Writing, Memoir Reading: Se non è vero, è bon trovato 80
SCOTT BROOK
Photographs 1933, 1916 86
Labertouche 89
TANYA RING
A Mannequin is Without 93
enlightenment 94
Sublimation 95
Mother Earth 96

ANNETTE TREVITT
  Deb Simpson … 97
MOIRA RAYNER
  Remembering Moira. … 102
NOEL C. TOVEY
  Little Black Bastard … 105
ANNETTE TREVITT
  My uncle … 117
SUSAN VARGA
  memory and exile, exile and memory … 124
MARION M. CAMPBELL
  Hanging on his word … 133
KATE LAMONT
  Delicious … 151
NANCY BERG
  Camp Ellis Beach … 153
ROSSLYN PROSSER
  Writing + Memory = Memory Writing … 157
KATE HISLOP
  Re-membering: a Line of Thought Reviewing the Colonial … 174
TANYA RING
  Control and Release … 188
ANNETTE TREVITT
  Myra … 192
ANNE BREWSTER AND HAZEL SMITH
  ProseThetic Memories … 199
MARIA ROBINSON
  Ethan's Angel … 212
CARMEN LAWRENCE
  A Nation in Denial … 226

MELISSA LUCASHENKO
Memory and Survival   237

Notes on contributors   240

Introduction

This collection of writings, initially, comes out of my own interest in the field of *memory writing*—writing that may contain multiple generic approaches, that may include biography and autobiography and social history and fictional conventions. Or, in the case of this volume, may also just be a new venture by its writer into writing itself or into a different form of writing.

Those books to have excited me over the last decade or so include Carolyn Steedman's *Landscape for a Good Woman*, Annette Kuhn's *Family Pictures*, Susan Varga's *Heddy and Me*, and all of W.G. Sebald's works. Especially in my rereadings, Maxine Hong Kingston's *The Woman Warrior: Memoirs of a Girlhood among Ghosts*, has dazzled as a spectacularly complex performance of storytelling. These books and their example of literary boldness were my starting point and invitation to the writers who follow.

I am excited, too, by these writings in Salt 15. There are likely to be many new names for most readers, or unexpected results from already known writers. I hope you enjoy them as much as I have.

Terri-ann White

Paul Carter

Little Places *Loculi*

1

The seasons of partings. Many forms of parting: the parting of death, the parting of lovers. We stand at the gate waving the dying farewell, bidding them prosper on whatever voyage they have to take. Our language hardly conceals our wish-fulfilment: to travel beyond the bourne, to come to the other side, to reach "home." So we speak, regretting we cannot travel together, keeping a firm hand on the tiller or in that labyrinth of ill-defined tracks, morasses, dark woods and deep crevasses imagined by Socrates be a guiding hand and support.

2

There should be an inventory of dead times. After all they have their structure. It might be likened to the profile of a wave about to break. These dead times are angles in the world where useless emotions gather, like the excess of light the dawn cannot place. Waiting breeds curious effects. You catch stifled sobbing in the walls. After the evolution towards full expression the high road splits up again, goes back to a braid of struggling tracks. You choose your route, and make no effort to rationalise the others. You give up the ambition to "pour out your heart." It is miscast, a metaphor, like the no less fluid conception of "slipping away."

3

In the canon of the Mass the prayer *memento mori* is twinned with the prayer *memento vivere*. Remember that you have to die; remember that you have to live. That is, the effort of dying is only to be compared with the effort of living.

4

If bodies cannot retain their souls, rooms cannot retain their bodies. Corpses are carried out; lovers arrive. The absolute indifference of waiting rooms to the passions that they stage: think of all the irrelevent settings of love and death. They are tombs. The lovers make love in defiance of the night; they sink into the gloom. And the dying man in his arms, mimicking the long sepulchred neolithic corpse still waves at the sky, still ignores the bed, the sloping wall, the shadow that will not be dislodged.

5

Concern, regard, consideration. Words that come from a root meaning. "A state of intense looking at an object."[1] It is a transient state. The fixed eye begins to smart and run. It slips through the vanishing point of focus. It enters the realm of Care – a word that comes from the same word as *Charon*.

6

Before that, let us dive into the harbour of each other. Underwater, in the entrails of the forgotten port, we will find tombs, perfectly sealed, whose contents, brought up to the surface, must instantly die. The selfishness of the lovers is not magical; their ecstasy cannot save the dying man. After making love he lies on his back, his arm extended vertically, his hand idly breathing, fingers opening and closing dreamily, like a sea-anemone. But she pulls his hand down to the chalice of her thighs and in their Hermaphroditus they drown.

7

One thing to sculpt a cadaver in stone; another, to chisel and polish a veil half-concealing it. To have stone preserve corruption is one thing; another, to have stone entomb itself. As if Death were caught signing its own Will and Testament. In the Chapel of San Severo (Naples) a handwritten card warns visitors not to touch the sculptured tombs because *gli umori corrodono il marmo* [perspiration damages the marbles]. Laying a hand on it brings stone to its senses. Memento umori.

8

To speak of the dryness. It is the mock slap of water under foot as you crush the crystallising leaves. Thus it is also the origin of wetness. The rain is drawn to stubble. Dryness assures bones and painting their fraternal eternity under the soil.

9

Rooms are the souls we evaporate into. Tombs, soul-houses – no different. To live under the sky, to shape an outer morality – but always the fatal split between consciousness and the soul-world of the everyday and every night. There is something ironic about the banqueteer raising his goblet. His gesture copies the outstretched arm of the sailor drowning. It foreshadows the recumbent's last failing purchase on the light.

10

Dreams fade from the curtain. What is occasionally recalled on waking is the condensation of what is already condensed – an oracular fragment staggering back down the slope to birth. The darkness is here. This is why it is difficult to see it. Taking the light for granted has been a great mistake. Supposing we were not dead, we inhabited another illusion. Like the one who confused death with not being.

11

To see as he saw is to feel the prickle in the eye. It corresponds to nothing in the visible field. It springs up from the scarred landscape of history. It is not past but a ritual of repeated passages, instinct with regret, with bitterness, with unfulfilled longing. The things he observed, and even painted, were all that lay outside him, what he could not grasp. You deny that he lived if you assimilate it to a pleasant, timeless view. He never saw "history." He is not represented by a life's incidents. His country was wherever he was. He knew even as he was known. As he could not be known by casual associations, this was what he knew.

12

Fugir a la Mort.[2] She ran down the road towards me, open-armed, weeping with joy. *Fugir a l'amor*. Leave this strange house, fly to love. The wind took the rest. "I run to death but death meets me as fast."[3]

I could lie down here until the lid of night slides over the sky, accompanying thought with writing's lyre. Could be at home here. You were the detour, the long road away. Here I can make the stones speak, and they do not oppose me.

13

The flesh is unimaginative. It keeps the old man awake at night with its repetitive and infantile needs. The nurse's hands massage the soul's passage. They help it to wriggle out from underneath the sheets of flesh. It is coming easily through the harsh breathing. There is no movement where there is no spirit. The figure who faces me in the morning is a glove.

14

You breathe slowly. You pay a renewed attention to the neglected rituals of everyday life. You face into the wind, saying less and less. You borrow the outer voice of authority. You understand that the renunciation includes self-indulgent analysis. You master the ticking of the clocks; you submit to the arrogant intrusions of the telephone. You let the rain do its weeping unresisted down your face. You cultivate an unbending aloneness whose heart is sweet – it does not speak, it waits more calmly than waiting, without expectation or irritation. It is without envy. It is unloaded of those fantasy reels, thoughts of those beyond reach. It slips into itself; the waters pour inwards.

15

I am painting a picture for the dark. You find its bone-bleached passages inexplicable. "They have no need of light there." No, but they cannot do without the dark. And: "Death is those things we see once we are awake." "There await people when they die things they neither expect nor [even] imagine."[4] One time I was very close to complete satisfaction when something began to irritate one of my eyes. An eyelash, a speck of something; dust. I do not know. In the same instant I was plunged into the abyss of despair.[5]

16

The fullness of renounced fullness collapses. The drowning swimmer sees life as a coast. Pain fissures the love that balmed the wound of parting. Under this torture love slanders the selfishness that goes beyond itself, calling it another form of selfishness.

17

Instant recall of snowfall. An anti-dawn of darkness breaks and through its dark white-out scratchlines of snowflakes matter-of-factly by the window, like people running after a train. In these days there is a strange earth-reflected pale light. He loses the urge to call. The telephone rings more rarely. Things settle down. He lives alone in the midst of nature's filtered sounds. Only sometimes at night, the thunder of the train racing south disturbs him, and he turns over, rearranging his bones.

18

John Donne to Christ: "Betray kind husband thy spouse to our sights, And let mine amorous soul court thy mild Dove."[6] Cremated remains of early Christians were placed in large underground tombs lined with niches, known as *loculi* (little places), "like those in dovecots."[7]

---

[1] Michael Balint, 'Friendly Expanses – Horrid Empty Spaces', *International Journal of Psycho-Analysis, vol XXXVI,* 1955. p.233, note 11.

[2] Auzias March, *Selected Poems,* translated by A. Terry, (Austin: University of Texas Press, 1976), p.40.

[3] John Donne, 'Holy Sonnets' I.1.3. Terry (op.cit.pp.20-21) notes that a number of passages in the Holy Sonnets recall the style and imagery of the XVth Century Catalan poet, Auzias March.

[4] Heraclitus, *Fragments* 21 & 27.

[5] Adapted from Soren Kierkegaard, 'Repetition' in *Fear and Trembling,* translated by H.V. and E.H. Hong. (Princeton: Princeton University Press, 1983), p.173.

[6] John Donne, 'Holy Sonnets.' XVIII.II.11-12.

[7] James Stevens Curl, *A Celebration of Death.* (London: Constable, 1980), p.43

Susan Midalia

My Father's Story

We stand looking down on my father's body. The chest is hairless and bony, the arms conspicuously thin, the hands folded decorously on the starchy whiteness of the hospital sheet. The familiar nose and chin, pointed like my own, are now oddly unfamiliar. The mouth is open, slack, obscenely lolling. It is the mouth above all which appals. They close the *eyes*, don't they, in deference to the dead and to those who look upon them? Why then leave this mouth agape, the careless revelation of an old man's toothless indignity? The body is utterly still. No gently rhythmic rise and fall of chest, no sudden twitch of a hand. This is negation, not rest. The curtain drawn around the bed protects us from discreetly curious eyes, but fails to shut out the drone further down the ward of a radio sports commentary, patients' conversations, the clicking of briskly purposive heels on hospital tiles. It all goes on, wrongly.

My mother puts her hand on my father's cheek and strokes softly back and forth, crooning, *No more pain, my darling. Now you are at peace.* Over the past month and largely unbeknown to me, she has seen him wither from a stout and hearty man, exhausted by insomnia and unrelenting pain. She has seen him fall asleep at meal-times, fall heavy with sedation over his bowl of soup, heard him say her name, feebly, again and again, in the dark hours of the night. She has ferried him to the doctor, back and forth. She has bathed him, fed him, helped him in and out of bed, herself unbearably tired and unable to sleep. Keeping watch, tending him, trying not to cry.

In the corridor, a nurse tells us that she will miss him too. *A lovely gentleman*, she says, *charming, always polite*. I thank her as I take the large plastic bag containing his clothes, his wallet and a magazine, and walk with my mother in silence to the car. Driving home, I see her face beside me turn suddenly red. Her voice spits, her vehemence is shocking: *Charming, my eye. Always charming to strangers, especially when he wanted something. They didn't have to live with him.*

Over the next few weeks I become a witness to my mother's anger. Refusing to say what is supposed to be said, she pours forth, more to herself than to me, stories of disappointment and humiliation, of minor cruelties and more savage abasements. *He would follow me as I swept the kitchen floor*, she said, *pointing at crumbs I hadn't noticed. He shouted at me if dinner wasn't ready on time. He called me stupid in front of my friends, what would you know, he said. He never touched me except when he wanted sex.* She told me of the time he brought her home from hospital, after her hysterectomy, when he had yelled at her for jamming the seat-belt in the door of the car. There in the driveway, in front of the neighbours, he had abused her as she struggled with her suitcase and her shame. Of course he was angry with her, angry for leaving him alone for two weeks to fuss and fume in kitchen and laundry at machines and gadgets which refused to work. While she lay in the hospital bed, weak from post-operative pain, he played the role of domestic martyr, unable to cope with his incompetence and dependency. The weak man turned bully. One of the neighbours had been so appalled by the scene in the driveway that she refused to speak to him again. She had told my mother later, *I just can't forgive him.* She didn't know the full story, but would it, after all, have made any difference?

There are other stories, similarly contemptible. There was the time, years ago, when he ordered my mother to wear two petticoats under her semi-transparent summer dresses. Or when he – the travelling salesman – cancelled the milk delivery because he suspected her of having an affair with the milkman, a story only rescued from risible cliché by the ferocious persistence of his accusations. He told her how to vote. At the dinner-table he would demand the salt, second helpings, complain about the fatty meat, gesturing imperiously, eating noisily, a boor as well as a bully. After his retirement, he restricted her to one weekly outing to the city with a friend. He would wait on the front steps until she came home; suspiciously and tediously superintending, he would always insist on knowing what she had done, how much she had spent.

In those weeks following my father's death my mother and I tie up financial matters, finalising the will, notifying the relevant government agencies, closing bank accounts. He has left nothing. Even worse, we discover undisclosed debts on his credit card, cash taken out to bet, and lose, on the horses. We have known about his gambling for years, but the size of the debt enrages my mother. To his manifest failure as companion and lover is added his failure – especially unforgivable for a woman of her generation – to be a good provider.

In one of our various trips to the city my mother and I stop in front of a florist's shop, silenced in mid-conversation by an unexpected proliferation of bright yellow blooms, scarlet bunches abundant and lavish. My mother says, deliberatively, *You know, he never once gave me flowers*. And there, on the noisy street, bodies brushing past her with busy intent, she is motionless and crying. I stroke her arm, thinking she cannot, surely, mean *never*.

The last time I saw my father alive was on the day before his death. Waiting for his operation, he was uncharacteristically self-effacing, even serene. At the end of my visit he accompanied me to the door of his hospital room. Shuffling with obvious difficulty, he played the part of the courtly European gentleman thanking me for coming, his voice surprisingly gentle. I was disconcerted by such graciousness and by the apparent possibility of transformation in the face of suffering. Later I learned it was the morphine he had been given for his pain.

Contemplating these images and narrative fragments, I am unable to construct a coherent whole. I am practised in the task of writing formal essays, not stories on my father's, or indeed anyone's, death. The trick of writing an essay, I tell my students year after year, is to know what you want to say before you say it. And don't try to say too much: confine yourself to the explication and development of three or four major points. Be selective without being reductive. And yes, in a literary critical essay, it is now permissible to use the first person pronoun: acknowledge your position, make it part of your ethical and political point. Confronted by my father's death, I am embarrassed by such confident glibness and the uselessness of my training. I cannot even be sure if his death is the real, the proper, subject of this story.

It began, I note, with my father's body, and a certain terse impersonality of tone. At one level such emotional detachment is easily explained, a self-protectiveness in the face of the reality of death. This body was after all my first experience of a corpse – its alarming conjunction of presence and absence; in the utter stillness of its persistent corporeality, an incomprehensible inability to revivify. But such impersonality also – perhaps shamefully – signifies my lack of regard for the man who is, it would seem, mourned by no-one. Like my mother, I cannot pretend to have loved him. I am unable even to respect him. This was a man for whom value was a matter always of dollars and cents. Who voted in the last election for the party which, after days of careful calculation, he estimated would offer him forty-nine cents a week more than the Opposition. Who thought his cleverness vindicated by making bogus insurance claim. Who often asked me how much I earned, but never once asked me about the intangible profits of my work as a teacher. Whatever sadness I feel, then, is for my mother, and for myself, as we grieve for the husband and the father we never had.

The night of his death, family members had met to compose a newspaper obituary and a speech for the funeral. My brother, always decisive and methodical, had taken charge, the well-meaning orchestrator of the required sentiments. He kept prompting our mother for words complimentary and consoling about her husband, our father. She offered merely perfunctory remarks and indifferent shrugs of the shoulder. At the end of an hour, my brother was able to note only that my father had been an affable, joke-telling travelling salesman, liked to debate current affairs and amused the neighbours with his loud barracking of the football on T.V. Visibly agitated by our mother's contempt, he ushered me outside and demanded, quietly, to know what was going on. *Good God*, he declared, *a man's life has to be worth something. There has to be more to say.* I am very fond of my brother, but was unable, and perhaps unwilling, to console. *You have to understand*, I told him, trying not to sound like the patronising sister, *how difficult it's been for her all these years*. She isn't sorry that he's dead. It was the closest I was able to come to feeling sorry for my father. At the funeral, my brother gave a speech which was amusingly anecdotal, and which earned praise from all those witnesses, like myself, who would have struggled for good things to say. I understood that the speech was for our mother's sake and for the sake of appearances, and was grateful.

My mother is one of those women for whom widowhood is a second chance. Since my father's death two years ago she has travelled to Europe, with money I discover she has secretly, surreptitiously, put aside over many years, ludicrously small amounts from the housekeeping, from her own wages, from her pension, and now finally and triumphantly translated into a single airline ticket and a return after forty years to the picturesque beauties of her homeland. I am in awe of such tenacious duplicity and mildly outraged by its necessity.

These days she makes regular trips to the city and sees much more of her family and friends. She has also been released from the daily tyrannies of domesticity. She eats when, what and where she chooses and allows the crumbs on the kitchen floor to rebelliously accumulate. Most importantly, perhaps, she has found her voice. Uncowered by husbandly insults, she has discovered the pleasure of offering her opinions to attentive listeners. She proves to be an entertaining storyteller, with a gift for mimicry and irony. She only occasionally speaks of my father, when, contemplating the perplexing ambiguities of loss, she has wondered aloud if she should share the blame for the failure of their marriage. Did she worry too much about money, set too much store by economic security? Might a different kind of woman have made my father happy? Perhaps, after all, he was right, that she simply wasn't smart enough for this university-educated man. A few times she has spoken of feeling lonely, and on one occasion was tearfully overcome by a sense of the awful waste of two lives. But mostly she remains angered, if now more mutedly, by his injurious disrespect. Although her mantelpiece displays a photograph of my father as a conspicuously handsome thirty-year old, her stories continue to be fuelled by a sense of injustice and a refusal to sentimentalise her past.

What is there, then, in all of this for me? Whose story is it anyway? Two years after his death, I am conscious, if only from a naggingly persistent sense of filial duty, of the need to do some rough justice to my father's side of the story. Was it all bluster and bullying, petty selfishness and tyrannical self-pity? Am I so unmoved, so unmovable, that I cannot conjure up some moments, any moment, which might represent that monstrous ego in a kindlier light? I recall, reluctantly, the two occasions on which I saw him cry. I come across him in the living room, where he sits with a magazine on his lap, wiping streams of tears from his face. I am twelve years old, and vaguely unnerved by this strange spectacle, this unmanning of the patriarchal bully of my childhood. He looks up and blushes and, in faltering half-sentences, explains that he has just finished reading a story about the death of a family pet. It is a St Bernard, he tells me, just like the one he had as a child in snowy Europe; a dog, it would seem, of lovable largeness and tongue-slurping devotion, who daily accompanied him on family errands, was known to everyone in the neighbourhood, was patted and fussed over and mourned for years after his death. I note that the magazine on my father's lap is *The Reader's Digest*, and, already the literary snob, I register contempt for the sentimentalism of both the text and the reader. So young, and so stonyhearted.

I recall a second scene of distress. I am alone in the kitchen with my father. He tells me that my mother has gone to the country for a few days to stay with a friend. I am fifteen, and acutely conscious not only of the loud argument the night before – voices sharp and bitter, denouncing and angry, behind their bedroom door – but also of the many silences, the glowering faces and stubborn withdrawals, all the corrosive markers of years of marital estrangement. My father is pacing the room and running his hand through his hair. *She says it's all my fault*, he says, more to himself than to me. *She says she may never come back.* Suddenly he stops and looks directly at me, asking for something, perhaps, which I can never give. His eyes are full of tears. *You know*, he says, *in all these years, she never once came to me. Not once.* I am both stranded by adolescent embarrassment and strangely touched by his old-fashioned turn of phrase. She never once came to him. She never, in modern parlance, initiated sex. She never showed him that she wanted him, never made him feel desired, desirable.

The moment passes and he goes from the room. Years later, now, I wonder if this is where it all began, where it all started to go wrong. In the bedroom, inhibited and emotionally inept, their sense of inadequacy and disappointment turned outward into mutual resentment and recrimination. She never came to him, he came to her only as a blundering intruder. Poor readers, both, of their own and one another's bodies.

There are other memories, fugitive and incomplete – half-recalled half-sentences, a single image, a gesture – which offer some dimly apprehended sense of paternal affection or pride. I recall my father standing, drenched with rain, on the side-lines of a hockey field, yelling encouragement to his unathletic daughter. There is a compliment on my dress for the first school dance, a beaming face at my wedding, and an awkward cradling of my first baby. But these fragments fail to move me; they are after all the unexceptional memories of conventional female milestones, in which my father merely performs a series of unexceptional and conventional roles.

There is a more intensely realised memory of an outing in the country on one of his travelling salesman's trips, in which I sit proudly beside him in the front seat of his brand-new car. Even now, thirty years on, the sharp smell of vinyl evokes the sense of a special day, me and my dad driving on long country roads, the red dust whipping up around us, farm gates being opened, dogs running alongside the car, a lime-flavoured ice cream at the end of the journey as a reward for my patience. And there is my graduation day, when, round and replete with pride, my father boasts of his prize-winning daughter to several anonymous dignitaries. Besuited and slightly tipsy, endearing and embarrassing, he hugs my mother several times and waves his wine-glass in the air.

But mostly I recall his arrogance, his anger, his profound indifference to the hearts and minds of those who might have loved him. I remember the hour before his return from work, which my brother and I would savour resentfully before the arrival of those demands, complaints, criticisms; which drove us to our rooms. The afternoon teas with friends, when my mother's social pleasantries were derided, shouted down. Never asking after my children, except to inquire about their scholastic success. Proclaiming his opinions, banging his fist on the table. All that noise, the fury and the tedium of it, the inability ever to pause, to hear us, to listen.

I am left with a final memory of my father. It is a story only recently discovered by my mother, who has in turn narrated it to me. It seems that on the night before his operation, he telephoned an old acquaintance – someone he hadn't seen in over fifteen years – to say that he wasn't going to make it. My father had no close friends; indeed, like so many men of his generation, whatever emotional links he had with others had all been forged and sustained by his wife. Unlike my mother, he had retained no connections with the Europe of his youth. I knew from his boasting of the existence of much older and successful siblings – a doctor, a lawyer and a priest – a professional triumvirate whose ghostly presence he occasionally invoked as proof of his intellectual superiority, and to lament the wealth that might have been. He had never corresponded with them since leaving his homeland; he didn't know whether they had ever married, had children, indeed whether they were still alive. Years later, an old man in an altogether different country, he had chosen to call a virtual stranger, called late at night from the payphone in the cold and silent hospital corridor, given his name, exchanged greetings and said he knew he was going to die. In barely a whisper, out of the blue. The bewildered acquaintance had asked a few questions, found a context. He had pieced together a medical history of sorts: an infected toe which had stubbornly refused to heal, gangrene, weeks of debilitating pain, and now the impending amputation which is the not uncommon fate of the elderly diabetic. He remembers offering some garbled sympathy and the required pep-talk, and the conversation, such as it was, trailing off into embarrassed silence. And of course my father's intuitive and dismal prediction was right. He didn't make it. After months of massive doses of pain-killers, his kidneys were barely functional. His heart, already weakened by years of angina, had simply given way.

When my mother finally got to hear this story, she was both puzzled and vaguely piqued. Why had her husband called this man in the middle of the night? Someone he hadn't seen, hadn't spoken to, in fifteen years. What did he hope to achieve? Why hadn't he called her, his wife, in his final hours? In the face of such terrible questions, I could offer only platitudes. *Sometimes it's easier to talk to strangers about such matters,* I suggested. *Perhaps he didn't want to worry you. Or perhaps he was simply confused.*

∼

Today I am driving home from work along the river and listening to the radio. It is one of those clichéd days in May: the warm sun streaming through the car window, an afternoon breeze gently scudding the water, the white sails of yachts puffed out proudly against an impossibly clear blue sky. The voice on the radio is familiar: a former current affairs broadcaster and interviewer, herself being interviewed about her professional and personal life. She is speaking about one of her programmes – I remember it as the long-running if rather predictably entitled "The Search for Meaning" – which featured many high-profile public achievers: academics and intellectuals, political activists, business people, artists, even a flamboyant socialite who was surprisingly articulate and emotionally astute. I register scraps of conversation as she speaks now about her *own* search for meaning: her former marriage, her childlessness, her conversion to Catholicism, the difficulties of solitariness and the pleasures of solitude. And I am lulled as always by her gentle, indeed mesmeric, voice. It has the calmness I remember from her radio days, a sense of conviction without complacency, of unassertive faith, perhaps. She sounds, I find myself thinking, like a woman whose serenity has been earned.

And then, as her interviewer signals the end of the programme, she is asked, finally, how she would like to be remembered after her death. As I drive along the river, feeling the warmth of the sun, I see the sails of the yachts and the blue of the sky, and I know in my heart what she is going to say. *As someone who loved . . . and was loved.* I wonder, momentarily, whether her pause is merely a rhetorical trick, part of the skill of the public performer aiming for emotional effect. But the sentiment, for me, sounds real enough. This, I feel, is the voice of a woman who knows herself to be blessed, who pauses to give silent thanks for the gift of loving and being loved. And suddenly, unexpectedly, I think of my father, calling from the hospital telephone, alone and whispering. I see his face, pale and bony, his frail hands barely able to move the old-fashioned dial, his thin legs beneath his checked dressing-gown. Did he feel himself to be someone unloving and unloved? Did he know himself, on that last night to be, finally and fearfully, unblessed? And because I see him there so clearly, and because I will never know the answer, will never know if that was after all his real question, I find myself at last able to cry.

Beth Yahp

Thursdays

Let's go together on Thursday. Together up the narrow stairs, so steep it's knees having to lift almost chin-height, one after another, stair by stair. *Why so slow? Hurry up, don't waste time.* Up to the long corridor, lined with cubicles all the way to a distant window, where sunlight falls in weak squares. Wooden partitions stop short of the ceiling. There are the usual piles of newspapers and plastic bags bulging with mysterious contents by each door. A cough from one of the cubicles, the soft whirr of a sewing machine. A radio down low. Empty bottles stand sentinel along one wall, braided in cobwebs. Here's the doorway, hung with a floral curtain. A red ribbon on a hook to tie it back. We'll lift the curtain, peer into the shadowy interior. *Come in, come in.*

Uncle Wong, a few strands of hair straddling the shiny dome of his forehead, beams through horn-rimmed glasses. The height of fashion, 1964, and like him, seen better days. *Come in, don't be shy.* His needle is poised at the apex of the thread's extension before he nips it free. Glint of a golden tooth. *Ah, sit there. Good, ah? Soft-soft. Just finish yesterday. You like? Special for you.*

The cushion is good for sinking into, after the usual moment's shyness, clinging to Nellie's skirt. She shakes herself free. It's just the right height, softness, plumpness, and placed under a row of dresses whose skirts tickle the tips of ears, the tops of eyebrows like an extra fringe. *Stay there, be good. Mr. Wong, usual time. No, no, on time-one. Be good, don't make trouble, hah?* The curtain flutters. A page from the Hong Kong filmstar calendar by the doorway curls upwards, then falls lazily back. Click-click-click of receding heels.

Uncle Wong, still beaming, holds up a finger. *Shhhhhhh.* He holds out a tray of bobbins in a chocolate box, still smelling of chocolates. Last New Year's present from Nellie, from Cold Storage in Singapore, where Uncle-Daddy bought so many boxes for Nellie and Nellie's family. Uncle Wong crinkles the paper cups still smelling of long eaten turkish delight, almond whirls, hazelnut creams. He fingers the cardboard cover still smelling of Singapore big stores. Singapore airconditioning.

Ah, you ready to choose?

As usual, it's a pointing finger drifting over rainbow colours, hesitating here and there, lifting away completely to tap at a cheekbone or chin, and then darting back. Peeping up at the slow bead of sweat which darkens the wrinkles running down Uncle Wong's neck. There's the Thursday smell of rosewater from a spritzer he keeps by his elbow, of strings of mothballs hung between the shimmery dresses. And a heavier, sour smell. Dust motes hang suspended in a blade of sunlight from a knothole in the wall, and a hawker's cry hangs also: *String hoppers! String hoppers, guaranteeeee frrressshhh!* The Hong Kong filmstar smiles sadly through her coating of dust on the calendar, one arm stretched forwards, hand delicately poised. Let's choose now. And the pointing finger finally chooses—as usual—pink. A papery rustle of laughter.

Ha—ha—ha—how come Uncle always knows what you choose?

A burst of pink on the tongue and a pink smile from ear to ear, sucking on the sweet always to be found nestled under the pink bobbin. Watching the slow bead of sweat seep into the rolled-up towel slung around Uncle Wong's neck, and then it's time for the usual whispered questions. In spite of Uncle Wong's *Shhhhhhhh.* The sweet wrapper carefully smoothened between pointing fingers and thumbs.

Uncle Wong, why you not married?
Ah, yes, I'm married. Long time married!
Where's your wife, Uncle Wong?
Ah, she's over there, you didn't see her?
Why she so quiet, Uncle Wong?
Ah, she's sleeping.
Uncle Wong, how come daytime she's sleeping? How come she's not helping you?
Ah, she's very tired.

Uncle Wong also looks tired, two enlarged pouches swimming in the lower halves of his glasses.

Ha—ha—special for me, like spare tyre, extra pair of eyes!

He squeaks on his tiny stool, needle flashing in and out of the material spilling from his lap. Shimmery. Soft to the fingertips, and the cheek. Let's try it. Tiny beads are stitched to a white satin bodice with even tinier stitches, seashell whirls secreted one inside another—but none of them pink.

You like, ah?

Uncle Wong's new cushion is embroidered with a giant waterlily, so lovely it's a head vigorously nodding, hair flying up and down. It's good for sinking into. And bouncing back up. Rainbow coloured carp kiss their bubbly lips through waterlily leaves. Gold-threaded fins.

Ha—ha—ha—it tickles!

The sweet, even sucked slowly, slow-motion tumbled over the tongue and under it, into each cheek pocket and out again while staring pensively up at Uncle Wong's extra pouches of eyes, is fast disappearing. It tastes of strawberries, like strawberry pink cough medicine in Uncle-Daddy's office, pink like rosebuds sprinkled all over Nellie's Thursday skirt. Like the ones sprinkling the little skirt now spread so daintily over Uncle Wong's new waterlily cushion, with little knees making hills under them, nicely together, two joined-together little hills.

In the street the Thursday fruit seller calls to Nellie. *Young Sister!* The Thursday paperman jostles the crowd to let her pass. *Where going, Young Sister?* The beggar man raises his matted head. Even the busiest meehoon seller stops dunking his noodles. *Young Sister, so pretty today with your baby sister.* Nellie raises her chin, her black eyes flashing. She likes having a baby sister, tells everyone it's a baby sister, even Grandma, who stares back at Nellie with narrow watery eyes. Nellie click-clicks away to the bus stop with her head in the air and a smile peekabooing, so quickly it's little legs having to skip after her, over the piles of dirty dishes and the open drain. *Hurry up! Why so slow?* It's little legs of a baby sister swishing in a Thursday dress just like Nellie's, but smaller, with a round collar and puff sleeves. With its seams hand-stitched, like Nellie's, its cloth-covered buttons made to order by Uncle Wong. And always sitting like Nellie, *Remember, hah? Be good, always be a lady. Hah?*

Uncle Wong, is your wife pretty?

Ah, she was beautiful once.

Prettier than Nellie?

Ah, Nellie's very pretty, but my wife prettier, yes . . .

Prettier than Hong Kong filmstars?
Much prettier...
Prettier than me?
Ah, almost as pretty...
How come you have such a pretty wife, Uncle Wong? How you found her?
Ha—ha—ha—Uncle Wong was handsome once!
Uncle Wong's Thursday laugh half-shoots out, then is half-swallowed, halfway between a cough and a croak. *Ssshhhhhh!*
As soon as the sweet is finished, he presses a finger to his lips. *Shhhhhh.* Let's be quiet now. He reaches towards the bed piled high with pieces of abandoned dresses, bolts of remnants like a mini Great Wall of China, blouses with their necklines crooked, skirts with snaggled piping. Zippers lockjawed in grimaces of metallic teeth. In the narrow space between these and the wooden partition of the cubicle reclines his sleeping wife, wrapped in a blanket of red and yellow towelling in spite of the afternoon heat. Her little feet protrude from the end of the bed as stiff as boards and still wearing their embroidered slippers. A strand of cobweb swirls lazily over her, a pair of houseflies buzz hovering just beyond Uncle Wong's reach. There's a smell of camphor mixed with new cloths and old cloths, chemical dyes in their pungency, dresses once danced in, twirled giddily, sweat-stained bodices releasing their heady mix. And a sour, stronger smell. Uncle Wong spritzes rosewater at the flies.
Uncle Wong, can I see your wife?
Ah, she's over there, you can see her sleeping.
Can I go and say Auntie hello?
Ah, later, she's so tired now. You know, Auntie Wong, she works so hard.
Harder than you, Uncle?
Ah, much harder.
Harder than Uncle-Daddy at office?
Ah, I think so.
Harder than Grandma at market?
Just as hard.
Harder than Nellie?
Ah, yes. I believe so, yes.
Harder than Uncle-Daddy's first wife?
Ha—ha—ha—much harder!
She needs a holiday, then, like Uncle-Daddy and Nellie.
Ah, yes...

Seaside holiday.
Yes . . .
Singapore holiday.
Yes, yes . . .

Uncle Wong lifts out his bundle of special cloths from a beautiful lacquered box by the bed. Where gold threads and silver threads and ruby-bright buttons and emerald-trimmed ribbons glisten like jewels. *Shhhhhh.* We'll be quiet now. Here are gossamer dragonflies, flittering from the lifted lid on thin wire frames for the bridesmaids. Here are webs of pearl and pursed netting for the babies' christening gowns. Black beaded lace for the widows.

Now time for you to work also.

Time to choose between a fluttery scrap of chiffon, Nellie's birthday present, or a stiff square of cotton for Uncle-Daddy, criss-crossed with stripes. Nellie can use hers to signal the minibus or a taxi coming home at night, or slip it into her neckline when the day becomes too hot. Uncle-Daddy can pull his from his pocket at office, so handsome against his white hospital coat. He can use it to dab at a trickle of pink cough medicine. Ha-ha-ha loud and echoing, not at all like Uncle Wong. *Good girl! See, that wasn't so bad!* While beside him Nellie smiles and taps the toe of one foot. *Stay there, be good. Stay there, hah? Don't move.* So it's legs kicking at the high chair legs, shoe tips tilted upwards, it's eyes roaming from the silver tray cluttered with shiny instruments, to the dividing screen shivery in the corner, to the jar of rainbow-coloured sweets on the far side of Uncle-Daddy's desk, with a rainbow-coloured lid, and little arms too little to reach them. *Don't move.* Uncle-Daddy can dab a red tremor of perspiration from his lips.

Now Uncle Wong spreads the small pieces of cloths out over his knees. And over two little hills of rose-sprinkled knees. *Remember? Always a lady.* Taking time, never rushing to choose. So it's the pointing finger hooking itself on to a lower lip, pulling the lip forwards in contemplation. Someone coughs and someone spits in one of the other cubicles, someone joins in a radio love song down low. Shall we choose a bright floral pattern for Grandma, its four corners knotted to fit over her head as she goes selling from door to door? Keep off the roadside sun. Or a red satin square for Uncle Wong's wife, as red as the beadwork of her slippers, as red as Nellie's lipstick. Let's choose. Uncle Wong carefully holds each piece up to the sliver of sunlight, turning it this way and that. He peers over the tops of his glasses, his eyelashes as neat as his stitches. Wobbling his extra pair of sewn-up eyes. Already beaming.

Ha—ha—Uncle Wong always knows!

Take it, in carefully wiped-first hands. Pretend pouting to hide the excitement of the needle, re-threading last Thursday's thread, which is pink from the pink bobbin. Uncle Wong leans forward, showing his long gold-edged teeth. Like magic, since last Thursday, the outsized knots have unravelled, the uneven stitches re-stitched themselves straight. In the blade of sunlight inching its way across Uncle Wong's cubicle the clusters of roses on Nellie's birthday handkerchief have grown in number since last Thursday, like roses in the neighbour lady's garden before Grandma snips them for market. There are rosebuds raised pink and rounded as little sweets. Good to run a pointing finger over, to peep up at Uncle Wong, pretend tasting them. *Mmmmmmm.* Good enough to keep in each cheek pocket, leaking a taste of strawberries on the tongue. Tiny green leaves, prickle-thin thorns.

Ha—ha—ha!

Uncle Wong, so pretty!

He holds up his needle and squints through his glasses so the thread slides through in one go. A double flick of his pointing finger double knots the other end. *Careful, sharp-sharp.* Then as usual he nods, beaming, stretching out his arm as gracefully as the Hong Kong filmstar on the wall. His needle flashes silver to go with his gold.

Uncle Wong, how come . . .

Shhhhhhh.

Time to work now. Uncle Wong pulls his thread as far as it will go. Then he brings it back. Forwards, and back. Forwards, then back. We'll work now. And as usual rosebuds blossom beneath his veiny hands. As usual Thursday afternoon stretches before us, drawn out upon the thread's silken extension, first his, then mine, in tandem. The thread's assured return. It's this movement, forwards and back, stitches itself to my memory: graceful, economical, reliable as breath, and absorbing the encroaching press of all the days which are not Thursdays, all the afternoons spent here or there with this or that Uncle or Auntie while Grandma scours the market for errands and it's *Don't make trouble!* in a roomful of cousins, it's lips pursed tight to a chorus *Baby sister, my foot! My eye, baby sister! My ass!* it's hands held tightly together too proud to ask again for orange squash *Cannot ask nicely?* it's a chorus *He did! Ask Grandma! He did!* it's little knees bunched together on the doorstep *Always a lady* too proud to ask nicely-again for the toilet it's a haze of mosquitoes and it's not Thursday and some not-Thursdays Nellie has no handkerchief to wave at a minibus or taxi, it's Nellie not noticing the time passing, Nellie with no taxi or minibus fare on the other side of town.

The flies flicker through the thin sunlight that has cut its way across the floor and now climbs up the opposite wall. Shadows deepen their way towards us from the jumble of material spilling from the room's hidden corners, from the bowed dress-racks above us, the tumble of remnants and rejects on the bed where Uncle Wong's wife sleeps. The lazy afternoon traffic outside heaves purring and honking to evening. This Thursday Nellie will be late as usual, click-click-clicking up the stairs with her black eyes flashing and creases in her petal-strewn skirt. She'll stand just inside Uncle Wong's doorway, her compact flicked open, wiping at a red corner of her mouth. Not noticing the suffusion of rosewater Uncle Wong spritzes just before she enters, a pink spray falling to the ground in dark spatters, or her birthday handkerchief hidden hastily away behind his back. She won't notice the porcelain pale feet of Auntie Wong poking out from the bottom of the bed, still in their lovely embroidered slippers. Or the smell beneath the smell of roses. Nellie won't notice the delicate stitches Uncle Wong has perfected over the long afternoons and days, not-Thursdays, spent hunched over scraps of material in a cubicle just like this. His needle lifting, piercing. *Shhhhhhhhhh!* With a locked door instead of the floral curtain and a chorus of Uncles and Aunties *He did, I tell you! A cushion over her face . . .* Nellie will snap her fingers. *Hurry, now. Don't be slow, hah?* She will flutter a dollar into Uncle Wong's hand.

Uncle Wong, your wife woke up already?
Hurry.
Ha-ha-ha!
Can I see her, please?
Ha-ha-
Don't be slow, I said.
Uncle Wong?

Now?
Bye-bye!
Now?

ANGELA ROCKEL

Remember: A working definition of blessing

This piece was written in early 2001 as part of the Universal Beatitudes project, a song cycle drawing on the theme of blessings or *beatitudes*, initiated by composer Raffaele Marcellino.

1   Saw the shadow of earth
    cross the face of the moon.
    Moon looked red
    in the little light that reached it.

    Saw my judgement
    cross a country of strangers.
    They looked frightening
    (I don't understand them);
    they looked dangerous
    (they don't want me here).

    Blessed are you
    who know where your own shadow falls.

    I breathe the smoke of your feast,
    you eat up my life.
    I am the ground underfoot,
    I am your neighbour.
    You do it because you are able,
    you do it because I am far from you,
    you do it because you think there will always be more.

1 I say blessed are you
when you meet me,
who give back
the shine of my own life
quietly turning.

2 Lost in the gap that waits
in the ribs of the world,
loose in that place
I stumble
towards a heartbeat.

Now, here in the light and noise
of my first day,
give me a place that will teach me –
bind it into my new bones –
power to bless.

I turn my will to your good –
this is power to bless.
You turn your will to my good –
bringing a change in the world's hard weather.

3 Stretch yourself out
in time, in space,
be a meeting of strangers.
Be blessed – you have no choice,
you will surely be wounded.
We opened a door that was always there,
followed the howling down,
crowding to serve the thing that flails
in the weightless space of our terror.
We soothe it with chunks of ourselves,
promise to call down our children,
feed it their juiciest years,
the days of their love songs.

Lie down,
let memory grow
like a thorn-tree from your chest,
its shade the unregarded ground
where breath and speech can come
to scatterlings from all the worlds.
Tongues of leaves and air
call up the rain,
spiny shoots push trampled earth,
another planet turns its unlit face
towards the stars.

Fist turns on itself,
a closed world.
Happy are you,
sore and afraid as you are,
who open your hand to bless.
Happy are you,
clenched so long
in a whirlwind of ashes,
who open to calm and shine back the life
of another face.

4 Earthlight, moonlight,
light of an ancient star,
turn with me now
as darkness settles the hollow bay,
sweet layers pressing down,
fresh over salt.
Curls of light from the boat's prow,
chaos of light, the bow-wave.

Knife-edged, lines burn in the wake,
green flames, haloes and sparks
from every moving thing.
See what life attends us;
we, with our answering clamour,
our dark star riding the swell.

From the wreckage,
footprints, silver in ashes, lead away –
after winter, something can happen,
ground rising in steam like a dark loaf –
lives are coming up,
trumpets and bells from underground.

Prickling with lights, the town flinches
where its past presses in too hard,
fits too tightly, rough wool and lousy.
Flashing evening to itself across the water,
its stories are shifting. Wind twists
meanings of floodlit landmarks;
the belltower scattering changes;
new pink watch house and hotel.
What are these places? Everything echoes,
the dead and those not yet born returning,
speech in fragments like a gust of bells.

In the winds of the equinox,
all our flags are ribbons.
Between equal weights of night and day,
in the whip of this air,
I feel their rags flick past my face,
loops and turns mapping in air
old paths that still run to the water,
thumbprints that fold into new whorls.

Earth and sky have moved again in sleep;
dark limbs, joints of light
flung in patterns we didn't see before.
Yesterday an eye opened in my breast;
worlds are rolling there,
the city a struck bell
retold in this fracture or wound,
new sounds from these pieces.

5   There's a voice that breaks from us –
words and the howl of what can't yet be said.
Our mouths and hands are full of blood –
closed to injure,
let them open now to bless.
We wait, we turn, we call –
speech from all that is – a little thing,
like a hazelnut in the palm of your hand.
Hold, breathe, bless.
Eyes gleam from scrublands returning;
wandering brightness, spreading arc of shelter;
small proofs – an age of destruction passes.

Robyn Ferrell

The Kingdom of God

Conchology, the study of shells, tells us that the shell is made by the mollusc, who is a shapeless creature in search of a shape.

It is strange to think that the beautiful rigid architecture of even the simplest shell is the product of a slug. There is nothing apparently beautiful (even something repugnant) about the slimy mass of the mollusc, creeping around on one large foot that doubles as a head. But perhaps art is produced to make up for what is lacking, as a compensation. Was the artist ever beautiful? Did anything beautiful ever need to create?

What conchology studies is not the filigree chambers and pearly laminate of the shell. It overlooks the pleasure of the shell, because that is an art, in favour of the scientific, which is to say the biology of the mollusc who made it. Detailed observation and intelligent guesswork reveal the parochial social life of the mollusc. What it eats, and how it reproduces. The shell is a function.

We know how the shell is formed; it hardens out of the mollusc's mantle, a growing edge sculpting a wrap in ever-widening whorls. The shell is its memory, each whorl a testament to growth and experience, and in the end its shroud.

The conchologist believes the markings on the shell, its colours and codes, to be a result of minerals in the organism, or else, of its waste. But this only goes to show how little we know about the mollusc, and indeed how little science grasps life. When forming around oneself the mask that will become one's representative, when creating the shell that is one's ambassador and interpreter, surely the question of how it will look to others becomes, for the mollusc, paramount?

Like love, shell collecting is about attention to detail. I used to make collections of the variegated limpets, shaped like chinamen's hats and with intricate spidery signatures on their backs. Also of black nerites, which shine like black and white marble when wet. I put them in arrays on the sand, so that I could see the difference and the repetition in them, like people in a crowd.

The best times for shell collecting are within an hour each side of the low tide. I have found angel wings and brown cowries, abalone and the shells of sea urchins. Banded Dog Whelks and Quoy's Turrid, the Glabra Mitre and the Fragile Air Breather - even Roadknight's Volute! Naturally, they didn't come with names. They came aimless and orphaned, hollowed husks of souls. I consulted a chart of 'Common Shells of Australia', to give them a home in their after-life. I am reminded of the place I lived as a child. It reminds me of being a child. I remember my mother, going ahead of us on the beach, falling with a cry of triumph upon the Tiger Nautilus. 'Look what the storm has fished up!' There was plenty of booty after a storm. She also found a Russian cool drink crate, which made a tidy occasional table. When we went digging through the seaweed, however, in sea-smelling armfuls, our father protested. 'Put that down! Little scavengers!'

My grandmother used to make things out of shells. Scavenging was accepted practice among the ladies of the church. They used to glue shells on the headpieces of dolls, and sew them onto the corners of a potholder. No surface was safe from decoration. That was a life that needed embroidery; there was something being compensated for in that molluscal activity. They too produced beautiful conventional rigid elaborations, through their faith, on seemingly shapeless lives.

My father was a lay preacher in the Baptist church. Before we went to sleep each night, he came and sang our prayers with us: 'Gentle Jesus meek and mild/ Look upon a little child/ Suffer my simplicity/ Suffer me to come to thee'. I think of Jesus Christ as a serious child-like man, with a good ear for music.

The church building was of undecorated brick, with long lights suspended on cloth-covered cords from the beams, and pews that gave off a sad old smell. At the front of the church there were no brass censors, nor gates, nor clergy in gowns. They pulled the wooden floor up from time to time, to immerse the converts in the baptismal pool. It came as a surprise to see a pool of water there, a piece of Hollywood lowered onto a dusty stage. The baptisms seemed melodramatic when contrasted with the more puritan features of the building and congregation. The converts came out in Cecil B. de Mille robes, yet it was a sin to wear lipstick. A theological democracy was practiced in which all participated, but this did not result in tolerance.

The congregation appeared to inhabit a left-over pocket of time; the dusty thirties, with its smell of wood and cotton, persisted in that church well after those fumes had been dispersed elsewhere. It was the old ladies who kept it alive, wearing rayon shifts and hair nets and hospital-strength orthopaedic shoes. They were all widowed, and still mentioned the Depression.

Mrs Grace, who lived in the brown house across the road from the church, had a singing voice so old it shook on the high notes. She clung, rocking, to the back of the pew in front as she sang, the many rings on her fingers appearing to have fused with her flesh - they were surely never removed. Her hat was decorated with white net, and her face powder finished at her jawline, leaving her neck to fall in folds toward her chest.

On occasion she played the organ, her feet pumping vigorously in a rhythm unrelated to the melody line. Every breath the organ took was a labour and consequently, every note a complaint. '*What* a friend we have in Jesus'.

The Baptist church smelt of decay. It was a place dedicated to the contemplation of sin and suffering, and its favoured penance for life was boredom. I remember long Sunday mornings of dreariness, sitting in the dark pews until, on a cue from Mrs Grace, the Sunday School filed out, selfconsciously clattering down the aisle as the servers took up the collection. I remember how browning eucalyptus leaves and hot grasses smelt, in the long hour between twelve and one, which we spent in the shade of incurable country town misery playing behind the hall.

Falling in love is like returning to childhood. We might sit side by side in a car on the way there, and the drumming of the motor, the repetitious landscape of paddock and gum, might draw us back into sentience. Time would become huge and engulf us. It would slow irremediably so that half an hour is experienced like a long afternoon, and the taking of meals and snacks creeps into childhood times. Tea at five o'clock.

I fear your company could dominate the small space we are in. My thoughts would sound like shouts in my head, my face would turn toward you, and I would be overly-attuned to each inflexion in your posture. Your profile would daunt me. I would feel observed. Falling in love threatens to return me to a world of overpowering feeling, of bodily chaos. But I can hardly bear to be shaken and rattled by that feeling, especially since experience tells me that feelings pass, even violent ones that lay claim to necessity. Being that close to someone else is terrifying as much as it is desirable. The loss of oneself to another threatens annihilation. This is why with you, whose body wrenches me back to childhood against my will, I need to be quite scrupulous. I need to employ all the second-order graces of maturity; tact, compassion, discretion and restraint.

To return to childhood, we would need an old weatherboard house like my grandmother lived in. There are copies of the Baptist Hymnal and the *Golden Wattle Cookbook* in the bookshelf next to the old organ. The organ was made in Indiana, and one of its stops is called *vox humana*. On the back verandah, there are two old wicker chairs, from which you can look across to the hill on which the town is built. At night, the lights of the town spread over its shoulders, and in the morning the sun rises in the crook of its arm.

Does childhood suggest to you plenitude? This was not a childhood like that. Grass was more often long, and roads unsealed, running beside vacant land. When my grandmother married, they still went up and down Grey Street in a horse and cart. Cooking was done on a wood stove, and laundry in the copper. She was still hanging her washing on a line suspended from two wooden poles that leant and swayed. She had a tin clock with a ship on it, in full sail. The key for winding it hung behind the clock, on a small hook. From her kitchen came the sound of the divine service on the radio and the smell of roast mutton.

Her house was built by my grandfather and some of its curiosities were his own design, some a necessity. But she grew the fig tree that could be seen from the kitchen window and the hydrangeas on the fence line, against the swamp. He favoured ramps over steps, perhaps because they were easier to build. In the morning and the afternoon, she heard his shuffle on the ramp, and the clip of his feet on lino, and the banging of the screen door. 'Here Skip!', he sang to his mildewed dog. Skip was a dog who would rush forward in excitement at small provocations, like children, and knock into them lovingly with his heavy hairy body and his dripping tongue and slapping tail. Skip had an unpleasant grin, something like a wolf.

Childhood is like the sea-green world of dreaming. When I remember life as a child, it is like grasping for the ephemeral and yet vivid images of a dream on waking. Those memories have a quality of strangeness about them, as if they did not quite belong to me, not in the way that, as an adult, purposes and intentions feel like my own. Rather, childhood happened; childhood was like being dreamed.

There was no sort of plot to it, outside the obvious stages that mark growing up. Existence passed by without a discernible coherence, and one thing happened after another in a contiguity that was both inexplicable and impossible to argue with. They say children are full of wonder, but this isn't quite right. The beautiful innocence of children comes as much from their incurious acceptance of the bizarre, the momentous and the nonsensical. The weight of not understanding so much of what surrounds you engenders passivity and a readiness to believe.

The child's body is melodramatic, and caught up with mortal questions. In dreams, you can feel again the body you had as a child. That body had fascinating sores, and vivid diseases, whose symptoms were medieval - fevers and pox. Things happened to that body that never happen now. Stubbing the top off a toe, letting blood go everywhere, letting the inside out. Grazing the knee or elbow so that the gravel left a needlepoint of drying scabs.

Other people - usually adult - disturbed one's body as a child, in more or less comforting or violent ways. No one licks a hanky and rubs marks off my face these days; I am almost never taken roughly by the arm and dragged. No one reaches out peremptorily, barring my chest, to shield me from oncoming cars, nor do they cradle the back of my head in the cup of their hands. In adulthood, this body recedes, and trails a wake only in dreams.

There is so much that must be ignored, in order to tolerate normal life! Childhood, the labile sensual time, must be given up. This is so sad an undertaking, so reluctant a parting, that you can no longer even acknowledge that you have done so. You are obliged to forget.

That time was too rich, it was too hard to live at that level of sensate disorganisation, drowning in response. Becoming adult is like getting your head above water.

And only then, can you afford the common nostalgia that characterises most memoirs of childhood; the pale imitation of what was a violent and passionate way of life. It is the tincture left in maturity, a stain of what was originally blood-red and ungovernable.

The circumstances of the town called on its inhabitants to engage in theology, and many of them failed. Perhaps the place was too grand for ordinary habitation. Abjection coloured small human attempts to live. At first, on our beach, there had been only fibro beach houses, which were little more than shacks. They were corralled by inane shell-fringed garden beds or left to spill over into sad pigface growing in sandy soil. The residents drew their water from a corrugated tank beside the house, and when it ran low in summer it was a matter of carting water in trailers from the pump-house near the beach.

Once the town water supply was connected, there came suburban villas with ocean views, proclaimed by a road sign as part of a Beach Estate. Modern bricks were lumped together in some godawful mess of domestic pride. Two-car garages! Before the Trinity? Its contemptuous judgment could be felt.

It might seem, from an outsider's perspective, ridiculous for any in such a small and backward congregation to have convictions as to eternal life and the nature of suffering. But there is something dour in the circumstances of that town that develops a metaphysical talent. When they read from the bible, it was in order to make sense of it. They *cared* about religion; they cared about God and the truth of God. They grappled with the truth in scripture, because they really felt that something hung on it.

There is something intimidating in the wide reaches of the Sound, which can be seen from every vantage point; and being seen everywhere, thus sees. Like the eyes of God, it exercises a kind of surveillance. Grandeur is a word often used to describe the landscape in this part of the coast, but it is more alarming than this. The Sound is deep and deceptively blue when calm. It is kin to the Southern Ocean, which lies behind it, feeding it on antarctic currents. The sucking of the surf and the smashed-up rocks below the cliffs can engender horror. The brown headlands are not responsive to eulogy. If this is not god-forsaken, then it is an old testament vision, not a god of love but a god of vengeance.

Then, occasionally, the sun would come through clouds and strike the sea in biblical shafts of light, imbuing the place with useless portent, giving life the appearance of significance. Everything was mixed up in my head with God. God was real and frightening; whose place this was; whose mysterious ways moved over the water like the weather coming up from the Southern Ocean. Most days, there was only brown heath-covered headlands and the disorienting sight of the sea in all directions. Moody skies, squalls, bleak sunlight breaking through briefly. It was a labile place, on a ground of loneliness - majestic and somehow incomplete.

The salty wind was not kind to the small lives which clung to the cliffs, or dug into the unpromising soil. The native species were consequently humble and defensive, occasionally suppliant, like pigface and the self-effacing flowers of the several kinds of heather. In winter, that wind blew too cold for encouragement; in summer, it fanned the aggressive flames of bushfires, ignited spontaneously from natural resins. The fires would bellow over the headland, turning the tenants - snake, lizard and wallaby - out of the bush and onto the road. That place was a hard mother, a severe father.

Childhood was this old testament place, with the book of Judges, of Deuteronomy and of Kings. The words themselves are old enough to become things. I handled them, I knew their texture, but only later did I learn what they represented.

Fear of the place provoked in the faithful a desire for a sign from God of comfort. They sought the protection of words, mumbling under their breath to fill a void which would otherwise frighten them witless. The power of words was everything. The Baptist finds his solace in the sweet reason of the New Testament. John told them: 'In the Beginning was the Word, and the Word was with God, and the Word *was* God . . . ' And in this beautiful word-god, the Baptist finds a friend. He is not christened, but goes into that baptismal pool under the floorboards in a believer's baptism, when he is of an age to take Jesus for his own 'personal saviour'. It is the sweetest desire he can imagine, the desire to be saved.

Those useless nonconformists, the Baptists! Their absurd desire to dissent made them disagreeable and dogmatic; their desire for personal salvation was a demand for intimacy with the divine that other humbler denominations do not expect. To know the word of a god, who was only known by his word, means to take the necessity of explanation on oneself. And John said that Jesus said: 'You shall know the truth, and the truth shall make you free.'

But did he warn them that this was less a blessing than a curse? Truth is a net thrown over the world; Jesus instructed his friends to be 'fishers of men'. And if you slipped through the net? Was there a deeper truth to be had, or was there only the opacity of the terrible deep - sunless, uncomprehended, uninhabitable?

Three islands stand in the Sound: Father, Son and Holy Ghost. Our beach commanded the most arresting view of them, from where the formal properties of their union were revealed. The sea stood for what lay outside the net, of what might not be caught and snatched in the way of comfort from God's creation and held, like the islands, in the arms of the sound. The sea was beyond meaningless, it was the truth that passed understanding.

I am not a city girl. Augustine held to a catholic promise, of a City of God, but the Baptist doesn't hope for cosmopolitan salvation. He is too lonely and ignored. He has no faith he could be redeemed at the centre of a spiritual commerce as mighty as its earthly model, Rome. Instead, he would hope to ascend to the shore of some bay by the celestial sea, and talk intimately until eternity with a select group of friends. Twelve in all. In Baptist heaven, each would be an apostle, a Peter or a John, in honest sandals at the water's edge.

There was God the Father, and then there were uncles. An uncle marries someone's sister, disturbing the incestuous comfort of the family, making strangers kin. The town was populated by uncles and aunts, a veritable congregation of relations.

Uncles were like being dealt a hand of jacks; there was the one of hearts, of spades, of clubs. 'Jack of all trades, and master of none', my grandmother used to say. They would have the car radio out of the dashboard on any Sunday afternoon, gizzards twisted on the grass as they experimented with the question of why it didn't work.

The Jack of Hearts, who was too young, married a girl from church. They lived in a large dilapidated house with little furniture. Their marriage was similarly provisional. That was the first marriage I ever heard of breaking up, like a ship breaking up on rocks. More like the glue coming apart on cheap chipboard shelves. There were grey smears on their old doors, above the handles, made by his careless, unwashed, unloving hands.

Before they broke up, they had a child. She was conceived before the wedding. 'She was born with a hole in her heart', I heard my mother telling Mrs Grace after church. I had hold of her hand, swinging on it, which she just tolerated. 'Can you imagine it?' Mrs Grace tutted, 'We must pray for them.'

I could imagine it, somehow, most vividly. Nothing seemed more plausible than that, being born in such circumstances, you would be born with a hole in the heart.

The Jack of Clubs worked in a service station among the oils and deodorisers and carpet squares. He wore a blue overall and wiped his hands on a cloth when we came to see him. He came down cashed up from being up North once and took me to the revolving restaurant in the top of one of those office buildings in the city. 'You're a scholar and a gentleman', he said, proudly, ignoring gender. From the thirty-third floor I could see the inky river and the suburbs lapping at its edges. By night, it looked glamorous.

He needed to give love and to receive it. His spirituality was sex and a good hymn and hard work. It was all rolled into one unpretentious bundle, tied with an old rope, and slung in the back of a decaying ute. He had idiosyncracies; a passionate erudition about early-model BMC cars, an intuitive grasp of machinery.

The Jack of Spades flirted with the wrong side of the law, and had a pedigree of insulted women and disenchanted employers - these were unjust failures. He couldn't keep to the project of mocking up a life; he was too honest, paradoxically. He never could finish anything. He was attacked always by a fatal loss of faith in himself at the eleventh hour; having set out into a project with bombast, he'd find it seeping away, like water running through sand. He got embittered, which didn't suit him, and his buoyancy deserted him. His hope curdled.

He was last seen driving a grader out the back of some mining town, from where life must really have looked desolate. But what was it? Perhaps this lame streak came from beauty, from the too-thin skin of a poetic nature to which guile and pragmatism were really toxic. There was no tolerance for this kind of masculine temperament in the town. Accustomed to overlooking his own capacities, he wasn't silent or a lover of solitude - he was anxious to oblige and would enter into social intercourse at every opportunity. Being alone probably didn't suit him at all, out on that grader. He was savaged by life, it expelled him, and his misery was made to look like madness. Surely, in other times, there has been a use for the tenderness of such a romantic man?

I wish I could write a simple story, of other people's lives. But that, in the present circumstances, would not be honest. One writes like this, confessing, to draw another in. I talk to you, hoping for an answer, like waiting for the answer to a prayer. Haven't rafts of human survivors called out in distress across dark water? I believe I am not alone in this. Company is the only remedy for the metaphysical loneliness my father's town engendered.

A woman, once she becomes pregnant, can be overcome with jealousy. Jealous for her own pristine body, entangled now beyond help in another helpless life. A woman could be jealous for herself, and might experience some early moments of outrage, that something is elbowing its way into her body. It will not be the last of its claims on her.

In the womb, I was not resting. A baby is a plastic substance, yet to be extruded into human product. My gestation was a period of purer introversion than will occur again before my death. I was obliged to close my eyes and clench my fists with concentration, materialising the potential bequeathed to me in the cipher-like gene. Word made flesh.

Making myself, a Herculean labour, leaving no room for pity. I had to fight tooth and nail against the human receptacle I grew in, while living off that flesh, to be stronger for the fight with it. Parasite! The baby *in utero* is fighting for its life, and the battle is with its mother - because if you think mother and child are joined in a common enterprise you oversimplify.

How the next generation must tear itself a corner off the page that went before, mutilating the finished smoothness of the parent, throwing her beginnings and endings into doubt! Generation is the simplest of stories, the most sparse of narratives. Can you say the whole plot was scripted before the event, in that little text of a gene, in that marvellous microchip that science tells us is lodged in every fibre? Or is there some room for interpretation?

At my birth, opinion was equally divided. 'She has his eyes', 'She has her mother's mouth'. I grew to look like them both. I became a perfect condensation of them. I came to represent the square of them, and to stand for their compromise.

In the terrifying space of infancy, I am powerless, and completely dependent on a giant with a giant's strength and giant's breath. It suggests all kinds of fantasied horror. But it would be worse to be abandoned, left to shift for myself. The world is not a safe place.

There was no philosophy in my infancy. Things were on the contrary very plain and unvarnished. Uninviting surfaces. Mothers resent philosophy. The idea of a mother is of a figure of mythical potency and thorough ambivalence, domestic banality and received wisdom.

Can anything compensate the disgruntled giant for the loss of her own ends? No wonder I fear the maternal, the voracious, murderous maternal, whose resentment I can feel through the crocheted rugs and flannel rompers, in every tiny pore - and can even sympathise with, intellectually. Why would a creature willingly sacrifice for another creature, in a world where sacrifice is only used against her? And all the other things not done! The smooth, glorious plains of experience, and here she is buried under a pile of nappies, tied to a being with a moral claim so much more evident than her own.

Poor mother! The excrement of social order, the detritus of bodies, all the things she desires to forget - powerlessness, abject fear and confinement - while she and her child are imprisoned together. I remind her of herself - not the self she likes to think of, but the needy, greedy, cunning side that she abhors.

My mother, offended, said: 'When you were a baby, I often used to just stare at you in your bassinet, you were such an angel.' Yes, the child is also a wonder, a miracle, a precious fragment of herself. It is the piece that must not be lost again, the celestial, sacred part which she clasps to herself. I don't doubt the sweet anguish of a mother. Mothers glimpse in the figures of children their own lost art. This makes children seem glamorous, for a self-possession of which the adult has been robbed.

I was born to ambivalence; to me, it is mother's milk. I remember that first delirious space, which was intimate and violent. The infant's way of life is a primitivist's, and ruled by the law of the jungle. Like Hobbes's mordant portrait of the state of nature, infancy is 'solitary, poor, nasty, brutish and short.' The child brings its own nightmare into life with it; fear propels it through the first voluptuous jungle to the clearing of self-consciousness. The psychoanalyst Melanie Klein claims the infant is a delusional paranoic upon whom reality gradually impinges. The mother is part of a primal fantasy, and all objects are more representative of threat than reality. Instincts are in full sway, their aggression and their desire are as yet ungoverned. Notions of being murdered, killing and eating are commonplace and the child experiences every attempt at training and care as a violation or seduction.

My mother, unaware she was a murderous tyrant, would say shortly, 'If you do that again, I'll smack you.'

So I was born with a Machiavellian sense of things. It took persistence to prise from me my native intuition, to separate me from myself. But they wore me down, so that at last I disavowed it and gave it up. I took on the conviction that the world is a nice place. The word 'nice' was tattooed on my face, a fatigued and fatiguing smile.

'Oh, you were as good as gold', said my mother. Was I exceptionally duplicitous, doing nasty childish things behind her back? Or was I practiced at denial from an early age? Perhaps I was governed then, as now, by a powerful fear of losing love. Warns Melanie Klein: The very good child is headed for trouble. She has adopted renunciation as a solution to conflicts, but this is untenable in the long term.

The baby isn't human, it's a supernatural being. It is impossible to read its gnomic expression. The baby is sweet-smelling, even its poo and its white, curd-like vomit. A world of women and babies is as it sounds; cramped and smelling faintly of sick and other organic things. A world of food preparation, of crumbs and mashed cereal smeared on things. Stickiness. Boredom. The smell of baby soap.

The world of infancy is a world of equipment, with many instruments of confinement. I was wedged in the high chair, shut into the cot, like a Coolgardie with its cage of flywire, buckled into a harness and lead down the street. In time, I confined myself. 'Take me to bed!' I would scream in panic, because the television program was rated 'A' for adults, and I feared corruption.

Originally I was an incandescent creature, the advent of a mystery plump in the middle of everyday life. But one's star wanes. In time, another baby came and I was suddenly a whingeing little girl, who was just showing off to get attention. I was all-too human, and the baby a magus from yet another star. I was told to go and play outside.

Outside was exile, although there was a tree and a swing. I felt discarded, like a bit of paper blowing down the street. Now my mother was always taking care of the baby and I had to tiptoe around, so as not to wake it up. Babies are tyrants.

What are the features of mothers? Very large white bras. They have nappy pins in their lapels. When they have a baby to nurse, they undo their clothes and show their fatty breasts. They have smells, the many smells of mothers. Warming the milk up, bathing the baby's little head and nape of neck. The baby has frilly singlets and booties on its formless feet. It is delectable, edible. It looks like a goblin or a fairy.

Klein lays great emphasis on the primal scene in an infant reality. It provokes fearful pain and jealousy. I think of a little plastic purse I had, which was clear on one side, so that the coins inside it were visible. I was fascinated at being able to see what was in it. Klein would say the coins were babies in mummy's tummy - how many more were in there? The arrival of a new baby means less love, if love is measured in concrete terms like getting attention. The new baby is already a more successful rival.

Children know immediately the singificance of small, eye-catching details, like coins and purses. They know to extrapolate.

Sometimes my parents made to escape, as if the serious spirit of the place oppressed them, as though the elaborate meanings of the Sound had become overbearing. We went 'over east'.

In the coastal towns of the eastern seaboard, life appeared lush and relaxed. Islands did not sit in judgment, there were no forlorn bays. We would set up camp in caravan parks near ocean beaches or oyster-clad inlets, and eat fish and chips sitting at picnic tables by the running tide. Things were not missing from these places. Then, a kind of sensuality would become evident, in hot tarry roadside stops or sandy camping grounds. Rivers had mown grassed banks, and municipal furniture and shops and bridges. Whereas our river had only melaleuca scrub down to the waterline and not a soul for miles, the water draining via collapsing inlets into the inevitable sea. These escapes were in the nature of the metaphysical; to surmount by a huge effort that early childhood place of confinement and misery.

But when I mentioned the loneliness of the town to my mother, she denied it, surprised. 'Oh, we weren't lonely!' she exclaimed, as though this would have somehow discredited them. 'You had an imaginary friend, dear. Her name was Mrs Smith. I used to hear you playing with her, under the clothesline. This was in the days before they had child psychology.'

This prosaic companion was with me in the back seat of the old Peugeot, as we crossed the Nullabor plain in the week before Christmas. It was hot and flat, and the corrugations in the unsealed road caused the car to shudder, loosening the grip. Fine dust drifted into every crack and corner, and life kept up a perpetual motion, a sort of predictable insecurity, to which I was obliged to surrender.

Mrs Smith and I kept a weather eye on the world from our commanding position on top of rugs, pillows and camping gear. If Mrs Smith found conditions cramped, she didn't think to say so. But, 'Mrs Smith was wondering when we were going to get there', I reported to the front seats, leaning through the gap between them, and; 'Mrs Smith says she'd like a toffee'.

My mother would open the glovebox, releasing clouds of dust, and producing the tin of toffees her sister always lent to the expedition. 'All right, but suck this one.'

'Don't give her any more of those,' my father growled.

'Last one, then,' said my mother, pacifically, handing it back over the seat. 'For Mrs Smith.'

I ate enough toffees for both Mrs Smith and me, on the Nullabor, out of the blue tin with deers on it. In reality, I had only the baby with me in the backseat. Being in love can be quite lonely; when you are my lover only by proxy, we feast on fantasy until we are both sick. The problem with Mrs Smith was, she wasn't real. How stubbornly she failed to materialise; and how even God remained invisible.

Writes the psychoanalyst Winnicott, of imaginary friends: 'These are not simple fantasy constructions. Study of the future of these imaginary companions (in analysis) shows that they are sometimes other selves of a highly primitive type.'

In the crisp world of psychology, the imaginary easily becomes sinister. The fear no doubt is that you might leave the reality of the situation altogether, in pursuit of a beautiful ghost. It is feared that the imaginary is easier than the real, and that 'other selves' are more enticing than the ordinary people around one. Shall I leave the ground with you, my phantom, my psychotic secret, and fly around the room with a scream of delight? Or will you answer me, and bring me back to earth with a bump?

My mother and her sister were like other selves. My mother's sister was a mirror image of her; everything was the same, only the other way around. Where my mother was sure of herself, her sister was tentative and hung back; where she was impatient, her sister was quick to sympathise. 'Oh, you poor thing', she would say, with conviction.

Together they made a Greek chorus, a circle of speech out of which an emotional reality issues. If their responses seemed apparently opposed, it was because they came from a shared conviction of what life was. They knew both roles, and could play both parts. Sometimes, it was her sister who was momentarily acid, and my mother who comforted. And when it came to commentary, on other people and what was to be done or concluded, they were in complete agreement. 'Oh, yes!' 'Isn't it?'

One called, the other answered. They swore that as children they had hated each other. My aunt told stories of the shocking torture my mother used to inflict on her, because she was older and therefore could. My mother always received these allegations sentimentally, with a laugh, and confirmed what a beast she had been and what a hiding she'd been given. My aunt married a farmer, and lived out of town on a farm. My mother told her sister that she appeared to have a good life. But my aunt replied sternly, 'You were never satisfied. Someone else's grass always looked greener.

You are my imaginary friend, my ideal reader, the one to whom I address my intimate asides, and with whom I share little moments when I am alone. No-one thinks to mention how being in love is like having an imaginary friend. I carry you about with me, to witness the moments when I am at my best. You understand me; our conspiracy goes back a long way. I have invented many pasts for us and bestow upon you the promise of many futures. You are good company.

Perhaps all friends are imaginary. Said Aristotle, a friend is another self. Friendship is at least based on the supposition that you are sufficiently like me to want the same thing. I place you in the space between the comfort of solitude and the distress of loneliness. You hold my place, like a finger in a book.

We have the beginnings of intimacy, when one writes and the other reads. Would it be better to preserve a reticence between us, which we can come to love in each other? In which we can sense, in bare outline, the shape of things to come. And yet, love involves of necessity an encounter. How can I reveal myself to you, without merely exposing myself? Can I hope, in making these revelations about my history, to have shown you something of yourself?

I am ambitious for this liaison. You will be my witness, and take the reluctant confession. I mean my story to be a gift to you. More than a testament to my predicament, and a catalogue of anxieties, *I mean you to have it*. I address it to you with love. I expect it to be a burden on you, as it is on me, something given to you, in that other sense of a fate, that you may not have wanted. It is an ethical thing. I feel I must make you a present of these reflections, since they reflect on you too. If I am like I am, it is because of what you are. If I want you, it is because of what you want of me. We are bound up in each other.

It can become awkward. I don't want to force you to watch the spectacle of myself, nor could I bear to see your attention wander. You must come close enough for me to whisper in your ear. For you to enjoy the tickle of my breath on your cheek as I do so. We must be side by side, so that we only see each other partially - the whites of the eyes, the hairline - and are most aware of textures - the soft cheek, damp lips. There is no help for it. We must be lovers. This takes time.

If romance lends itself to a story, it is probably because of this proximity to time - the time it takes for the imaginary to become real. True lovers become stripped back, closer than skin to skin. As close as: history to history, innocence to innocence, faith to faith.

Going to school is the first big break with the family scene, which has been the little citizen's whole world until then. But the child must now replace the indulgent, partisan, unreliable attentions of mother, father and siblings with the relentless, continuous indifferent pressure of civic authority. In an influential psychoanalytic paper, on 'The Role of the School in the Libidinal Development of the Child', Melanie Klein reflects on first encounters with writing instruments and the regimentation of learning. She notices the context in which, for the child, these inevitably take place, going through the looking glass, into a public world.

In the classroom at the Infants' School, the letters of the alphabet were printed on laminated cards and strung along the tall south-facing windows. The room was always in a kind of gloaming. The walls were partly lined with dark jarrah planks, and the floorboards were the same dark colour. This - and the eerie realms of things yet to be known, presaged in those letters - gave the classroom a haunted quality.

The classroom held other fears, and the risk of humiliation. There were reprimands for talking in class, and the punishment was having to sweep the deep verandahs with a giant's broom. There was a peg in the washroom which had my name beside it, looking stiff and unfamiliar. My raincoat was lost among many others in the forest of pegs. I was one among many.

In my mind now, the school has a gothic grace. Nothing in it was simply there; it was never reduced to a front path lined with rose bushes, or a mere corridor ending in glass doors, for everything was charged with feeling. Like animists, we gave to those objects all the meanings of the terrifying encounters with the public world, and each object was imbued with dread, with exaggerated glamour and the fear of one's insignificance. The architecture was daunting - dark wood, high ceilings, long windows, all much larger than a child's scale and authoritarian and remote.

I was touched when it was pointed out to me that they had provided child-sized desks and chairs for us, since it showed that they realised that children were a smaller body size. It showed that they had made a close study of children. But the concession did not reassure me, because they had not modified the other features of the rooms, and there was nothing domestic or homely in the chilly brick buildings. I was forced to conclude they intended that the rest of the place should intimidate us.

I don't remember the other boys and girls as clearly as I remember stationery. The crayons with new points, in their red box; the counters pushed out of perforated card. All these things were proof of a strange institutional generosity, with which I remain fascinated. They gave you things. The books, the crayons at the beginning of term, we received as presents. How else could we think of them, so deliciously new-smelling? The coloured plasticine, the paints, were toys masquerading as work.

Education itself was a gift from an unlikely, unfriendly source. Gradually I learned that institutions could be said to love you, in their way. They loved you for yourself - anyone could drink the school milk which was provided in small child-bottles (even the children who came on the bus from Ellicker). No doubt, this free milk every morning first persuaded me of the value of democracy. I went from fear at the impersonality of the school, to a kind of gratitude for being entitled to certain things merely by virtue of being in a system. It seemed almost naive on the part of the school, as though a lofty father couldn't see what a little minx his daughter was, what a rotten brat his son.

The roses growing in a bed in the front yard of this school led all the way from gate to door. They were pink and red. At the gateway to the public world, small proofs of love. The credulous blind generosity, shown me by schools and other public institutions, has continued to be a blessed relief from sticky personal intimacies.

The desire for magic led me to keep a fairy in a box. While books gave a sense of being in company with others, playing alone at the beach reinforced solipsism. Playing alone, it seemed nearly possible that there was a fairy in the dark cavity of the shoebox, and she would be revealed by carefully lifting the lid. She was naturally too quick for me. I took my occasional friends onto the sandhills behind the beach, however, and swore them to secrecy about it. They, too, tried hard to believe.

Sometimes, if I was playing alone on the sandhill, I would look out across the bay and believe I could fly, like Aslan in the Narnia books, over the sea. I would have gathered all the islands to me, like the Shepherd gathers His flock. How persistent is the belief in fairies! What else is the personal God, the hope for the resurrection?

This meditation is predicated on you, on the chance that you might hear. Am I keeping a fairy in a box? Or can I hope that at the surface of my words, a film can form, like the skin on milk. For you to lick up, my love. Some children hate the skin on milk, or custard, and other liminal things, but I know you are not squeamish like this.

What pleasure was suitable for children? Children were allowed to eat and to read. But the books on the bookshelf, seemingly so innocent, were in reality dangerous. They created worlds of wish-fulfilment for which I will not forgive them. Even as a child, my guilty pleasure in reading showed I was aware these fictional worlds were narcotics for the insufficiency of my own boring afternoons. I knew their satisfaction was phantasmic, and not real, while I wished passionately to believe that there was a world possible in which trees grew cream buns, or where gold keys opened onto rooms of treasure. How seductive I found those worlds to be! How alarming to notice as an adult that they still shape my expectations.

When we were very young, it was the dainty world of Christopher Robin, a world of artless cheer and harmless grief. Nothing more serious than loathing rice pudding. 'Oh, *what* is the matter with Mary Jane? She's perfectly well and she hasn't a pain and it's lovely rice pudding for dinner again ... ' The dry wit of the English was not considered wasted on children, for which I am grateful. Character was never inconsequential, and yet no one need ever be taken seriously. Life was preserved in its romantic eccentricity, a secure world where idiosyncracy was not frowned on.

But the world of Winnie-the-Pooh was a harsh one of natural selection, in its way. The donkey was depressed, as donkeys might be, since objectively they were awkward animals. Though Owl was wise, it was a bear of little brain who was best loved. So it seemed that life, in as much as it had a point, was pointless and unfair. Winnie-the-Pooh fostered fatalism and apathy.

From Enid Blyton, I learned to force cheerfulness, and to insist on a happy ending. An Enid Blyton story wouldn't leave life alone, as Winnie-the-Pooh might, nor let the chips fall where they may. Instead, a communal concern was taken over morals in the Upper Fourth, and Muriel was always a 'brick' for not 'ratting'. Friendship was its highest endeavour, the sensible hockey-playing kind that showed quick sympathy in a hand-squeeze and some brisk advice to 'buck up'. Introspection was not encouraged, unless it was the kind that inspected conscience and found there the right thing to do. This world of loyalty and decency was a serious misrepresentation, then as now, encouraging expectations of justice and equality that could only be disappointed. Enid Blyton was a poor preparation for life.

And what of the Narnia chronicles? Of all the hard-cover volumes, their spines now fading and the gold lettering effaced, these were the most treacherous. They were the most beautiful. C.S. Lewis proposed worlds of wonder, where life was ruled by deep magic. There was a cold black-and-white forest at the back of the wardrobe, while the sea at the end of the world became shallower, greener and clearer as they waded. Narnia was not a safe world - it was often perilous - but it was meaningful, and nothing happened in Narnia that didn't have metaphysical significance. Narnia was full of signs, subtle, divine, of good and evil. It was all underwritten by the passion the story cherished for its hero, Aslan the Lion-Messiah.

Aslan came across the sea, and his warm breath carried children across the sea. He wasn't vanquished by the violent execution ordered by the Witch, despite being flesh and blood. He was resurrected.

Narnia books were too potent for children, for they engendered such strong desire for virtue, truth and beauty I doubt it could ever be requited. From the Narnia books, I learned to prize meaning above anything. I was taught that, however terrible, life might at least be understood. And isn't that the frailest hope I hold? To inculcate in children the pessimism of Milne, the social justice of Blyton, and the faith of Lewis, is to develop in them a propensity for disillusionment.

On the Nullabor, there was no shade, except what was created under the galvanised iron at Ivy Tanks. Ivy Tanks represented a kind of purgatory, a transit camp between worlds. The tanks were filled from a bore, which was driven by a windmill that clanked in the wind. My father filled the canvas water bag that hung on the grille of the car. He drank out of it. He topped up the radiator from it, to prevent the car overheating.

In the driving conditions on the Nullabor this was always likely. The Peugeot, my father boasted, was to be found at one time on safari all over the French deserts of North Africa. Almost certainly, then, it was to be found halted near a tree with the bonnet up and steam escaping. The cap must be taken off a boiling radiator with great care, to avoid violent jets of rusty water spewing all over the bush mechanic. Water should be added with the engine running, being careful not to crack the head. Anxiety clouded the temperature gauge as it pushed up into the red.

Overheating was more than a frustration entailing delay, expense and recrimination. It was like a malaise the car developed, or a sort of madness that came upon it. Out there on the Nullabor you were a long way from help. In the noon of a hot day, it was impossible to imagine relief. Overheating was a fear of any extravagance of passion that could not be satisfied, fear of how it would make life intolerable to want so badly and not to receive. It was fear of burning, unrequited, and of thirsting for things that could only be found as mirages in that desolate place. This is a fear of one's own daring, a dread of aspiration. I have learned that there are places other than that parched one, where you can slake thirst. What looks imaginary from Ivy Tanks- the ambitious mirage - can be real elsewhere.

My parents' life together seems, in hindsight, lonely, simple and unsatisfied. But I inherited their circumstances as eternal verities, instead of as they were - impermanent periods of transition in the story of long and complicated adult lives.

There came a time when they ran out of road. On the Nullabor, the January heat was unrelieved. My father had no intellectual objection to offer, because he could not refute the proposition that they were not happy. He knew it to be true. It was only that it seemed to render a lifetime of other propositions redundant. What did it mean, for example, for the vow he had made, 'forsaking all others, to cleave only unto you'? He waited for God to speak, but he heard only silence.

It was concluded just beyond Ivy Tanks, at a place stripped back to the bare minimum: sun, dirt, horizon. 'Let us pray', said my father, to his tiny congregation, and he dropped his head into his hands. But what could we pray for? That He would will the deconsecration of this marriage, the decommissioning of an ideal? That He should approve this loss, even the forcible extraction, of a faith? No.

Strange, though, how the night that followed seemed to be a blanket, thrown around shoulders in rough comfort. The stars came out, and I identified the constellation, the Southern Cross, strung on a rosary of several million stars.

'I don't think I can go to Sunday School any more', I said, speaking as a realist. 'I don't think I believe in God.'

No more trailing down the gravel shoulder of the highway to the red brick hall alongside the church and next to Wesfarmers. The spines and quills of the farm machinery could be seen from the window, behind the cyclone fence. No more handing out the guides to Bible study and tracking down the sickly-sweet authority of pious scripture, my first scholarship. Never more to feel the simple fellowship at beach camp, singing 'Be present at our table, Lo-ord; God is love' and meaning it.

Much like the moment, several years later, when my boyfriend and I were kissing in the car in the driveway. 'Come in, please,' my father called, from the front door. His broken form was sanctified by the halo of porch light, an impotent angel. 'Go away,' I called back. And he went. That night only confirmed my loneliness.

But what woman wants to be a law unto herself? I read Nietzsche; truth is hard, error is cowardice. Oh my beautiful God-Father, my heart weeps inconsolably for you. Come back! I will obey! But the damage was done.

My scepticism had overborne that faith, like paper wrapping around stone. But still occasionally a line from a hymn came upon me, like a saboteur. Always sung, with a poignancy that can't be got rid of. Scissors cut paper. Faith is a habit not easily unlearned. Stone blunts scissors. I began to believe in love.

Tony Birch

Ashes

When my grandmother died, just two days before her ninetieth birthday, she was buried with her husband, Liam Cochran. He had killed himself forty-five years before her own death. Therefore my grandmother was to spend half of her life with my grandfather as a memory she lived with each day.

My grandfather had slipped away quietly one morning while my grandmother slept peacefully in their bed. He walked across the hallway into the bathroom and gently closed the door behind him before removing his underwear and folding it over a wooden chair in the corner. He then knelt over the bath and cut his throat, 'so not as to create a mess on the floor' a coroner's investigation later surmised.

Liam's suicide was regarded as sufficient a crime to deny my grandmother access to his life insurance. In a state of anger, sadness and disbelief she took to the task of raising her young daughter, finding paid work during the day and spending her nights alone at the kitchen table. Without fail Sunday morning was spent at Liam's graveside, both cursing him and desperately searching for his touch once more.

She had pre-paid for a double plot at the Royal Victoria Cemetery so that she could lie with Liam again when her time came. She often reminded me of their impending reunion when I went with her to the cemetery where she tended the flower-bed covering Liam's grave. Her loyalty and love for Liam remained unchallenged for close to a decade until she met and fell in love with Jack O'Hea, a local scrap metal dealer who charmed my grandmother during negotiations over the sale of a queen-size brass bed. After a long courtship Jack eventually moved in to her neat two-storey terrace, nominally as a boarder.

Why my grandmother failed to be open about her relationship with Jack I am not sure. She could have married him if she'd wanted to. There was no need for a divorce. And no real scandal. But if she ever considered doing so she never mentioned it to anyone.

Most issues with her and Jack had an element of secrecy attached to them. We were never sure why that was so. But I now know that it was out of the guilt she carried with her from sleeping with a man other than her own husband, even after he was a long time in the ground. As she was so certain that she would one day be reunited with my grandfather my grandmother suffered the sin of adultery from the day that she took Jack O'Hea into her home. Her visits to Liam's grave allowed her to remain loyal to him while not denying herself the need to live a life other than that of an eternal widow. When I was around five years old I went to live in my grandmother's house with my own mother. I had no father to speak of. My mother had never discussed him with me and without knowing why I did know enough not to ask who he was or where he had gone. I had heard occasional quiet comments in the presence of various relatives that I had been some sort of 'accident'. I misinterpreted this as indicating that my father, whoever he was, had been the victim of a disaster that had killed him.

I enjoyed my grandmother's house. I loved the sounds of voices and footsteps moving up and down the stairway. It made my mother happy also, to be home with her mother after several years of living in stark government housing flats with no family.

I was happy there, with my mother, grandmother and Jack, particularly Jack. He would spend each evening in the brick laundry in my grandmother's yard scrubbing the grime that had attached itself to his overalls during the day. He would then polish his work boots until his reflection appeared in the toes before washing and shaving himself in a small wooden-framed mirror that hung above the laundry trough.

In warm weather Jack would sit underneath the peach tree in the corner of the yard wearing pressed trousers and a white undershirt while reading the evening paper and smoking roll-your-own cigarettes. When it was cooler, particularly during the winter months he would sit in his room looking out through the window that faced into the back garden. He kept very much to himself, never going to the pub after work and he only drank alcohol on special occasions, such a Christmas or christenings.

Jack would often bring stuff home that he had collected from empty houses; toys that he would repair and repaint and then present to me, comic-books, old tennis balls and once a full-size leather football, scuffed and darkly bruised with age and wear, but a real football none the less.

I was fascinated by Jack's habit of taking tobacco from a tin and rubbing it vigorously between his palms before rolling what he called a 'whippet', a slim, neat cigarette that he would light and smoke with purpose between his orange-brown nicotine-stained fingers.

I would sit under the tree watching Jack roll and smoke cigarette after cigarette. And each night my grandmother would come into the yard and give him a cup of tea with the standard formalities.
'There you are, Jack', she would comment seemingly disinterested as she placed the cup in his hand, 'a good day on the road?'

It was the same question every evening, absent of any familiarity. They appeared suitably distanced from each other, playing the roles of landlady and tenant. But there was much contained in this exchange. My grandmother could have easily placed the cup on the upturned fruit-box alongside Jack's cigarette tin. But she didn't. As she handed him the tea-cup they would touch with a briefness that made the gesture hardly detectable. But it was there, in the near smile on her face before she withdrew again into the kitchen.

I slept in a small room between the kitchen and Jack's room. He would read each night until very late before turning off the light and sneaking past my room, through the kitchen to my grandmother's bedroom at the front of the house.

This was the pattern of their relationship for 15 years or more. And it would have remained so for longer had Jack not begun to cough his lungs up most nights after he had finished smoking under the tree. It got so bad that he finally went into the hospital, coming home two weeks later with a piece of paper in his suit-coat pocket informing my grandmother that he had only six months to live.

One morning, soon after Jack came home my grandmother, who was in the kitchen making breakfast, asked my mother to take Jack's tea and toast into his bed. My mother picked up the tray and began to walk out of the kitchen toward the back of the house.

'No love', my grandmother called to her, 'he's up in my room.'

Nothing more was said.

And it was in my grandmother's bed that Jack remained for the next months before he died. Sometimes, when the weather was particularly good he would pull on his dressing gown and sit under the peach tree slowly rubbing, rolling and puffing as I watched transfixed as ever. But for much of the time, particularly in the final month or so of his life Jack stayed up in her room listening to the radio or sleeping.

In the final days of his life a doctor who had visited him each week advised my grandmother that she move Jack to hospital. But he did not want to leave her at all now and stayed in her bed until the moment he died.

I did not see him at all during the last weeks of his life. I was kept out of the bedroom. On the day of his death I arrived home from school as Jack's body was carried out of the house by two ambulance officers who had been called when he had stopped breathing.

His body was shrouded beneath a sheet. As they went by me I could see Jack's hand hanging limply from the stretcher, with his darkly stained fingers close enough to touch. My final memories of him are of those fingers and the eyrie sight of the ambulance disappearing out of the street with the two heavily tinted rear windows resembling the large black eyes of some sort of mechanical monster. I did not go to his funeral but I knew there was an argument between my grandmother and Jack's family over the burial arrangements. His family wanted Jack cremated, which to my grandmother was an act of horror. They won the argument as she had no legal rights to Jack's body.

So a little more than a month after his death a small brown parcel arrived at my grandmother's house. I noticed it sitting on the kitchen table and looked at it for some time before picking it up and shaking it in order to ascertain what was inside. It rattled with a dull thud. My grandmother, who had been in the garden came into the kitchen as I was holding the box to my ear.

'Put that down', she yelled at me with surprising anger.

I quickly returned the box to the table-top but continued to stare at it.

She immediately felt bad for yelling at me.

'Sorry, sorry', she whispered. 'It's just that Jack's in there, in the box. Don't shake him too hard.'

Overcome with fear I pulled back from the table.

'Don't be frightened, love. He can't hurt you. Never hurt a fly when he was alive, Jack, so he's in no condition to do any damage now.'

She looked at me again as she picked up the brown paper parcel from the table and placed it on the shelf above the kitchen stove.

'He can stay up there while I fix tea.'

And there Jack stayed, for many years, wedged between the tea caddy and a spice set that my grandmother had bought at a church fete but never got around to using. I knew it was only Jack's ashes that sat up there but with my grandmother's words 'Jack's in there' revisiting me from time to time I often thought of him being trapped in that box.

This created its own haunting and a profound sense of fear about death more generally. I could not sit in the kitchen without looking up at Jack and becoming anxious. My mother was particularly uncomfortable about his ashes sitting on the kitchen shelf and suggested that my grandmother find Jack a more suitable resting place.

'One of those lawn cemeteries, mum. You can have your ashes in the ground, with a plaque over the top, and a sort of vase buried in the ground to arrange your flowers. There's one out near the airport. Looks real neat and tidy. Better than the Victoria, all the broken headstones and weeds. Bloody morbid place.'

'It's a cemetery. It's supposed to be morbid. It's not a fun parlour. Nothing wrong with where you father is, nothing.'

She looked at my mother with real pain on her face before turning to Jack.

'And Jack, he's not doing any harm up there. Bury his ashes? That's a joke, a real joke. I wanted him buried before all this but they wouldn't have it. No. But they were to mean to pay for anything more than the postage to have him sent here through the post. What a joke. He's staying here, up there. He's happy there.'

My mother attempted to reply, apologetically I think, but my grandmother had already left the kitchen and walked into the yard. My mother gave up and walked through the house and out into the street. I sat at the table looking up at the shelf above the stove wondering if Jack O'Hea would really be happy next to the tea-caddy. While she was in that house Jack's ashes rarely moved from their home on my grandmother's kitchen shelf. Occasionally she would take everything down for a dust but Jack would quickly be put back in his place once the cleaning was done. She sometimes spoke of purchasing Jack a more formal resting place and even mail-ordered a brochure from a funeral company displaying an array of urns, both ornate and austere. But she never got around to doing anything but leaving him where he was.

But Jack was not neglected. In fact in addition to talking about Jack more openly to others after he died, my grandmother spoke more and more to Jack and less to others around her. My mother and I moved out and into a flat around the corner from my grandmother just before I was to begin High School. My mother felt that I needed more space and privacy so as I could do my homework. This seemed pointless to me as I never did homework and did not take up the habit once I started High School.

While we were at my grandmother's I watched cartoons on television most nights after school and when I wasn't doing that I played football. My mother worked at a newsagency in town until closing time so she did not know if I was doing any work or not. And after we moved to the flat I continued to have tea at my grandmother's each night and she never bothered me about homework at all. I helped her with the crossword of a night and that was enough for her.

While we were siting at the table or if she was at the sink doing the vegetables she would be talking away to Jack as much as she talked to me.

'They knocked over Tilley's today Jacko. No one bothered to strip the place. Lead, copper, the lot, all gone. Bulldozed everything and shovelled it onto the back of a truck.'

She would be doing the dishes after we had finished eating.

'Ran into Solly today', she would inform Jack, 'he hasn't worked for six months. His hip is gone, getting up and down, up and down from the truck. Wants an operation, but he can't afford it.'

She would look up at the parcel and pause for a moment as if waiting for or listening to Jack's reply.

I was happy enough to listen to her one-way conversations and as she got older I imagined her relationship with Jack to be amusingly eccentric and evidence of mild and harmless dementia as her memory faded.

As her more open attachment to Jack grew my grandmother visited Liam's grave a little less. It seemed that with both Liam and Jack both dead she was able to find a balance in her relationship with the two of them, absent of her earlier sense of guilt.

I continued to visit her each week after I had left home myself. One night as we sat at the table while she announced the race results to Jack, I patronisingly asked her what he said to her in reply to her comments.

She looked at me curiously.

'What are you on about? What you mean?'

I knew immediately that I had asked the wrong question but mistakenly assumed that this was the result of her being embarrassed about hearing voices or some form of forgetfulness.

'Doesn't matter, Nan.'

'Oh yes, it matters. What do you mean, what is Jack saying?'

She looked up at the parcel, seemingly astonished.

I stumbled for words.

'Jack ... um ... Jack', I pointed to him, 'what does Jack say, you know ... you know ... when you ... ah ... talk?'

'Talk? Talk?'

She began to laugh, almost hysterically.

'Talk! Don't be silly, love. Jack's dead. Dead as a door-nail. He don't talk to no one. I talk. I miss him so I talk to him. But he don't talk back. Don't be silly.'

She sat back in her chair and continued to laugh.

In the weeks before my grandmother's death she was admitted to hospital, suffering great pain as a result of kidney failure. She was incoherent for much of the time but knew enough of what was going on to ask a request of me. I had been siting in an armchair next to her bed as she slept. I was watching the evidence of my grandmother's life appear in the regular blips and lights of the electronic heart monitor.

She called to me weakly.

'Love ... love.'

I moved toward the bed.

'Jack's ashes. You know where they are?'

Of course I did. I thought that she was going to ask me to bring Jack into the hospital to be with her.

'When it's over . . . when I go you let Jack rest there with us. Put his ashes in there with us. Liam won't be too happy about it but he'll have to get used to it. Please.'

On the day my grandmother was buried the sun was shining. The open grave was surrounded by a mound of clay. The gravediggers had generously removed the plants from the garden that my grandmother had lovingly attended to for many years. The plants were temporarily placed in pots so that they could be replanted later.
Her coffin slotted neatly into the hole and was gently eased down to where Liam's bones were lying somewhere below.

Just before the gravediggers and their shovels began to go to work I unwrapped the aged brown paper that surrounded the cheap plastic sealed container that had housed Jack for so many years. I leaned forward before letting his ashes rain down gently and knock on the lid of my grandmother's coffin.

I now tend their garden-bed and often take my children with me. They play among the laneways of graves and look into the faces of the photographs of the dead, mounted on the black marble headstones in the Italian section, their gold-lettered inscriptions documenting life and death.

As I weed and water I think of the three of them down there together, with the bones of my grandparents and the ashes of Jack O'Hea fusing together, to become one.

When I leave the cemetery my two young daughters ask me many questions in their curious innocence.

'Is this where the dead people live? Do they sleep here? Do they get wet and cold when it rains?'

We drive slowly out through the overbearingly ornate cemetery gates.

'Dad, do they talk to each other, all the people here? What do they say? Do they talk to each other down there in the ground?'

Daniel Brown

Norma Desmond as star-sign: Being and being seen in Billy Wilder's *Sunset Boulevard*

Norma Desmond, the pivotal figure around which *Sunset Boulevard* (Wilder, Paramount US, 1950) turns, lives and kills in accordance with the ideology of the Hollywood star: "No one leaves a star. That makes one a star." But she also puts her faith in the stars in another sense. Astrology determines Norma in her big decisions to employ Joe Gillis, and to send her film script of *Salome* to Cecil B. De Mille on a particular day: "De Mille is Leo. I'm Scorpio. Mars has been transitting Jupiter for weeks. Today is the day of greatest conjunction." For Norma Hollywood stars have a mythic status and destiny akin to the star signs of astrology and the titanic movements of the planets it interprets. The mythic ideology of the star defines her character, and she voices its dicta to herself in low tones as sibylline utterances: "Great stars have great pride."[1] Indeed she expands this ideology into an entire world that she inhabits. It merges with the deterministic cosmology of astrology to furnish a tragic fatalistic universe, one which both clashes and coalesces with that inhabited by the screen-writer Joe Gillis, the film's star-crossed lover.

From the time she first enters the film, looking down on Joe from her balcony through her dark-glasses and a bamboo blind, the ex-silent screen star Norma Desmond has the prerogative of sight. She is identified with sight and wants to be its object on her own terms. She articulates this desire in the filmscript of *Salome*, which she writes as a star vehicle for herself that is meant to re-launch her career. It is based upon Oscar Wilde's 1892 play *Salome*, the first version of the story to include the Dance of the Seven Veils. Wilde's play articulates Norma's fantasy of being constantly looked at and of being begged to perform again. Most of the characters in the play are obsessed with looking at Salome, including Herod ("I have looked at thee and ceased not this night"[2]), who pleas with her to dance for him, promising her anything she wants in return. Salome is in turn obsessed with looking at Iokanaan's body (much as in the film Norma maintains an interest in Joe's body), and in exchange for performing the Dance of the Seven Veils receives Iokanaan's decapitated head on a platter.

Wilder knew Wilde's play from his early days in Vienna, in Hedwig Lachmann's abridged translation for the libretto of Strauss's opera *Salome*, while his co-writer and the director of the film, Charles Brackett, the theatre critic for *The New Yorker* from 1926–8, would also have known it as a young man, probably in the original French. The choice and use of Wilde's *Salome* as the ground for Norma's filmscript (and character) signals the film's self-conscious interest in aesthetics, identifying the ground of this star with the *fin de siecle* ideology of "Art for Art's sake" as well as making the related observation that the type of the vampish female silent star can be traced to the stylised theatricality established by the play and more particularly by Sarah Bernhardt, for whom Wilde apparently wrote the play. Salome is identified from the start of the play with the moon, forming a composite identity with it which is figured as dead, "a woman rising from a tomb" and predatory, "like a mad woman, a mad woman who is seeking everywhere for lovers," as well as "looking for dead things."[3] Such analogies establish Salome's identity as the *femme fatale*, and by extension furnish a gloss for Norma's characterisation as the vamp who shades into the vampire. The moon is dead in the sense that it draws its light, its semblance of life, from the sun's light. It is a decadent vampiric symbol of art as parasitically drawing its life from an external source, absorbing and reflecting light from other bodies, from the living audience. Norma Desmond's stardom is like the moon – she is like a dead star which gains its semblance of life from another light source – the light of the projector as it pierces her "celluloid self."[4]

Norma is identified with photographic stasis, fixed in a past age like the ubiquitous pictures that memorialise her and make a misnomer of the "living room" which contains them. But this room is also a cinema, and its transcendent images of Norma, like the vampire she is likened to by critics of the film,[5] assume a semblance of life only in the darkness. If, as Roland Barthes argues, photographs function as *memento mori*,[6] then the moving pictures that share their silence-of-the-grave have the ontological ambiguity of the Undead. Norma Desmond's "living room" of silent pictures privileges stillness over movement. This is clear from the rather impassive motion picture footage from *Queen Kelly* that she shows, but also from the sequence which precedes this screening. In this scene the camera pans over the framed photographs on the long table and the piano, – ". . . a gallery of photographs in various frames – all Norma Desmond . . ." "More Norma Desmond and still more Norma Desmond,"[7] – it pans over them as if to deconstruct the illusory movement of the cinematic image itself, which occurs when photographic images, "frames," are presented to the eye at the more rapid rate of twenty-four per second (as they are in the screening that immediately follows this sequence). The static image is prior to the moving image here, and indeed stillness is at the heart of the moving image of Norma's profile in the footage from *Queen Kelly*, just as it is in the arrested temporality of her Miss Havisham-like existence within the house. The face of the star shines in an eternal stasis – "Stars are ageless, aren't they?" – and is, as the footage from *Queen Kelly* and Norma's final closeup serve to highlight, sustained by its repeated presence on the screen: "You see, this is my life. It always will be."[8] The protensity of cinema is reduced to the melancholy and futureless stillness of the photograph.[9]

Norma Desmond enacts this paradox of stillness within movement through her characteristic circling gestures and poses which arch around the still aloof point of her face, a face that is veiled, made-up and later treated by "an army of beauty experts"[10] to correspond to the idealised static form that is enshrined within the living room. Throughout *Sunset Boulevard* Norma's character, her cinematic being, is defined imagistically by such circling motifs. Early in the film, Joe observes that "she sat coiled up like a watch-spring,"[11] the cramped gothic claw of her hand turned in on itself and her body. In other scenes she arches her arms above her head, or around Joe's head or body. Other circling movements associated with her include the spinning umbrellas and walking sticks of the "Norma Desmond Follies," and the recursive circling of her tangos (both without and with Joe) and the flourishes of her hands. The rolling exotic arabesques of Norma's musical theme, which Franz Waxman based upon the tango, rush in to meet her distinctive personal choreography in the New Year's Eve party and subsequent scenes. Originating in the physical expressivism and grace required of the silent star, her poses and gestures now enact Norma's self-enclosure within her nostalgic fantasies and the house on Sunset Boulevard. They emblematise her closed world, like the hermetic economy of the fan-letters and the picture signings with which she answers them, a short-circuit engineered by her protective servant Max Von Mayerling. Norma's circling movements and poses are both an aggressive occupation of space, a symbolic marking out of the larger subjectivity that belongs to the *arch*-star ("the greatest of them all"), and a defensive buffer to preserve the fragile being at its core from the outside world. They are in effect the Seven Veils – multiple, softening and obscuring, barriers to external reality – movements which gesture toward her incarnation as Salome at the close of the film.

The camera that Norma gestures toward in her final closeup vindicates her self-identity as the star. The camera lens offers to Norma her reflected image, her double, much as its surrogate does, the mirror that she becomes increasingly obsessed with toward the end of the film and at which she sits "staring at herself blankly"[12] before the staircase scene. It is the gateway to "all those wonderful people out there," who she reaches with the reflected images of herself that the camera records. As a dead star Norma shines with a light that is not her own; she comes to reflexive self-consciousness of herself only through the eyes of others, through the recognition of the audience and her fans. This crucial relationship between Norma and her audience is demonstrated through the forged fan-letters, which she answers by signing photographs of her face. The letters provide Norma with objective recognitions of herself as the star, a reflected image that becomes concrete in the form of the photographs that she is called upon by her "fans" to reaffirm and authenticate with her signature. As she directs her gaze in the final closeup toward the ambiguous space of the camera she replicates and fulfils this image of herself. Both Salome and Narcissus, Norma gestures toward the reflection of her own head arrayed on the convex platter of the camera lens by which it will be eventually delivered up (via the analogous lens of the projector) to her public. While Joe Gillis, insofar as he has been recently killed in accordance with the will of the heroine, corresponds to Iokanaan, he is forgotten by Norma in the final scenes: it is not his head that she is dancing for here, and moving towards as if to kiss, but her own – the image of the star that she imagines her audience identifies with. The only images of decapitation that the film presents are the pictures, photographs and footage of Norma's static and aloof face; her various closeups. The ultimate object of her passion, "her celluloid self,"[13] is like that of Wilde's Salome, fixed as in death.

Norma Desmond's circling, obsessive stasis is the key to her abstract cinematic being. Her hand and arm movements, which are most clearly articulated in the closing scenes, are centripetal, self-enfolding. Such movements suggest a vortex as they gesture around the still centre of her face. The close of the film marks, as Joe observes, Norma's apotheosis: "The dream she had clung to so desperately had enfolded her . . ."[14] The definitive gesture of self-enfoldment through which Norma articulated and defended her dream of stardom has swallowed her up. The film ends with her sublime dissolve into the stillness at the centre of the vortex of her movements, the heart of light that constitutes the star. With this final nihilistic dissolve it is as if Norma enters the aperture of the camera lens and collapses it into unfocused light. Her being is reverberantly spectral, like that which the Young Syrian ascribes to Salome in Wilde's play: "She is like the shadow of a white rose in a mirror of silver."[15]

Norma is characterised by *kenosis*, a complete emptying or lack of an original selfhood, a capacious absence or hollowness that provides the foundation for an entirely artificial selfhood, so that the fulfillment, the complete presence and expression, of her character occurs with the mad scene at the close of the film, when she becomes the composite Star-Salome figure. Like Wilde, she understands that selfhood is not original and innate but something that has to be created. The paradigm for selfhood in *Salome*, as elsewhere in Wilde, is art. Iokanaan's body is transmuted by Salome's words into jewel encrusted statuary: "Thy mouth is like a branch of coral that fishers have found in the twilight of the sea, the coral that they keep for the kings!," "Thy body was a column of ivory set upon feet of silver."[16] Similarly, the structured and shaped eroticism of the Dance of the Seven Veils that Herod demands of Salome furnishes the full expression of her being, after which she is killed.

Norma regards her self as an object of artifice, not only through the meticulous and individualistic clothing she wears, but more radically in the way she subjects herself to "a merciless series of treatments, massages, seat cabinets, mud baths, ice compresses, electric devices"[17] in order to hone her image as the "ageless" star. Such gestures of self-mastery are discussed by Michel Foucault in his late works, where he sees them as the model for the independent creation of selfhood. He traces the principle of self-mastery to the classical Greeks, arguing that such rulers as Nicocles based their political authority upon the austerity with which they formed themselves as ethical subjects.[18] Self-rule is a precondition for the rule of others here, much as Norma's self-disciplining as the star is understood by her as the precondition for her capacity to hold sway over her fans: "they want to see me, me, me! Norma Desmond."[19] Her creation of herself through her beauty regime, her circling gestures, and the screenplay she writes for herself are all directed towards her ultimate incarnation as the princess Salome, a figure of the star as a female oriental potentate who will, she believes, exercise power not only over Max and Joe but a vast constituency of fans.

Norma moves from her position of self-mastery to mastering Joe. Rather like Wilde's Salome, who through her words transforms Iokanaan's ascetic body into a work of art, Norma treats Joe as raw material, as a body to shape and enhance. As Iokanaan to her Salome, Joe is for Norma primarily of aesthetic and erotic interest. She appears to retain him as an ornament languishing on sofas or "on a rubber mattress in the pool." Norma towels Joe's back after his swim, and elsewhere admires the way that the shape of this back, enhanced by the clothes she chose for him to wear on New Year's Eve, describes a "V from his shoulders to his hips": "Perfect. Wonderful shoulders. And I love that line." She likes to dress him up and wants to embellish him with "Nice big pearls."[20] Whether as a clotheshorse or an accessory to melodrama, Joe is consistently constructed and construed aesthetically by Norma as the surrogate leading man. She domesticates him to fit in with her visual aesthetic, drawing him away from his dynamic aesthetic of narrative to incorporate him within her static world. Of course, when he reasserts his independence towards the end of the film, Norma shoots him, and his body falls back into the swimming pool, arresting and completing the narrative trajectory that defines him.

Death transforms Joe into a de facto star, bathed in liquid light and accosted by gawping crowds and the flash bulbs which grimly preserve and multiply his image ("They must have photographed me a hundred times"[21]), thereby furnishing a macabre set of photographic portraits to parallel those which comprise Norma's shrine to herself in the "living room." Joe's static image supersedes his life here as "Photographers' bulbs flash in rapid succession"[22] over his corpse. He is captured and contained within his transparent medium here, much as the photographs of Norma are held in their frames by the more reluctant liquidity of glass. Norma "stands exultant in the strange light from the pool" after shooting Joe, seeing both herself and her lover now to be "ageless" together, united in a sort of *liebestod*. Joe, who a few minutes earlier rejected the clothing and jewelry with which Norma had tried to make him her leading man, telling her that he doesn't "qualify for the job,"[23] is fixed resolutely within her world. He has undergone the Hollywood equivalent of a "seachange," with the agelessness of stardom furnishing a parallel myth to the aesthetic deathlessness of poetry, as if he were cinema's answer to Milton's Lycidas. Parallel to the aestheticism of Wilde's *Salome*, in which Iokanaan is both killed as a result of Salome's words and transformed by them into everliving art, Norma completes her aesthetic mastery of Joe by killing him. From this point she assumes a purely cinematic being, which is emblematised by the copious glitter that covers her clothes and face in the final scene as she descends the staircase as Salome. Norma's being, this detached and delusive play of light, corresponds to what Foucault refers to as "the sparkle of the outside," which he locates at "the very core of language"[24] in late nineteenth-century literature. The effect of these "spangles" is to literally highlight Norma's aesthetic autonomy from interiority, a depthlessness that is parallelled in the use of language in Wilde's *Salome*, where words generate and play upon the surface, uninterested in the possibilities of substance or positivist fact. Like Wilde's Salome performing the Dance of the Seven Veils, Norma is as the composite figure of the Star-Salome pure spectacle, art that is the antithesis to life: "The spectacle in general, as the concrete inversion of life, is," as Guy Debord defines it, "the autonomous movement of the non-living."[25]

For the Foucault of the second and third volumes of *The History of Sexuality*, the self is not simply formed through his earlier reductive categories of power and knowledge, but has some agency through what he calls the process of "subjectivation," which Deleuze defines as "the relation to oneself." This is why the Greek principle of self-mastery is so important to Foucault, because it allows him to see force not simply as something that is exercised from outside in acts of subjection, but as something which a self can choose to fold back upon itself in order to form its own subjectivity. "The most general formula of the relation to oneself is," Deleuze writes, "the affect of self by self, or folded force. Subjectivation is created by folding."[26]

Logically that which is folded here, in subjectivation, is necessarily the "outside." Deleuze develops his broad concept of the outside from Foucault and Blanchot as the unthought, that which cannot be thought. In Deleuze it is identified ultimately with death and madness, the two categories which thought cannot think. The outside which normally cannot be thought by the characters within their film, because it is the very ground of their being and verisimilitude, is defined by the production codes and anticipated audience demand and taste. Norma decides herself what the public want of her and constitutes herself accordingly. She consequently breaks the most fundamental and abiding conventions of realist movies, that characters act without self-consciousness of their filmic existence. Norma of course always behaves with this peculiar self-consciousness, as an object of artifice. All of her movements, the clothes she wears, the way she speaks, and most tellingly the form her madness takes at the end of the film, demonstrate her perpetual readiness for the cameras and the audiences for which they furnish the proxy. Her writing of the "Salome" script is a recursive gesture of enfoldment akin to the circling physical gestures by which she focuses and reiterates her identity. Indeed, as the final scene of the film indicates, the script appears to have been written to furnish opportunities for just such balletic expressivism.

Norma's subjectivity is the hollow interior defined by the fold of the outside, the enfoldment of her dream of stardom. She accordingly sums up her being in relation to the conditions determining the film's production, the outside to the film which we see and she inhabits: "You see, this is my life. It always will be. There's nothing else – just us and the cameras and those wonderful people out there in the dark."[27] At this point she threatens to pass out to the audience through the camera and projector lenses, which valve-like usually allow only the one-way traffic of the audience's gaze and the imaginative engagements with the characters that this facilitates. Her direct address to "those wonderful people" the audience near the end of the film and her movement toward us in the subsequent closeup sequence impinge upon the sanctity of our safe refuge "in the dark." The camera's loss of focus registers the fact that Norma has literally overstepped the mark, that she is moving into the space occupied by the camera and the audience, a breach of the distinct spaces and ontologies of film characters and audience that is reminiscent of the menacing claustrophobic shots that are a staple of the horror movie.

The lens that finally focuses upon Norma belongs here to both the Paramount newsreel camera, which will bring to cinema audiences the sort of publicity that Joe anticipates "would kill her,"[28] and, for Norma (and indeed in fact), a Paramount movie camera that will perpetuate her role as a star. The closeup and fade-out mark her death, the dissolution of her discrete cinematic identity, and the end of the world of the film: the last flickering rays of Sunset. The end of *Sunset Boulevard* parallels the close of Wilde's play, where Salome's triumph ("I have kissed thy mouth, Iokanaan, I have kissed they mouth") is both apocalyptic ("*The stars disappear. A great cloud crosses the moon and conceals it completely*")[29] and the cause of her execution by Herod's soldiers, the point at which the curtain falls. "People like Norma Desmond," Charles Brackett observes, "fade out with a bang, not a whimper."[30]

With Norma Desmond's extreme "closeup" both she and *Sunset Boulevard* itself punningly close up. She becomes most clearly recognisable here as a being that is created *ex nihilo*, drawn out as light from darkness in the figure of the star. Norma's abstract cinematic being is summed up spatially by the trope of enfoldment, constantly gesturing towards the hollow core of the star into which she effectively implodes at the close of the film. The full expression of Norma's being occurs as a madness that Joe diagnoses; "the dream she had clung to so desperately had enfolded her." Norma's subjectivation, the line that enfolds, is so strong that it constitutes her madness, an irredeemably solipsistic style of meaning-making. Norma has her being as a fold in the cinematic material, the ideology of the star that furnishes "the baseless fabric of this vision."[31]

End notes

[1] Brackett, Wilder and Marshman, *Sunset Boulevard: The complete screenplay* (Los Angeles: University of California Press, 1999), 121; 74; 70.

[2] Isobel Murray (ed.) *Oscar Wilde*, The Oxford Authors (Oxford: Oxford University Press, 1989), 328; 324

[3] Murray (ed.), 328; 301; 311; 301.

[4] Brackett, Wilder and Marshman, 42.

[5] See John Orr, *Cinema and Modernity* (Oxford: Polity Press, 1993), 165.

[6] Roland Barthes, *Camera Lucida: Reflections on Photography*, trans. Richard Howard (London: Jonathan Cape, 1982), 92-97.

[7] Brackett, Wilder and Marshman, 42.

[8] Brackett, Wilder and Marshman, 122, 126.

[9] This contrast is elaborated by Barthes, 89-90.

[10] Brackett, Wilder and Marshman, 98

[11] Brackett, Wilder and Marshman, 31.

[12] Brackett, Wilder and Marshman, 122.

[13] Brackett, Wilder and Marshman, 42.

[14] Brackett, Wilder and Marshman, 126.

[15] Murray (ed.), 302.

[16] Murray (ed,), 310; 328.

[17] Brackett, Wilder and Marshman, 98.

[18] Foucault, *The Use of Pleasure*, The History of Sexuality, Vol. 2, trans. Robert Hurley (London: Viking, 1986), 172-4. See vols 2 and 3 *passim*. See also Gilles Deleuze, *Foucault*, trans. Sean Hand (London: Athlone Press, 1988), 100-1.

[19] Brackett, Wilder and Marshman, 42.

[20] Brackett, Wilder and Marshman, 73; 53; 54.

[21] Brackett, Wilder and Marshman, 123.

[22] Brackett, Wilder and Marshman, 9.

[23] Brackett, Wilder and Marshman, 119.

[24] "The Thought of the Outside," trans. Brian Massumi, in James D. Faubion (ed.) *Aesthetics, Method, and Epistemology*, The Essential Works of Foucault, Vol. II (London: Allen Lane, 1998), 151.

[25] Guy Debord, *Society of the Spectacle* (Detroit: Black and Red, 1983), # 2.

[26] Deleuze, 104.

[27] Brackett, Wilder and Marshman, 126.

[28] Brackett, Wilder and Marshman, 123.

[29] Murray, 329; 328.

[30] Charles Brackett, "A Matter of Humour," in Herbert G. Luft and Charles Brackett, "Two Views of a Director– Billy Wilder," *The Quarterly of Film, Radio and TV* (Autumn 1952), 69.

[31] William Shakespeare, *The Tempest*, IV, i, ll. 151.

Nancy Berg

Memory Writing, Memoir Reading: *Se non è vero, è bon trovato.*

Memory mediates between the past and present, recalling and often deceiving. It brings the past to the present, viewing this past through the perspective of the present. Memory can be manipulated by selection and coloration: what is remembered and how it is remembered. Writing can further shape the memory. Narration orders events, and in so doing, asserts control over them.

Writing freezes memory, distorting it by ordering, defining and concretizing it.

I am drawn to memoirs, fascinated by them, at times repelled. The luminosity of the language concretizing deliquescent memories into something solid, coherent. My New England discomfort with too much self revelation. Self exposure masquerading as introspection makes me queasy. The best of them make me envious. I envy the writers their memories, their abilities to recover them and their talents in conveying them.

The most compelling of these memoirs are narratives that are carefully shaped by invisible hands into a subtle weave of interconnected motifs, moments of recognition, and felicities of language. Any fragmentary quality is a calculated strategy. My memories are elusive like my dreams, momentary sensations, glimpses of color and motion, wisps of scent. Anything more concrete is a reconstruction imposed after waking in vain attempts to assert logic and even order on the fading vanishing images. I am paralyzed by the fragility of my memories, and my slippery hold on the truth.

Instead I delight in the beauty of others' memoirs, and am most intrigued by memoirs set in places that are simultaneously familiar and exotic to me. Their authors seem undaunted by the demands of accuracy, instead aspiring for a different kind of truth. Andre

Aciman's *Out of Egypt* (Farrar Strauss Giroux, 1994) is just such a memoir. The boy at its center is the only child amid an extended family. He serves as our first person narrator, growing into early adolescence by the end of the narrative. He is never identified by name, never called "Andre" or something else; we rarely see him with other children. His otherwise lonely childhood is relieved by a colorful extended family, the richly cosmopolitan city of Alexandria, and a lifestyle of unapologetic colonialism. Only in a later essay does Aciman reveal the existence of a brother, excised from the author's childhood memories, presumably for aesthetic reasons.

Near the end of the book the boy protagonist is suspended from his private school for his failure to recite an Arabic poem in class. The narrative tells of his mother arriving to collect him and light-heartedly taking him downtown by the tram, entertaining him with her recital of the names of stations. Describing the circumstances of its writing in a subsequent article, he compares and conflates images of his mother from within the story and from the time of its recording. "I did not lie about the names of the tram stations, but I did make up the scene about her coming to school that day. It doesn't matter."[1]

Each character in this book is more idiosyncratic, more vividly drawn, and wittier – in several languages – than the one before it. Almost larger than life, they are still credible figures. The memoir begins with a portrait of Uncle Vili: "soldier, salesman, swindler, spy." Samir Rafaat questions the curious parallels between Aciman's book and his own *Maadi 1904-1962: History and Society in a Cairo Suburb* (Palm Press, 1994).[2] He questions the historical veracity of Aciman's relation to this great uncle, asserting that the Vili character was based on one Maurice G. Levi. Fixated on Aciman's claim that his great uncle auctioned off the property of King Farouk, Rafaat contends that his research does not show any Vili Aciman involved in any such auction. He ends his recitation of evidence with the pointed comment: "The only entry under Aciman is one Elie Agiman who ran a massage parlor in Alexandria."

Not only does this last barb not meet its target – one senses that such a character would only add to the cache and quirkiness of the family portrayed – but his complaints are put into place by the author's nonchalant response, thanking the would-be exposer for his careful reading: "Yours is, needless to say, a highly interesting investigatory piece; it almost asks to be the subject of another book on [...] shady bankers and mock pashas!" Samir Rafaat comes off – in his own article – as pedantic; as a less capable reader of the breezy memoir; as someone Egyptians would dismiss as *thaqil al-damm* (literally "heavy-blooded," that is, lacking a sense of humor).

Edward Said wrote about his childhood in his recent book-length memoir *Out of Place* (1999). He was famously attacked by Justus Reid Weiner, an American born lawyer based in Jerusalem.[3] Claiming three years of research Weiner refuted Said's claims that he was born in the family home in Jerusalem, that he attended school there, and that he was aversely affected by the establishment of a Jewish state in what was until then Palestine. While some of Weiner's contentions can be explained away as cultural misunderstanding – for example, Said's childhood home was actually deeded to a member of his extended family – they are all geared toward questioning Said's identity as Palestinian and thus his authenticity as Palestinian spokesperson. The numerous articles written in the aftermath – including Said's own refutation – are ideologically charged. [4] The readers here are perhaps not missing the point, but they are missing the poetry.

In 1993 the Iraqi-born Israeli writer Sami Michael hit the best seller list and stayed on for an unprecedented fifty weeks with his novel *Victoria*, the life story of his mother. While the book garnered critical acclaim to match its popularity, it was not uncontroversial. Unlike the readers who flocked to community centers, schools, and auditoriums to hear the author, there were some who criticized the novel for its unvarnished look at Jewish life in Iraq nearly a century ago. They complained about the images of the courtyard described: the wretched poverty, the familial rivalries and the frank sexuality. Those who read it as documentary ignored its novelistic qualities and charms, instead questioning the author's ability to reconstruct the once glorious community in all its details. A complicating factor is the autobiographical nature of the novel. Michael has not made any claims otherwise, at times shifting between the name of the fictional character and its real life counterpart within one sentence. The author was more or less excoriated for not changing the truth – or at least not representing his truth in a more culturally acceptable way. Michael's personal memories challenge the collective memory of Baghdadi Jewry and that which has become accepted as part of the Israeli Jewish collective memory.

More compatible with the collective memory of Jews from the ancient Babylonian community is the novella *Laylat ʿUrābā*, [The Night of Hoshana Raba][5] by Samīr Naqqāsh. It tells the story of one family's celebration of the harvest festival Sukkot on the eve of their exile from Iraq. The frame-story narrator describes the evening twenty-nine years ago in the fictional past to an implied audience in a small coffeehouse in Israel. In this story the narrator's uncle constructs the family sukkah every year as part of a preholiday ritual. (The *sukkah*, a temporary home, is a boothlike structure erected as part of the celebration of the Jewish holiday of *Sukkot*.) The iterative sense of the *sukkah*-building ritual shifts almost imperceptibly to a specific occurrence.[6] The *sukkah*, and that night of Hoshana Raba, achieve a permanent existence in the narrator-character's memory, and the written text. Paradoxically, Naqqāsh's *sukkah*, is made permanent through the narrative discourse, the narrator's memory shared with his "fictional" audience in the frame story, and with his "real audience", readers outside of the narrative itself.

Naqqāsh's masterful use of the Arabic language reinforces the difference between the frame and the framed. It also contributes to thematization, tone and characterization. The characters presented in the framed story speak in the informal Jewish dialect of Baghdad. Their discourse differs in levels and styles according to their own personalities and backgrounds.

The language in the framed story differs from that of the frame; description is more lyrical, dialogue more lively. The narrator speaks Modern Standard Arabic to his implied audience who do not share a common background with him (nor perhaps with each other). This presents a contrast between the homey and familiar with the formal, reinforcing the contrast between the lyrical past and the nightmarish present. The sense of community is gone. Only this eulogy to the memory of goodness and family remains.

As part of his story, the narrator relates his encounter with a long lost relative in Israel. The old man is oblivious to his surroundings and the fulfillment of his lifetime fantasy to return to Rishon LeZion. The narrator then concludes his account of this sad incident with a disclaimer, "But this never happened." He denies its truth, trying to erase the uneraseable. The chance encounter is now part of the reader's memory, remaining palimpsest-like as part of the narrative.

The narrator begins his recitation by undermining his own reliability and the authority of his text.

> I might get confused or make mistakes. My memory might not be as reliable as the electronic variety, nor as precise. I am a human being discussing the bygone days. And when people talk about the past, they skip things. They don't necessarily put things in the best order.[7]

He has pre-empted any reader looking for factual accuracy at the cost of poetic truth. The narrative ends when our storyteller is "interrupted". His uncle – the one who built the sukkah year after year – is missing, and he must go and look for him. The story is left incomplete, the narrative uncorroborated; the past remains beyond our reach.

Memoir seems to straddle several genres: history, biography, confession, and fiction. It is intensely personal, collapsing the distance between the author (implied and biographical) and the first person narrator, leaving only the distance of time between narrator and protagonist. There is slippage inherent in the genre. The memoir lies between readerly expectations of factual accuracy, and writerly submission to the demands of the craft.

In reality, memoir is subject to many of the same rules as fictional narrative. Events are selected, ordered and presented from a particular viewpoint. The very linearity of narrative distorts a true time sequence; overlapping or simultaneous events must wait their turn. The narratives order memory, bring the past to the present, and make it permanent. They create memory, evoking visceral responses in their audience. They frame the memory by language, separating past from present, and readers of fact from readers of truth and beauty.

Notes

[1] Andre Aciman, "A Literary Pilgrim Progresses to the Past," *The New York Times*, August 28, 2000.

[2] Samir Rafaat, "Andre Aciman's Out of Egypt," *Egyptian Gazette*, December 21, 1996.

[3] See for example, Weiner's initial article "My Beautiful Old House and Other

Fabrications" in *Commentary*, September, 1999, and his follow-up "A Tale of Two Frauds," in *Academic Questions*, Summer 2000.

[4] See Edward Said, "Defamation, Revisionist Style: Commentary Seeks to Prove Prominent Palestinian Doesn't Exist," *Washington Report on Middle East Affairs*, October/November 1999; Christopher Hitchens, "Commentary's scurrilous attack on Edward Said," salon.com, September 7, 1999 (http://www.salon.com/news/feature/1999/09/07/said/); Jeff Jacoby, "The Lies of Edward Said," Front Page Magazine. Com October 2, 2000 (http://www.frontpagemag.com/guest-columnists/jacoby/)

[5] Samīr Naqqāsh, "Laylat ʿUrābā," *Yawm Ḥabalat wa-Ajhaḍat al-Dunyā*, (Jerusalem: al-Sharq al-ʿArabiyya, 1980), pp. 161-226.

[6] See for example, Gerard Genette's discussion of the pseudo-iterative in *Narrative Discourse: An Essay in Method*. Translated by Jane E. Lewin (Ithaca, New York: Cornell University Press, 1980), pp 121.

[7] Naqqāsh, p.163.

Scott Brook

'Photographs 1933, 1916' and 'Labertouche' are extracts from *Warren: a guide to decent*, a novel-in-progress based on the life of Reverend Hubert Ernst Warren who was a missionary-evangelist during the 1920's. In 1933/34 Warren led the famous 'Arnhem Land Peace Expedition'. See 'The Caledon Bay Affair' in Henry Reynolds, *This Whispering in Our Hearts*.

Photographs 1933, 1916

Three men in pressed white suits. White safari helmets. 'History in the making' you can almost hear someone say.
　A nervous laugh.
　And as the photographer from the Torres Strait Gazette peered inside the box, he held up three fingers. You uncrossed your legs, straightened your trousers. Tried not to squint in the sun.
Click.
And gosh . . . that it?
　—*Yesir. But don't getup chaps cause here we go*
Again. Click. Again. Peace Expedition to Caledon Bay, Nineteen Thirty-Three. Mission Party assembled at Thursday Island, prior to embarkation for Groote.

Better to tell people 'Arnhem Land', I mean no one has heard of Caledon Bay. 'Arnheim's Land' they used to write and I wonder if as a child it made you think of Rembrandt. Of queer looking men with earrings and cuffs. Another Australia, almost unthinkable.

In the photo Reverend Alf Dyer is looking as emaciated as ever while Donald Fowler, well he just looks comfortable. In the middle of the photo sits yours truly, and he's awkward I suppose because he knows his stuff. A reputation like that. Built up over years. It must feel like arthritis. Joints go stiff, your back starts to ache. You had to watch what went on behind it too. In 1928 a bad report from the Society's new secretary stung your sense of Christian loyalty. After a decade of founding the Groote Eylandt it was recommended you take furlough. A well earned break. An island in the south this time. Tasmania.

But it's the consistency that gets you in the end. The uniform behaviour that goes with being Superintendent. Not that you weren't flexible, able to adapt. You were good at surviving. Just think of all those years on the coast. The edge of the colony, standing in the sun and hoisting a red and blue cross. You were eccentric alright. Sang 'God Save the Queen' on an island off the coast and felt the loneliness of a double remove.

But awkward? Perhaps it's Fowler's arm wandering along the back of the bench, or just the idea that cameras make people uncomfortable. In London in the thirties they complained about cars and trains. Neurasthenia and the Talkies. In 1906 you stood in the rain outside Buckingham Palace and waited for the King but he didn't show. The curtains rustled and a face appeared, but it was impossible to say for sure.

But cameras, well. In 1916 you'd just sighted shore. Saw the locals follow you around the coast as you looked for a safe place to land. Waiting for you to come ashore. Funny, but it felt like they'd done this before. The scene of white men arriving. Much pointing and waving. First signs back and forth like semaphore. As the Aboriginal boys from Rose River towed you in you said you 'came in peace'. One of these translated for Umbarriri who translated for you. He told them, 'well these two fellas in the boat you see, we'll they're from God'.

Something like that. Back at the Roper River Ellie would write down the stories you told about these first excursions. She described communication on these visits was like Chinese whispers. Once Reverend Dyer tried to demonstrate 'Jesus loves me, this I know' and it came back as 'Jesus loves the hair on my chest like a Father loves his piccaninny'. After this missionaries knew not to point at parts of the body.

Then came the gifts. Always the gifts. You had to get things moving, but later you would be strict about these. 'Nothing-for-Nothing' became the motto, only trade. Shillings and Pence.

—Savvy?

—Youee

There was no hard currency back then so to supplement the Mission's hand-made coinage you used tobacco. You even made up a chart to teach about accumulation. Saving for the future and how anything could be accomplished if one worked like this. Columns above the names which you'd give out as you wrote them down, each blue square corresponding to a penny saved. One penny equalled a quarter of a stick of tobacco. Five squares equalled a tomy axe.

Yura Yankanar people would say when you placed it on the bench. The first Enindilyakwan phrase you got to remember. 'Paper talks'.

In 1916 Reverend Joynt got everyone to sit down on the beach. You had brought a fresh shirt and collar just for the occasion. The men were fascinated. Sleeves. Buttons. You were nothing like the Macassans. Telling stories all the time then handing out food for nothing. The Macassans were happy to come an go with the trade-winds, sailing from Sulawesi along the Indonesian Archipelago, stopping at Timor before crossing to the Gulf of Carpentaria, a land they called *Marege* where they would harvest trepang from the coastal shoals for markets as far away as China. Only rarely did they stay behind to marry, have kids, to live to old age and finally be buried on the coasts of the Arafura Sea facing Mecca.

But you, it would never have been clear who you were working for. You came and built this small hut for your tools, then left straight away. Totally crazy. Later, much later, when some men lead you back to their camp, you saw how the women used folding bark screens to cover their bodies. It made you think of Eve in Genesis. It was all very Old Testament this place. The vegetation. The birds. The rumours of caves where ochre paintings showed the crucifixion.

In 1916 you held the island's first service. The boys from Roper knew the songs, could explain the pictures. Even the smirks about a white man being nailed to a piece of wood didn't seem so bad. That's engineering for you. Plenty clever these balandas.

During the hymns old man T. even crooned along. Told the others to be quiet and sit still. So far so good, but then that old pull inside, down in your guts. A sense of the moment. You sent Umbarriri to the boat for the camera tripod, then disappeared beneath the hood like some puppet-show. Got everyone to huddle in nice and tight. Reverend Joynt reserved a space for you in the centre.

You were just showing Umbarriri how to set the thing off when it started. Shouting. Men picking up spears, throwing your presents in the sand.

In seconds the shore was completely empty. You followed through the scrub and pandanus trees, calling out to the birds, but no one returned. You laid out more gifts on the sand. A knife. A loaf of bread. A small picture of Jesus.

LABERTOUCHE

[T]his keeping of a diary by a nation which is something entirely different to historiography the narrowing down of the attention of a nation upon itself and the accepting of what is foreign only in reflection the acknowledgment of literary events as objects of political solicitude the dignification of the antithesis between fathers and sons and the possibility of discussing this the presentation of national faults in a manner that is very painful, to be sure, but also liberating the beginning of a lively and self-respecting book trade . . . [1]

I'm copying this out into a notebook, in the kitchen, and spend a while writing over the words 'father' and 'discussing'. The pencil doodles with the letters, emboldening them, until the lead starts to shine.

Perhaps all I'm after is more information. These days 'information' comes to mean a glossier picture rather than answers to awkward questions. Imagine Fox Mulder zooming in on a 21' Trinitron monitor; we see the same image at two hundred percent, five hundred, a thousand ... the picture disintegrates into pixels, a confetti of raw data. Once again the case is solved at the level of details, where 'the Devil' resides.

The sound of the phone ringing reminds me how far I've wandered from what I'm 'meant' to be writing about; a photograph of me and my father, en route to writing about Hubert. How do the generations relate? What connects them? It's hard not to fall back on detective fiction, that twentieth century companion to Psychoanalysis. Every 'I' is a Private Eye Freud might have said.

The answering machine intercepts, the recording of my girlfriend's upbeat voice enough to make you think there was a party going on. The machine clicks to the sound of a dial tone.

I takes out the photo album. Skips to the one of me and Dad. That's us, carrying a parachute over the grass. Another successful sky-dive in the mid-seventies. You can even see the white landing zone in the background. Dad's carrying the bulk of the parachute while I'm carrying the pilot-chute. I don't remember what a 'pilot-chute' is, only that that's what it is that I'm holding. A line dangles between our bodies like an umbilical cord.

Something a bit contrived about all this, but the moment is entirely innocent. The figures are uncomposed even if someone has found a composition. The gaping mouth of the child suggests he's talking, or singing, while Dad must have blinked when the shutter came down. We have the natural awkwardness of moving bodies that have been captured from time. Bodies that are made still through being made into a still.

It's the kind of picture you show friends feeling comfortable with the past it suggests. The candid shots are always best. From *don't point a camera at me* to *jee, how did you manage that?* we see-saw lives, animated by out-takes.

The photo was probably taken by my Uncle, dad's brother, who was both a sky-diver and amateur photographer. I entertain the possibility that the blur in dad's goggles could be him, but it's impossible to say. It's definitely dad's handwriting on the back though.

Feb. '77. Labertouche. Jump no. 101.

I phone Dad and ask him what 'Labertouche' means, thinking it must be sky-diving jargon. He tells me it's a place, 'near Drouin', two hours East of Melbourne.

—And what's a 'pilot-chute'?

—It comes off your main-chute. There's this vacuum behind your body, when you're falling.

Dad tells me the pilot-chute pulls the parachute across the vacuum. Out into the slipstream.

—How does it do that?

—It's spring-loaded.

—Oh. Thanks.

—Pleasure.

I hang up and come back to the kitchen. Think how incredible the whole thing sounds. I start wondering about the connection between my dad and Uncle being sky-divers and the fact *their* dad invented the first inflight recorder, the so called 'Black Box'.

Did Grandpa's famous invention pull their attention skywards? Like a pilot-chute?

My Grandfather, David, wasn't into planes for their own sake. He began as a chemist at CSIRO when it was originally the 'Department of Supply', supplying the army with whatever it needed during the second world war. The story goes that David spent a lot of time blowing things up and putting out the fire, and somewhere in here he comes up with the idea of an heat-proof box that could take instrument readings. And then the idea – an after-thought? – of putting these in planes.

At the time the novelty went generally unrecorded. Australians weren't meant to have big ideas; they were 'lucky', not 'clever'. A memorable joke from the time: 'David, you'll get more expletives than explanations'.

'Black-box', David tells me, was the popular term used for a box full of gadgets. It was originally called the 'red egg'.

I wonder about David's father, Hubert. Unlike his descendents I have the feeling Hubert didn't like planes. A missionary-pilot in the Church Missionary Society spent a few years at Roper River and then wrote some novels about it, and in one of these books there's a reference to a certain 'stern missionary' who thought planes were a crazy invention. For some reason I've always thought this was Hubert. I guess I like the idea that despite his love of Modern things, Hubert too had his limits. There's always a fictional element to our lives, no matter how much we chase-up the leads. The name of the pilot-missionary was 'Langford-Smith'.

The fact is Hubert did take a plane though, from Launceston to Melbourne just after the Peace Expedition, but not before sending his family on the boat for safe measure. Or perhaps just to save money. It's hard to know for sure.

In any case, in 1934 Hubert bordered a plane to cross Bass Strait, a so called 'Holyman Airways DH-86'. The flight should have only taken a few hours. Time does strange things for those who are waiting. When you're waiting for someone time stretches *and* compacts. It becomes full of crinkles. The point is Hubert's plane never arrived.

[1] from 'The Literature of Small Peoples by Franz Kafka'. *The diaries of Franz Kafka: 1910—1923* ed. Max Brod (Harmondsworth: Penguin, 1964); p. 148.

Tanya Ring

A Mannequin is Without

Inside the car is an arm: full size, fake, mute, frozen in
silent gesticulation, dislocation, vain communication.

Cold sheen streetlight stares hard,
shunned by the indifference of perfect form:
painted nails, fingers long, thin, desiring,
dreaming filmic reproductions that flicker generic.

Sweating against the car vinyl, *you're one of my kind,*
all electric intensity friction attraction, the chemistry
of discarded, disposable, plastic-on-plastic abandonment,
synthetic lust, fetishised delight of consent oh-so manufactured.

Somewhere an acrylic mold aches with plastic loss
and somewhere else a one-armed girl stares wide-eyed
full of brand new sexuality, all Modesty Blaising
in the darkness of her own hermetic seals.

ENLIGHTENMENT

all you get are rebounds. And rebounds
of rebounds, rays weary and worn,

so thoroughly secondhand and been-around
or was that pre-loved? This,

that is all that reaches your eye all
photon and quanta, bits and flows,

gone so fast and so far it's tired and
used and not to be relied upon, these

beams right now all golden glissando
could be from a sun now dead and

you can't know, can't ever know, always
eight minutes and twenty seconds

from even this kind of truth.
Oh you can see the light, alright.

Sublimation

With one swift abstract leap
he renders his life the
chance coincidence of substance and light.

This sharp arc of thought
– gleaming intense –
pins him to the moment.

Objective acuity hurts. In fever
of pain he dreams pure form, white light
in an order at once mathematical.

Beauty Platonic. Certain, true, complete.
Discrete, and Meant.
Screaming bright, God he desires.

Mother Earth

He mused over how a bell-curve might fit the curve
of her hips. The ecstatic hyperbolae of her breasts.

The intense desire he had to measure every inch
of her skin against the constructions of men's minds,
flesh prickling against cold, alien symmetries.

Annette Trevitt

Deb Simpson

She looked at the divorce papers once again and folded them. She put them back on the step beside her and looked out into the yard. Debra Ann Simpson, Debra Ann the divorcee. It sounded like the name of a porn star. She poured another drink. Maybe I could move to the city and become one, she thought.

She rested the glass on her knee and watched the clouds as they moved across the sky like a herd of cattle. She wished to be taken away like that instead of being stuck on the ground feeling like she did. It started off as such an ordinary day but since the afternoon mail, nothing seemed ordinary.

Deb picked up the papers and unfolded them as if she hadn't read them before. They took her back; back to when he was always on her mind. She was thinking of how it didn't take much to be back there when the phone rang in the kitchen. She looked up; it sounded like it was coming from a house across the road.

It was her father.

"It's your mother, she's gone..."

A bullet entered Deb's heart.

"She's left a note."

"Oh, oh I thought you meant she was..."

Deb couldn't continue the sentence.

"No, no," he said.

"Where's..."

"On the kitchen table."

"No, where's she gone?"

"Who knows."

"What does the note say?"

"'John, Gone away for a while, yours Faye.'"

"I'll come over."

She pressed her hand hard on her chest. It still felt hot and sore. What was going on? Her mother had phoned yesterday but she just talked about the dog. She told Deb how she had to put the TV on during the day to calm him. Something she never did. 'I turned it on and then we sat on the couch and I fed him hot pasta with ham and cream sauce,' she said.

It was only now as Deb grabbed the car keys off the sideboard that she remembered her mother's favourite dish was Spaghetti Carbonara. She pulled out of the drive and onto the street. The storm was already over the hills, near where her parents lived, on the other side of town. She picked at the loose plastic on the steering wheel cover and thought again of how her mother hadn't mentioned anything to her. Deb knew that she hid things from her mother but she didn't know that her mother held things from her. It had never occurred to her that her mother was a person with secrets. As soon as she saw the house, her heart had the same piercing ache as it did on the phone. She parked her car in the drive and got out. She pushed open the side-gate and walked around the back, noticing that the dog wasn't around and that the yard was unusually quiet.

Her father was in the shed; he was always in the shed. He was at the bench with his back to her. She had always found old men's backs unbearably sad but this was the first time that she saw her father's back as an old man's. He turned around and she fought back tears.

He pulled the shed door shut and they crossed the back-yard to the house. Deb watched the clouds as they stampeded over the roof. They were low and dark, making it seem much later in the day than it was. He opened the screen-door for her and she walked inside, turned on the light and sat down. Her mother's note was on the table, folded like a restaurant bill, under the sugar bowl. Her father wiped his hands on his trousers and reached up into a cupboard and pulled out a bottle. He grabbed two glasses off the sink and while he poured the drinks, she picked up the note, read it and put it back.

He handed her a glass. They looked at each other, then he closed his eyes, had a mouthful of brandy, paused and had another. He'd drink straight from the bottle, she thought, if I wasn't here. They both drank too much. Deb told herself it was because her marriage had ended but that wasn't true. She had been drinking for a long time.

She watched his fingers tap against the glass. She didn't know what to say. She couldn't remember the last time she and her father were alone. She looked out the window and wondered where her mother was and if she felt lonely. The clouds were lower than ever. She looked over at her father and then at the frayed edge of the vinyl table cloth that she had been picking.

She was always picking at things. That's what her ex-husband told her, 'always picking at things, always picking at me.' And she remembered the night. The night at the Chinese restaurant where she had arranged a surprise birthday party for him. The place was full; extra lanterns were lit and his favourite dish of Duck with almonds had been ordered in advance. It seemed like a great idea until she sat down opposite him and saw the thunder in his face. She picked up a menu and opened it. Her head roared. The words on the page kept losing their shape, she couldn't read, she couldn't think, she couldn't lift her head.

She was nervously picking at the laminated cover when he said, 'Can't leave it alone, can you, SimO?' She put down the menu and looked at him. SimO? He had never called her that before. He looked as surprised as she was. Then his surprise turned into something else, something that she couldn't bear to think of; a way of getting away from her. She picked at the corner of the menu and watched a fish float upside down in the tank behind him. SimO.

The table shook. It was a moment before she realised why. She looked up. 'Dad.' His elbows were on the table and his head in his hands. She wanted to cry too. It was like that in her family. She leaned over and patted his arm.

"She'll be back."

The crying got heavier and fair enough; what did she know? She had no idea and wished that she hadn't said it. She finished her drink and poured another. Her father had cried in front of her before but not like that.

She picked up the note and re-read it in the same searching way as she had read the divorce papers. They didn't help her understand anything but that didn't stop her wanting them to. For the life of her, she didn't know where her mother had gone. Every time she thought of a place it was somewhere where her mother had already been and she couldn't see why her mother'd want to go back to any of them.

Secrets, now dreams; Deb didn't know that her mother had them either. She looked at the note again and then held it up to the ceiling light to see if her mother had written another longer message which might be imprinted on the paper but she hadn't.

The crying subsided. He blew his nose and wiped his eyes. Deb poured him another drink and screwed the top back on the bottle. She loved that sound of metal on glass and she also loved to watch her hand as it twirled around. It made her feel like a movie star. She winced. She hadn't told anyone that except her ex-husband. And when she did, he had rolled over and looked at her and said, 'You, a movie star!' and laughed. He was like that. Nasty.

She looked across the table. Her father was frowning at her.
"He had a vicious edge, love," he said.
She looked down at an edge of a checked square on the table cloth.
"How did you know I was . . . "
"The look on your face, you only ever had it with him."
She bit her bottom lip and felt her nostrils flare. Don't cry, she told herself, please don't. Her eyes stung. She wanted to tell her father that she was sorry she thought about him at a time like this but the divorce papers had come through and they reminded her of how things had changed. They reminded her of how much she had loved him and of how now she didn't; not at all. Not once she finally saw his meanness. She looked at her father. His head was low on his chest. She had never used the word love in front of him and didn't want to now.

Her father rubbed his eyes and placed his forearms heavily on the table. Thunder sounded in the distance. He sighed.
"Where do you think she's gone?" he asked.
"Don't know, I really don't."
"Did you know she was unhappy?"
"No, . . . maybe she's not."
"I should know shouldn't I? Whether she's happy or not but I don't. She's like you, keeps everything so close to her damn chest, takin' everything to heart . . . I should know, I should've noticed." Deb looked at her father but she didn't say anything. He was right. He should have known and she should have too. She thought of the TV being on, in the day time.

It was dark outside. She twirled the empty glass in her hands; her father was doing the same with his.

"You hungry, dad?"

"No, not really."

"Have you eaten anything today? Why don't we go to the Chinese place?"

"Nuh."

"Come on you've got to eat and you love their lemon chicken."

"That's true," he said.

"Want to? Do you, dad? We won't be long."

He put down his glass, nodded and stood up. He pushed the chair in under the table and walked down the hall. Deb watched him, then got up, rinsed the two glasses and put the bottle away. She looked at the note and wondered if they should leave one for her mother, saying where they were, in case she came home.

She was still thinking about it when her father came back into the kitchen. He had brushed his hair, put on a clean shirt and tightened his belt. The neatness overwhelmed her. She decided not to leave a note; she didn't want her mother to think that they took hers lightly.

She backed out of the drive and the first drops of rain hit the windscreen. She turned onto the street, put on the lights and the wipers and headed into town. It was pouring down. Through the windscreen, she watched the rain fall through the light in front of the car and remembered the divorce papers on the back step. They'd be destroyed by now. It must be symbolic of something, she thought, but she couldn't think of what. All she could think of was the word, drowning, but paper doesn't drown. She looked over at her father, at the back of his head, as he sat and stared out through the side-window; the seat belt was pulled tight across his chest. He had left the kitchen light on, filled the jug and put a teabag in a cup, just in case.

Moira Rayner

Remembering Moira.

My mother lives in St Andrew's. My strong, funny, frightening mother lives in a nursing home. Her rage to live has been gentled by age, injuries, illness and dementia, and possibly by having her immediate needs met immediately: she was always demanding. I love her. I am like her, and we always clashed, but she is only sometimes the fiery mother I remember, though she seems to notice no difference. My mother lives in a nursing home in Western Australia, because she has lost and is losing those parts of her mind and memory that make us socially adaptable: her recollection of the recent past, the manners that smooth relationships and let us share dining rooms and public space. My mother lives in a nursing home in Western Australia and talks constantly of New Zealand, which we left nearly 40 years ago.

My mother has often told the same stories about her family and childhood. Her father, my grandfather, used to tell me about his, and I am sorry now that I can only remember flashes of them, not the whole once-familiar tale. The staff always laugh in the right places at my Mum's stories. They say, and I think they mean, they love her. My Mum seems happier here, in the place she fought not to enter, than she has been for years. She has, I think, decided to accept what she can't change – she never lacked courage – but she is also getting medication now, for the chronic sadness, anxiety and confusion that blighted the last 18 years of her life, before the dementia crashed in. My mother is in a home now, partly because she would not let it be treated. Angry, irritated, anxious, confused and losing judgment she began to fall over, again, and again. Each broken bone and torn skin took longer to recover and a greater emotional and mental toll. Finally she broke a hip, and lost her mind and her independence. In a Perth nursing home she talks sometimes about her childhood and her sisters and brothers, and of the New Zealand where we were all born and her family settled 162 years ago. Her memories are why she would not contemplate, let alone consider being treated for, a mental illness, which chronic sadness is: because of the family legend about the psychiatrist who married her sister.

My mother has always told family stories. Sometimes she doesn't remember what she did yesterday, or is unsure about who we are or where we've been. She often greets me with enormous joy, for instance, because she thinks I haven't seen her for months, and that I still live in London. Some memories are intact: she remembers with exquisite exactitude how to infuriate my sister. Some are lost: she doesn't really remember where she and my father lived, though she remembers to be angry with him, but not why. My mother still remembers the family crises; her wedding day; the words, but not the meaning of the Welsh she learned (and to be proud of her mother's Welshness), and the words and tunes of the hymns she and her Scottish Presbyterian Minister father sang in the Presbyterian Church that no longer exists. Yet when Jocelyn, the only daughter of the family's legendary psychiatrist who married Mum's sister, visited my mother in St Andrew's, Mum not only had no idea who Jocelyn was: she denied she ever had the sister who gave her birth. My mother would 'never trust a psychiatrist' because the sister who married one, was the first in the family to die, pitifully young and in peculiar circumstances. Her husband, a man not much liked by the other sons-in-law, took her away and – so the family story goes – controlled and manipulated her, deliberately alienating her from her brilliant, sarcastic, clever, competitive and close-knit siblings, from her saintly father, her sensitive, sensible, managing mother. My mother's abiding, superstitious fear of falling into the hands of a 'Svengali,' a practitioner of psychiatry, comes from this story.

The story goes, that her older sister, Hope, made the long journey to her married sister's distant city and telephoned the young wife and mother, who was sitting alone in her home, unable to leave it because she had hurt her foot, which was being treated by her husband. They arranged, by telephone, to meet the next day, but when Hope called that morning, her sister's husband shockingly told her that she could not see her, would never see her, because his wife had died overnight and was not only being privately cremated, but that very morning. He had not told her family, and would not tell the shocked and grieving girl where her sister's funeral was to be. So Hope called the city's undertakers and found the church and the funeral party: the bereaved psychiatrist husband, sobbing over an open coffin where lay his young, beautiful, dead wife in her wedding gown, supported by the medical colleague who had signed her death certificate. She was cremated an hour or two later.

When he learned of this her father, my grandfather, made a single, emotional telephone call to the widower who 'killed his daughter': there was a single family discussion about 'calling the police' and a policy decision that 'it wouldn't bring her back'. Not surprisingly, the uncomfortable widower – if not actually accused, he must have felt it – cut himself and their only child completely off from my mother's family. He married his nurse some months later, and a few years on died himself, a quite young father, of a drug overdose: leaving Jocelyn.

Suspicion: a sudden death: an almost surreptitious funeral: a quick remarriage: the absence of a grandchild. This family myth has been taught me for nearly 50 years. My mother, in her nursing home and living in her moment, now does not remember the blonde young mother who died in her early twenties; nor her middle-aged niece, who as a child grew up cared for by a well-loved father, whom she also lost, who in his turn passed on to his child another legend, in which my grandfather was the villain. There is no absolute truth. I am the present owner of my living mother's dead sister's name: Moira. Moira is supposed to mean 'mother of God', as Mary does, and Morag, Marie, and May, a common sort of name, really, though rarer in distant Western Australia from the land where I was given it. My mother, in her nursing home, remembers my name, but in her mind, I am absent, even when I am sitting at her table, watching her read, as I am, today, writing about what I remember about my mother.

Noel C. Tovey

Little Black Bastard

I don't remember precisely how many times in the last sixty years I have invented and reinvented myself. I recently obtained all my files from The Far West Home, the Police, and the Welfare Departments of NSW and Victoria. According to these documents I was born in 1933 and 1934 and 1935. From my birth until 1941 I was Noel Christian Morton, from 1941 to 1946 I was Noel Christian Challenger; from 1946 to 1952 I was Noel Christian Morton again and from 1953 until now I have been Noel Christian Tovey. That's who I am, well that's who I think I am; at least that's who I believe I am.

I have also been known as, Choc, Nig, Darkie, the Abo Tondalayo, and the Poof.

Add to the above list the alter ego I invented for myself when I was very young. His name was Rohan Scott-Rowan, a white Anglo Saxon matinee idol. These were the perfect ingredients for that much maligned and now-jargonised phrase 'identity crises.' It was only when other people told me that I didn't know who I was that it became a crisis .We all knew who I was but I had great difficulty explaining us to other people. We have all contributed to the telling of Noel Tovey's story that began in Melbourne in 1933, 1934 or 1935?

I hadn't lived there for more than forty years. Eighteen months ago I was invited down to a theatre conference at The Playbox Theatre. In the morning newspaper I was reading over breakfast I saw an advertisement for a flat in Parkville that was for sale. I had been toying with the idea for some time of returning to live in Melbourne so I decided to go and have a look at it.

I caught the 57 West Marybinong tram in Elizabeth Street, to go to Parkville. Even as a kid I loved riding on the trams; they are heart the soul of the city. I purchased a ticket from the faceless vending machine and settled down for the long circuitous route I had chosen.

The Tram travels a short distance up Elizabeth Street and stops. I'm oblivious to all the shouting and traffic noise. I'm enjoying staring idly out of the window thinking of other tram rides in other times. My gaze wanders above the canopy of 57 Elizabeth Street and I'm surprised and thrilled to see still intact a window with a gold and black silhouette portrait of the legendary 1930s Musical Comedy star Stephanie Deste painted on it. Gone are the words "Stephanie Deste Salon de Beaute." They have been replaced simply by the word Hairdresser. Stephanie had a weekly radio programme and was the beauty guru to every Melbourne housewife. Her daughter Toti, named after the opera diva Toti Dal Monte and I became good friends in the 50s.

Suddenly I'm a little boy again. Now I see only the ghosts of buildings that were once real to me. Collins Book Depot where I worked when I was 15. The manager's name was Charles Dickens and it was there I met Chesca who became my soul mate and introduced me to the Ballet. Next door was the London Hotel. I sold newspapers outside the public bar when I was 12 and two prostitutes I knew, Patsy and Jill, always made their sailor boy friends give me a tip. Now Robertson and Mullens bookstore, Mary Hardy and I would go there at lunchtime to meet John Muirehead The three of us were inseparable and besides John was the only one who had a regular job and money for lunch. As the tram crosses Bourke Street I see a refurbished Magill's bookshop. In a lane at the back of the main shop was the storeroom where I applied for my first job as a newspaper boy.

Luckily one of my mates had warned me about the boss, Fred. He liked to grope you as he adjusted the straps on your leather money bag and used phrases like "aren't we big for our age." I suffered the groping, I feigned innocence and pleasure and got the job. On the other side of Elizabeth Street on the first floor above Pellegrino's Catholic bookshop with its array of missals, rosary beads, holy pictures and other necessities for a suitable entrance into heaven was the Borovansky Ballet Studio. I spent many happy hours there.

La Trobe Street is the next stop. The old majestic Argus building is still stands sentinel on the corner. I worked here as a 'galley boy' after my trial. My trial was big news in those days.

There is a lot of noise and everyone's pushing to get on and off the tram at the next stop. It's the Queen Victoria Market and market day. My sister Mag and I would come here on Saturday morning when we were very young and hungry because we knew we could get broken biscuits and spotted fruit for nothing and if we had a penny we could buy a jam donut.

The tram turns left into Victoria Street. The Central Hotel on the corner is the beginning of what I now think of as Mumma's way home. Mumma was barely five feet tall, she had had polio as a child which left her with one leg considerably shorter than the other and she walked with a decided limp. She had short straight dark hair and a small a pretty face. Her drinking habits had changed considerably during the time Mag and me were living with the Challengers in Burren Junction. She was now a periodic alcoholic, that meant 2 to 3 weeks of total alcoholic oblivion, one week of feeling crook and drinking endless bottles of lemonade which I bought for her on tick from the corner shop. This was followed by weeks of recriminations and alcoholic remorse and promises. Every day she would say "no more drink for me, Noely boy." It was during these periods of sobriety that our lives were comparatively normal. I made a big effort to go to school and Mumma made a bigger effort to stay sober. Mumma worked at Parker Toys in West Melbourne and she always went to the market on pay day. I spent my North Melbourne years dreading Fridays because if I walked into the house after school on a Friday afternoon and got this strange inexplicable feeling of emptiness then I knew Mumma had busted on her way home and was doing the pubs in North Melbourne. The British Hotel was a particular favourite. The tram rattles its way up Victoria Street passing The Victoria Hotel and St. Mary Star of the Sea convent where Mumma went to school. The Three Crowns Hotel on the corner of Errol Street is a now restaurant and the Town Hall Hotel has been tarted up in blue and pink paint. The old picture Theatre where I would go on Saturday mornings has gone but not the memories. I loved westerns and I always wanted the Indians to win. I thought there must have been millions of them because no matter how many were killed each Saturday morning there would be just as many the next week and the week after that.

The tram turns left at The Town Hall, passes The Court House Hotel, swings down Queensbury Street into Abbotsford Street. Crossing Arden Street I can see the North Melbourne Football ground. I was footy mad, I sold drinks and lollies on Saturday afternoons and made enough money to take Betty Pollock to the pictures in Newmarket on Saturday night. Two tickets, two Peters Dixie ice creams, two Polly Waffles at interval and two hamburgers with the lot on the way home. I was desperately in love with Betty Pollock.

We pass the North Star and British Hotels and in the distance there's the North Melbourne swimming Baths. I think I can see Clarrie Foster still bouncing up and down on the end of the diving board. Clarrie was small and very athletic with a great body and in the vernacular of my day 'a good sort'. He would spend hours bouncing up and down on the end of the board going higher and higher each time and then when everyone was looking he would do a one and a half forward somersault in the Pike position into the pool as we all shouted and applauded . Clarrie and I were the same age and we both thought he looked like Cary Grant, especially in his Wesley College uniform.

No two boys could have had more different home lives. He once jumped into the creek at Fern Tree Gully and pulled me to safety after I had fallen out of a tree chasing a possum. Clarrie was the only real friend I had in those days.

The tram slows down in the traffic opposite Miss Alice Cullen's House. Miss Cullen taught me elocution at St. Michaels when I was twelve. Old habits die hard and unconsciously I started reciting out loud a little poem based on the vowel sound 'A.' When the man sitting opposite me says *Pardon*? I pretend I didn't hear him and that I am perfectly sane.

I knew at a very young age that one day I would get out of North Melbourne. Maybe I would go to America and join the Indians or become a film star but wherever I went I knew I didn't want to be or to sound Australian so I practised everything Miss Cullen taught us. That's when I invented Rohan Scott-Rowan. He stayed with me for many years. As I grew up and got older so did he. He told me that he would be rich and famous one day and buy all his clothes at Bukley and Nunn and eat all the time. I desperately wanted to be him.

I would stand under the mulberry tree in the back yard before an imaginary audience and three cats and recite all her exercises for the voice A "Ann met an ant, and an ant met Ann, Hello said the ant, Hello said Ann," B "Boys boots are big so when boy jump, boys big boots go bump bump bump." One Saturday morning when I had finished my recital I heard applause coming from inside the outside dunny which was near the back gate. It was Mrs Molloy. Later she said to Mumma "Geez Win, Noely Boy has a lovely speaking voice."

This tram terminates at the corner of Flemington Road and Abottsford Street opposite my old school St. Michaels. There are so many bad memories here. Even though I was quite bright, I always had to sit at the back of the class and I can still feel the burning of the broad leather strap on my hands after getting six of the best from Sister Mary Isidore for being late. I was a devout Catholic in those early years of my life. Religion saturated everything I did. I could recite all the catechism by heart and sing the mass in Latin. God and the Devil were everywhere. They fought huge battles for my soul. Often I would sit in church when things were really bad at home and ask God to explain my life for me.

I couldn't understand why everyone got drunk and became violent and why I was always being called a little black bastard and being beaten up by the other boys. One time I had my nose broken. But God never did answer my questions. Sister Mary Louis who taught Mumma at St. Mary's was still teaching grade three at St. Michaels in her late seventies. She made the only memorable statement I can recall from my brief time at school. She said "Now children I want you to remember that you were all born to die, and when you do Jesus will be waiting for you at the gates of heaven." I crossed Flemington Road and got on the Parkville tram. I'm still thinking about St. Michaels when the tram driver announces that the next stop will be the zoo.

Opposite the zoo is where The Royal Park Welfare Depot for Children was, I think, part of it is still there. I can hear voices from the past, Mag's voice, my voice, I'm crying, it's raining, I'm cold and I don't know where we are. Mag is saying "I'm here, I'm here, everything's gonna be alright," but everything wasn't alright.

The tram finally arrives in Parkville and I get off at Park Street. I'm disturbed by some of the memories I've been having and I'm asking myself if I'm doing the right thing. Am I ready to live in Melbourne again? I go to see the flat. It's too small.

I need some time to think, so I go and sit in the park and discuss my situation with some magpies that are nearby. This is not an unusual thing for me to do as magpies are my totemic self and I have always believed that they are the embodiment of my ancestral spirits. It is a beautiful day, the old feller gum trees are whispering in the wind to each other and the magpies are singing to me. I know then and there that Melbourne is indeed where I want to live. I am part of Melbourne, I know every nook and cranny of the place. It is my home and something that has been missing from my life for many years. I also know that today is the day for me to spring clean the memories of my youth and exorcise the ghosts of the past.

I walked down Park Street to Sydney Road and caught the East Coburg tram that goes to Bell Street, I want to stand outside Pentridge Gaol again. I was an inmate there during my trial 50 years ago and two of the most traumatic experiences of my life took place inside those walls.

Looking out of the tram window as I ride up Sydney Road is like watching a travel documentary. I doubt if there is a more multicultural area in the whole of Australia. The names of the restaurants and shops are so evocative: La Paella, The Sri Lankan Village; The Mediterranean Delicatessen; The Muslim Women's association; Sartoria Manduca; Pummaklale Bakery; Curry Valley; and many more.

The Mechanics Institute, built in 1868, is now a community theatre. Halfway up Sydney Road I get off the tram, as all those Middle Eastern and Italian food stores demand to be investigated. I am instantly struck by the friendliness of the people, there is an air of village and community life here and compared to Sydney where I've been living for ten years the cost of food is very cheap. I go into a Lebanese grocers and I buy some dates, bread and beans. The young girl says thank you in her best English when I pay her and I reply *Shucrun* in my best Arabic and we both smile. Sandwiched between The Sun Yee Cafe and La Massate Trattoria is Herbert's Home Made Pie Shop. It is obvious from the facade that it was there long before the multicultural Invasion of Sydney Road. Displayed on old-fashioned trays in the window are vanilla slices, apple slices, rock cakes lamingtons, fairy cakes, custard tarts and, joy of all joys, real coffee scrolls. Now I know I'm home in Melbourne.

The coffee scroll is to be enjoyed with your morning coffee and is as the name implies a scroll of delicious sultana and mixed spice laden dough which has the consistency of a bun when baked and finished off with a dollop of very soft pale pink icing on top. There's an art to eating a coffee scroll. First order your coffee, then start uncoiling the scroll from the outside, this releases the intoxicating aroma of cinnamon and gradually eat your way to the centre and finally savour the piece with the pale pink icing on it.

I can't resist so I go in and buy a scroll and then set about looking for a coffee. Almost by accident I find Maria's Coffee Shop. It is hidden in a narrow pedestrian walkway to a car park. I smell the coffee first before I see the shop which is very small with a few baskets of coffee beans in the window. Inside there is a 1950s espresso machine and several shelves of jars filled with sweets all labelled Maria's Lollies. There are a couple of red plastic tables outside to sit on so I ask the young woman behind the counter for – *un cappuccino per favore*. She then asks me *lei Italiano?*

No sono Australiano, I reply, *ma mi piace molto Italiano.*

By the time she's made the best cup of coffee this side of Naples I have told her that I lived in Rome in the 60s and that I have forgotten most of my Italian. She has told me her name is Mariella and that I can come any time and practice my Italian with her. Feeling that my emotional batteries have been recharged by the friendliness of the people and the enjoyment of the coffee scroll ritual, I begin the walk up the hill to the Gaol. When I arrive at the corner of Bell Street and Sydney Road the first thing I see is a huge Real Estate hoarding which says: Welcome to Pentridge Village. The most exclusive new residential precinct in Melbourne" I don't know whether to laugh or cry. I walk a little further and see the gaol which has been closed for some years and is soon to be redeveloped as a holiday resort for poltergeists. I'd forgotten that when the city fathers of Melbourne had Pentridge designed in 1856 they instructed the architects to build them a replica of an English mediaeval Castle in granite. This morning it looked like an outdoor set for the local amateur production of *Camelot*. I go searching for someone who may be able to let me have a look inside.

When I turn the corner I see the roller spikes on the end of the wall and instantly I'm in the exercise yard again with a group of boys all about my age. It's raining and we're huddled under the corrugated tin awning which is also the latrine eating our lunch. We're staring in silence and disbelief at a boy who has climbed up onto the wall. He was brought in this morning. His face is bruised and swollen. He looks as though he's been badly beaten up. He is crawling toward the spikes. The guard in the lookout turret fires a warning shot over his head, the boy speeds up his crawling and the next shot fired by the guard hits him in the upper thigh. Blood spurts out of it like a fountain and splashes down onto the yard below. Several of the boys throw up and a guard takes us back inside to our cells. My cell was probably even smaller than I remember it. There was no bed. You were given four blankets and slept on the floor. These had to be folded each morning in a particular way. A bucket with a tap over it was in one corner and there was a small window that was too high up to see out of. I still suffer very badly from claustrophobia that began there. It was there that I contemplated suicide the first time. I was sent to Pentridge Goal at the beginning of my trial in 1951 the year they executed Jean Lee for her part in the brutal murder of an old bookmaker. She was the last female to be hanged in Australia.

Late one evening after lights out the guards erected the gallows somewhere near my cell. I could hear them practising the mechanism of a trap door. I don't know how long the rehearsal lasted but in the quiet that followed I decided that I wanted to end my life. I felt hopeless and worthless and I wanted to die. Usually in the past I had been able to rise above whatever situation I found myself in by laughing it off or getting angry but tonight I couldn't laugh or get angry, I was just a scared little boy. I started crying as seventeen years of my life passed before my eyes in a torrent of bad memories. I'm sure my sobbing would have echoed throughout the world had not the walls of my cell been deliberately made to absorb all human emotion.

I cried and cried until I had no more tears. Sometime before dawn I thought I heard the trap door again. I panicked and had difficulty breathing then I felt something in the cell grab me and I heard voices yelling at me from inside my head, "Did you ask to be born in the slums of Carlton?" "Did you ask to be born black? Did you ask to be raped and abused by Uncle Josh and Arthur Challenger from the age of four?" I didn't know what was happening to me. The voices got louder and I thought I was going mad. I was so exhausted I passed out. Next morning when the banging on the cell door by the guard woke me up I lay for a few minutes thinking about the voices. I knew that what they had said was true. None of this shit was my fault. They were telling me that there was a better life for me somewhere out there in the world and I became determined to find it when I got out of Pentridge.

I heard those voices again in 1989. I came home to recuperate from an operation I'd had in London to remove several growths in my nose and head. It was early in the morning and I was sitting on Bronte Beach thinking about my future. I had spent the last three years running away from London and myself. In February 1986 after 16 years together my friend , partner and lover Dave died of an AIDS-related brain infection. I had given up my work and nursed him watching as he developed severe dementia and loss of bodily control knowing all the time there was nothing anyone could do for his condition, I spent nine months watching him die. I wanted to end his life for him but I couldn't do it.

I met Dave in 1970 when I was in the much-publicised production of Kenneth Tynan's Nude Revue *Oh Calcutta* at the Roundhouse in North London. Dave had come down from Yorkshire for a job interview and bought an overpriced ticket from one of the Touts outside the theatre. We met briefly in the bar after the performance and I invited him home for supper.

I had just finished a long and happy relationship with a well-known actress I had first worked in 1961 in a production of "Grab me a Gondola" at The Gaiety theatre in Dublin. In 1968 she played the lead in "The Boy Friend" at the Comedy Theatre in London for Sandy Wilson and myself. We had the same agent and singing teacher and were very close friends. We had been sharing a flat in Holland Park since 1966.

Considered the couple most likely to succeed we announced our engagement. The newspapers ran big headlines *Girlfriend finds real boyfriend in the Boy Friend*. We enjoyed all the publicity and the parties but we both knew that we were never going to get married and that eventually we would have to move on which we did. We are still very good friends.

Dave returned to Yorkshire next morning and wrote me several letters. I was his first homosexual experience. He got the job he'd been interviewed for and when he came down to London he moved in with me.

Six months after Dave died, Mag telephoned me and told me that Mumma had joined him in the Dreamtime. I came home for the funeral, stayed a few days had a misunderstanding with Mag and returned to London feeling depressed. I no longer wanted my gallery. I was exhausted and very angry with the world and God. I couldn't and wouldn't grieve properly for either of them.

The sea at Bronte that morning was flat and calm, suddenly from out of nowhere a 'whirly whirly' wind came off the water, it circled me and in the whirling sand I heard the voices; this time they were saying *come home, it's time to come home.* Later that day I called my solicitor and agent in London and told them both that I intended to close my gallery and return to Australia permanently. Having decided to come home I became very apprehensive about what I was going to do when I got here, I'd had a good career in London and had lived there for more than half my life. I always knew that one day I would want to return to Australia but now I wasn't sure how I would fit in. I had never really been accepted before I left there and from the first day I arrived in Europe I went into a thirty-year period of total denial of my black inheritance.

This morning sitting there on the beach I knew it was the right time for me to reclaim it and the only way I could do that was to come home and involve myself in the community.

Today I stood looking at those spikes on the wall for some time and I shook my head in disbelief at the brutality of the system 50 years ago. It's time for me to move on and I have a strange feeling of achievement as I walk down Bell Street to catch the tram to Carlton. These memories are mine and I've earned the right to live with them. It takes an unmemorable twenty minutes for the tram to reach Lygon Street where I get off.

I was born in the Women's Hospital, Carlton, on December 25 1934. The third child born out of wedlock to Winifred Ann Tovey and Frederick James Morton. I can in all honesty claim the title *little black bastard* that was so often bestowed upon me during my formative years. On my father's police record he states that he is an American Negro and that he was born in England. I have no exact date for his arrival in Australia but Mumma told me that he arrived here as a young man and joined an all-black minstrel show. I believe he was also in the chorus of the now-famous Oscar Ashe production of "Chu Chin Chow" at the Princess Theatre in 1912 and "Show Boat" in 1927.

He enlisted in the 1st Australian Imperial Force at Holsworthy NSW in 1915 and was shipped out to the Middle East at the age of 26. He learnt to ride while he was stationed in Egypt. He wanted to join the Light Horse but was rejected on medical grounds as he had a slightly withered hand. Instead, he played the piano and sang in the Anzac Hostel, the Officers' Mess in Cairo.

He was discharged without his medals, and, back in Australia, in 1918 at Collingwood he married Irene Kathleen Morton. She was a vaudeville artist from Tasmania. Unless she had died he was still married to her when he met Mumma.

The first born was Fred then Marion (whom I called Mag) then me, followed by Claudia and Francis. Fred was four years older than me and he was the first to be taken away by the Welfare at age ten to save him from "a life and career of vice and crime." He was uncontrollable at home and he told the Welfare Inspector that he didn't want to live there.

In 1997 the University of Melbourne, where he had lectured, named a communications award in his memory. He had a successful career as an attache for the Australian Embassy in Holland and France. On his return to Australia he became a radio and news editor for the department of Immigration in Canberra and in the 1980s he produced films for the Aboriginal Affairs department.

On Fred's removal papers in 1940 it states:

> Father street musician, poor home, drink and neglect. Mother Australian, father shows colour line. Boy beaten at school for dark appearance. Morton said his son could not go to school because he had no boots but when I questioned the boy he said his mother kept him home to look after the baby. I drew Mrs Morton's attention to the children's heads which were verminous.

Freddie was taken to the Royal Park Welfare Depot in the early afternoon but later that night he escaped and next morning began a day of great excitement when the police and welfare came to our house looking for him. He was on the roof of the house opposite hiding behind the chimney; one of the welfare men spotted him and a policemen climbed on the roof and Freddie took off. Mag and I stood in the street and killed ourselves laughing as Freddie jumped from roof to roof whooping with cries of joy until they caught him.

He was sent to the Silesian Brothers, an offshoot of the Royal Park Welfare depot in Sunbury, where he was well educated and looked after by the bothers. It was ten years before I saw him again.

Claudia was born one night at Aunty Myrtle's when Mumma was drunk. A few days later Mumma took off, leaving Claudia behind. She grew up believing Aunty Myrtle was her mother and it wasn't until she was an adult that she learned the truth. Aunty Myrtle's nickname was the Fuzzy Wuzzy: she was a big Aboriginal woman with a mop of fuzzy black hair and a face the colour that comes from years of boozing. She was an old girlfriend of my father's. She was obsessive about Claudia and so afraid of her being taken away that she never let her go to school.

We lived in Barkly Street Carlton. The house, as described in our welfare papers, was *an old two-storey house. The front room was clean and is used by the parents. The back room is used as a kitchen.* I remember the kitchen was very dark, with a black stove and old wooden table that Mumma would stand me on to smear my legs with a paste of treacle and sulphur to get rid of my scabies. It was also under this table that my younger brother Francis was found *in a pool of wine* according to his papers. He was eighteen months old when the welfare came to take him away and he remained a ward of the state in seven different institutions until he was eighteen. To this day I still haven't seen him.

The description of the house goes on. *There are two rooms upstairs, one contained a stretcher bed with a filthy mattress. On the floor was a wire mattress with a dirty flock mattress and dirty blankets. These beds are used by the children.*

This room had a broken window and on cold wet Melbourne nights Mag and I sat at the window and counted Yellow cabs that went by in the street below to stave off our hunger and the noise of the drunks below. The endless days and nights of misery for Mag and I were only interrupted by occasional visits from the welfare. For a few days after that there would be food in the house and we would be washed and clean. Mag was so much a part of my early life that my story is to some extent also her story.

ANNETTE TREVITT

My uncle

I was thinking of a Geography test that I just failed at school when a ute flew past. The driver waved and sounded the horn. It took a moment to realise that it was my uncle. I waved back but he didn't see; he was already fishtailing around a corner. I watched the back of the ute as it disappeared down the street and then turned around and continued to walk home. Tyres screeched in the distance as he took another corner.

The ute wasn't his. He didn't have one. He didn't have any vehicles. Not any more; not after his wife sold their Ford Falcon and then drove out of town in his Torana, five months ago. His lime-green Torana with black Naugahyde bucket seats, mag wheels, tinted windows and snow lights. Now he borrowed cars. He was a mechanic; 'the best one around' his customers said. He'd want to be, my mother said, for them to put up with the way he thrashed their cars.

I walked down the drive, looking at my shadow stretched out in front of me and thinking of the test again when I heard my father yell,

"It's plywood, Kay, fucken plywood!"

My mother said something but I didn't catch it. I snapped off a hydrangea flower and threw it behind some bushes and walked around the back. A door leant up against the side of my father's shed. A hinge was ripped off and it looked like it had been kicked in. It must be what they were arguing about. My uncle must have brought it over for my father to fix.

My mother was at the stove, rolling sausages around in a fry-pan, and my father was at the table, sorting through a pile of papers in front of him. It wasn't hard to see that they were bills; one look at his face told you that.

"All I'm saying Ron is -"

The screen-door banged shut behind me. My mother looked up, startled.

"– oh hello love," she said and went back to the pan, "where've you been, Cathy's? All I was saying, Ron, is it shows that he's not over her."

"Bullshit Kay, Lenny couldn't give a rat's arse about that woman any more."

Then my father looked over at me,

"Gidday sweetheart, how was school?"

I didn't answer. He didn't expect me to. He had already gone back to glaring at the bills but I knew his anger was with my mother.

"Has anyone seen the tongs?" she asked as she dropped a saucepan of peas onto the stove. Water spilt out onto a hotplate and hissed. She wasn't too happy with him either.

I walked into the TV room. We called it that but it was really the same room as the kitchen, only it had carpet. My father and his brother had put it down one Saturday while my mother and my aunt made sandwiches and talked and smoked and sunned their legs out the back. As I sat down on the couch, I looked at an edge of carpet that was too short. In my mind I always tried to make it fit properly against the wall so you didn't see what was under it. I hated seeing the lino. It was the last piece that they had cut and tacked down. They cared when they started out but by late afternoon, all they wanted to do was have a drink.

The sausages continued to fry on the stove and my father punched numbers into a calculator. I went to turn on the TV and then remembered that it was broken and that my mother wasn't in a hurry to get it fixed. She said it ate our brains. I looked at the screen for a moment longer and then picked up our atlas from the coffee table and flicked through it. I knew some countries from school but not many. It fell open on a map of the Mediterranean. I looked hard at Albania and told myself that I will never forget where it was and the countries that were close to it. But once my eyes wandered off and then came back, I couldn't find it.

I was still looking for it when my father stopped at the calculator.

"And as for the money, Christ! Talk about add insult to injury," he said.

My aunt had left $1500, along with the farewell note, for my uncle to put towards another car. My father always brought it up whenever she was mentioned.

"Has any one seen the tongs?" my mother asked.

"You can't even get a good set of tyres for that," he went on to say, "No wonder he hasn't got a car yet."

My mother slammed down the fry pan,

"What the hell would you know about the cost of new tyres with the clapped out rust-buckets you get around in."

She then went on to remind him that the only reason his shit-heaps, and his father's for that matter, stayed on the road was because of the hours of work his brother put into them. But my father wasn't listening. He didn't see it like that. He loved to brag about how he had never paid more for a car than the cash in his pocket at the time.

My mother pulled out three plates from the cupboard. She held them against her chest and stared at the corner of the cupboard as blue smoke rose from the fry-pan. Finally she put the plates down and went back to the stove. She picked up the pan and poured in more oil.

"What is it with your family and cars anyway?"

"Do you mind, I'm trying to concentrate," my father said, running his hand through his hair. He punched in some more numbers, paused, swore and then went back to it.

"Leave all that Ron, I'll do it, has anyone seen the bloody tongs?" my mother said as she opened and closed drawers, without really looking in them.

"The Millers! Now there you go," she said and threw open the last drawer, "there's an example. If your brother really wanted a car, he could've had theirs. They gave him first offer and -"

"He didn't want it!"

"He's surrounded by cars all day, he could buy anything and fix it, but he doesn't. He can't, can't you -"

A look crossed my father's face.

"She walked out on him Kay and don't you ever forget it."

My mother slammed the drawer shut and looked out the window. Her shoulders rose and fell. After some time she turned around and looked directly at my father.

"Listen knucklehead," she said slowly, "if he gets another car, it's like saying to himself it's over, she's not coming back."

"She's not."

"I know! Jesus Christ Ron, we all know that but he doesn't, he doesn't want to, he misses her for God's sake."

"What the hell do you know about what goes on in my brother's head?"

My mother dipped her hand into a pocket of her dressing gown and then the other before looking as if she only just remembered that she didn't smoke any more. She rubbed her face.

"They were married for 15 years of course . . ."

"Of course what? Clearly it meant nothing to her, she clears out without a second thought," my father said.

"She was desperate Ron."

"And she steals his car on top of it."

"It was a Torana! A fucken Torana, not a Lamborghetti."

"He loved that car."

"And he loved her," she said, looking at my father.

My father looked at her for a long time.

"I tell you, you don't know anything about anything," he said.

My mother threw back her head and laughed. She turned back to the stove and picked up the pan. She flipped over the sausages with a fork and then stuck it into each one. Fat sizzled in the pan.

"And you do?"

"There are just things that you don't understand; things that you don't get."

She laughed harder.

"And what are they Ron? What could they be?"

"That's it, I don't have to listen to this any more."

"Go then, see if I care."

With that my father stood up, grabbed the newspaper from the table and rolled it up as if he was about to walk straight out the door. But he didn't. Instead he stood and stared at my mother but she didn't lift her eyes from the fry-pan.

"Right then," he said and thumped the paper hard on the table and stormed out. Then he stopped on the back steps and said,

"And you don't know a fucken thing about cars either."

A few moments later the shed door slammed shut.

"How do you want your egg?" my mother asked as she cracked open one on the side of the fry-pan. The yolk broke and ran down her wrist.

She handed me my plate, put the tomato sauce on the coffee table and sat down, next to me, on the couch. We faced the TV as if it was on. She had the dressing gown on over jeans. She had taken to putting it on when she got home from work; more so now that she didn't smoke. As she reached for the tomato sauce, I noticed that the cuffs were frayed and grubby.

My father's dinner sat on a plate on top of a saucepan. My mother had covered it with the fry-pan lid and removed it from the heat. He knew it was there.

A neighbour's lawn mower got louder. My mother didn't seem to notice. She was thinking about something. She hadn't asked me about the test and I wasn't going to bring it up. I didn't want to tell her that I had failed. For some reason once the test was in front of me, I couldn't recall a thing. The more I tried to think of what to write, of what the words were, the more they got stuck in my head and wouldn't come out.

I rolled my sausage up in bread and tomato sauce. The lawn mower spluttered to a stop and in the quietness, I thought of my aunt. I liked her, so did my mother. She wanted her to call but she hadn't; my aunt hadn't contacted anyone since she left.

Suddenly a thought punctured my chest.

"Is she dead, mum?"

"Who? Leah? Lord no love, we would have heard that."

"How?"

My mother didn't answer. She continued to eat with the same small even bites, but her face looked different. Now she looked worried as if she, too, was caught up in a test that she wasn't sure about. Maybe she remembered; maybe she remembered what it was like to be in a car with Leah.

I did. And I thought of the last time I went to Griffith with her. The road was unsealed but that didn't stop her driving fast or make her

hold the wheel properly. She didn't seem to be concentrating and then, out of nowhere, she spun around and stared at me and said,
"I hate living here, I hate it, I'm screaming inside."
I looked at her but I didn't know what to say. All I could think of, were how her eyes looked small and dark, like a budgie's, behind the glasses. Then the car hit loose gravel and she had to swing the steering wheel around hard to get back onto the road. Her purse fell off the dash and everything in it went all over the floor but I couldn't move to pick anything up. Instead I stared at the door handle and held onto my seatbelt. The road roared beneath us and as stones hit underneath, I kept thinking that at any moment we will slam into a tree.
But we didn't. We got to town and, after my aunt went to the bank, we had lunch in a Cafe on the main street. We sat in a booth and I had a hamburger and then a lime spider with double ice-cream, while my aunt had a cigarette and a cappuccino. Everything was quiet on the way home and I remembered how whenever I looked out of the window beside me and saw my reflection, on top of the hills; I felt grown up.

I left the burnt bits of sausage on the side of my plate, along with most of the peas, and put it on top of the atlas on the coffee table. I didn't tell anyone about my aunt's driving that day or about what she said. I kept it to myself, but I thought about it a lot and when I did, like now, I thought of the word, disquiet. I liked knowing the word; I felt like I knew things, like I might be smart, like I had gone away too.
An electric sander started up in my father's shed.
"Your father must be hungry," my mother said and stood up.
She went to the sink and looked out. A breeze came in through the window and lifted her hair. I watched and wondered if she felt it; the movement was so gentle. I went and stood next to her and looked out too. The sun had nearly gone down behind the shed and the backyard was in full shadow. And the plywood door wasn't there any more.
I put the plug in the sink and turned on the taps and looked up, just as a flash of white light flared up and then vanished, like lightning, in the shed window. Silence followed.

"Christ! What was that?" my mother said, clinging to the edge of the sink.

"Ron!" she called out, "RON!"

He didn't answer. Everything was hot and thick. My ears roared. I couldn't move, nor could my mother. Then she flew to the back screen door and threw it open.

The next thing I knew my father was in the shed's doorway as if he had been there all his life. My mother turned and looked at me but I looked away. I turned off the taps. I wanted to cry. Some time passed and then my mother said,

"Have you finished with the newspaper yet?"

She sat at the table, opposite my father, and read it while he ate his dinner. Even though it must have been cold and soggy, he didn't look up from his plate except to pour more beer from his stubby into my mother's glass. My parents looked pale and yellow under the ceiling light. Their backs were rounded like two beetles. The pile of bills was still between them but pushed to one side. I looked at them for a while longer and then went to my room, closed the door and flopped onto my bed. I thought of the Geography test and wondered if my mother will remember it too. I wished that I could go away but I knew that I wouldn't. Where would I go? It was clear that I wasn't going anywhere.

A car drove by and the room lit up momentarily and then went dark again. As the sound faded away, I pictured my aunt streaking across the plains in my uncle's Torana. I pictured the GT strip that ran right over the top of the car; over the bonnet, the roof and the boot. My uncle had done it himself with masking tape and a spray can. The strip was a little off centre and there was a little kink in one of the lines. I knew; I watched him do it.

Susan Varga

MEMORY AND EXILE, EXILE AND MEMORY

My father said to me a few weeks ago, plaintively, only half in joke – "I was a refugee too, once. Could you pay me more attention?"

Monday, 10th September, 2001

A perfect spring day till now, but the clouds coming over. Such bursting forth in the garden, and much more still to come! The rhododendrons are starting, and the white freesias are earlier than usual, fat and fragrant.

Tonight, in the aftermath of the Tampa crisis, we resign from the Moss Vale branch of the Labor Party. But where to direct the energy now? Into fringe politics? Into visiting the refugees in detention centres? Into writing letters, articles, to try to put dents into the xenophobic selfish narrowness overtaking this country's citizens?

We went up to a rally yesterday in Sydney. Less than a thousand people.

Monday 24th September

Almost two weeks have passed since the suicide planes flew into the World Trade Centre towers in New York and into the Pentagon in Washington. Possibly 6000 dead and the world in turmoil and tension. In Australia, Reith and Co suggest that the asylum seekers trying to come here in leaky boats may well be terrorists.

My grandmother, aged sixty five, used a people smuggler when she escaped Hungary to join us here in Australia. She escaped from behind the Iron Curtain because there were no more visas out. She slept in disused factories and potato fields. She was given a hero's welcome when she arrived.

I came across a man called Kassak by accident. I noticed, stacked against the wall of a furniture shop in Woolhara, a set of collages that immediately said, Europe, 1920s. I looked for the signature – almost certainly Hungarian. Who was he?

Wednesday 26th September

America on a war footing. Such a self-righteous quest for vengeance. As if evil only began the day that America was hit at its (cold financial) heart. As if America has never done anything to contribute to the toll of unjustified suffering and death.

Everyone reads the papers, watches the TV compulsively, talks about the New York tragedy non-stop, HAS to talk about it, to relieve their anxiety and apprehension. Might our comfortable world collapse, either gradually or as suddenly as the helpless collapse of those hundred- storey twin towers? And there's a restlessness, in a lot of people, to DO something, anything. But no-one knows what.

The American empire is beginning to crumble I think, and perhaps our own safe country with it, and I have very mixed feelings about that. I wake up in this haven, the spring flowers more numerous daily, and one part of me just wants to enjoy this perfection a little longer, because bad and dangerous times are ahead. But another part of me is already rejecting this lovely, tiny piece of the world, impatient to be in the thick of the anti-war movement, protesting against the treatment of refugees, because that would be a way to keep sane and to keep one's conscience at bay.

Keeping one's conscience at bay though is not the priority – it's WHAT WOULD BE BEST TO DO? And I'm no nearer the answer than I was two weeks ago. I've offered to go to Villawood Detention Centre, I've gone to a protest meeting , will go to another. . . . Should we write a book on women refugees? Helpless, helpless.

I found out a bit about Kassak – a working class kid who left school at eleven and didn't read a book till he was eighteen. He went on to become the poet and painter of the avant-garde.

Kassak was an anarchist, if he was anything. He spent his life in a dogmatic struggle against ideologies, believing that flux, change and creativity were the only truths.

He wrote a thousand page autobiography that only covered his life to the age of thirty five.

Thursday, 4th October

The refugees have been taken to Nauru. Hastily erected tents and toilets in the middle of nowhere. Many refuse to get off the ship. The Government used force on some – two soldiers on each side, frog-marching distressed, shouting men. Howard still high in the polls – the more fascist he gets the more the populace seems to approve. Some estimates put the cost of his refusal to let four hundred plus people land here at over a hundred million dollars.

Today we read and write books about the Jews, homosexuals and gypsies of World War Two. Stories of desperate survival – hiding, false passports, bribing of officials to stay alive. We thrill with indignation, reading about the ships full of Jews turned back from the world's harbours. And can't see the parallels.

I sneak out to the garden a few times each day – marvel and pull a few weeds.

Kassak did a spell in prison once the brief Hungarian Communist regime of 1919 failed. He fled to Vienna as the rightist Admiral Horthy rode into Budapest on a white horse. In Vienna, so near, so far from his homeland, Kassak, unlike the middle class intellectuals in exile, could not speak any other language. He was desolate.

I discovered Rosika Schwimmer by accident, too. Rosika, who shares my birth name, was a Hungarian Jewish bourgeoise, turned feminist and peace activist. After the Communist Revolution collapsed, she also fled Hungary. She lived much of her life in exile in New York, battling for the rights of women, fighting the US Government for peace.

Rosika was short round, dark, and had huge presence. She fought all her life, often lonely, for causes.

Tuesday

No move from the US as yet. Blair is being their hawkish mouthpiece. In the newspapers a flood of information about places we've barely heard of before, because they may well be the new theatre of war - Kajekistan, Uzbekistan etc. I never knew that China had a border with Afghanistan. Pakistan's status as a pariah state is transformed now that the US needs it so badly. Much of the international community suddenly willing to see the Chechyna war not as Russian oppression but a war against Islamic terrorism after all. The whole world realigning. Things changing so fast that the newspapers can barely keep pace.

The first mention of a Palestinian state by America – a most interesting development.

Here and maybe all over the world the wave of fear about terrorist attacks is making Government crack down on security and thus on civil liberties. In Australia, increased power to ASIO, beefing up the SAS, powers of detention for forty eight hours without a charge.

When Kassak returned from exile in Vienna, he stayed on in Hungary till he died, in and out of favour with more than one regime.

I bought two of those Kassak collages I found in the furniture shop. They hang on my white wall, so he is never far from my mind. Am reading – skimming in parts – a book on Hungarian intellectuals in exile. Rosika has a couple of paragraphs. This compulsive activist for social justice wrote just one book apart from her hundreds of tracts and pamphlets – a work in English on the Hungarian fairy tales of her childhood.

Interesting to see Kassak from other angles. So far I've only met him through the autobiography I'm struggling through in Hungarian. I already see how he's going to come across – unbending, dictatorial, puritan in his own peculiar way. But a trail blazer, untrammeled by bourgeois expectations and behaviours.

Kassak sometimes reminds me of my friend, George Molnar. I was interested in George, reluctantly while he was alive, more so now I have the freedom of his death. George lived through the war in Hungary as a child. At fifteen and already a precocious intellectual, he came to Australia. Like me, a Holocaust survivor. He was forced to shed his skin and to take on others – Libertarian, political activist, gambler, public servant, philosopher extraordinaire. After that first exile from his birthright of European Jewish intellectual, he took on successive voluntary self-exiles, over and over, as if to relive the pain.

FRIDAY

Election called for November the tenth. For the first time in twenty years I don't care who gets in – it will make no difference to the issues that matter. Will I last in this enforced indifference? Maybe seeing Beazley trying to outdo Howard in warmongering and fearmongering will keep me to my resolve. How then to vote – Democrat, informal, Greens? Perhaps if enough people defect to the Democrats or Greens, Kim will finally realise that a Labor Party without principle is no party at all.

Fighting a constant feeling of weariness, wanting to retreat from the world. But that way lies depression, and moral failure.

I heard about Rosika Schwimmer from Les Strait, a a retired musician who teaches cello here in Bundanoon. In his family papers Les found a letter from Rosika to his grandmother in Hodmezovasarhely, my father's birthplace. Rosika may or may not be my relative.

Les Strait is a Hungarian Jew who arrived in Australia in 1939 before things got really bad. In his declining years he wants to be known again as Laci Strasser – he is trying to find his way back from exile.

Monday, October 8, 2001

The Americans have finally made their move. It's still night in Afghanistan so no-one knows the extent or the methods. Despite fears of counter attack, the predominant mood in America is relief. Even I felt a momentary relief that the daily waiting was over, then despair and dread. This will not be a war that can be kept within boundaries, physical or emotional.

There is no clear place to go. Who is the real terrorist? The arrogant greedy maxi-state or the fanatics with a holy war lighting their eyes? If it were merely about the inequality between East and West ... but it is far more complex. Racial and religious hatred are at the heart of it too, and as a Jew I stand on infinitely shifting and paradoxical ground. How dangerous it is to say that much of the Muslim world hates the Jews and the Americans for 'good reason'. Once they become the generalised 'evil doers', all kinds of thoughts and acts are justified against them. Yet so, too, with Bin Laden and his dedicated few hundred or few thousand followers. Hourly they are more demonised by the West, and so much killing will be justified in the name of rooting out their 'evil'.

And finally Australia is being plunged into the world-wide refugee crisis. We no longer feel inviolate or masters of our own fate. We are being swept into a chaotic world kicking and screaming. So reluctant are we to lose our undeserved paradise that we're willing to confuse refugees with the regimes they are fleeing. Most of us can't see individuals, each with a story, each with a family, all with an already dangerous and desperate journey part achieved.

The prevailing feeling is that if even one terrorist were to slip in with them, the rest must be sacrificed. I try to point out how many Nazis 'slipped in' with the Jews and other 'reffos' after WW2, but it doesn't do much good.

During the war my mother lived illegally on a false passport, pretending to be of another religion. Yet when she left Hungary she had one of the last legal visas issued before the Iron Curtain came down. Is she a law-breaking opportunist? Is she a heroine? She used money and courage. Is she better or worse than those who patiently waited for someone to help them? Those who patiently waited for death?

Two days ago, America announced an aid package for the starving Afghans. Today it bombs the same population.

What to do? What to do? Inaction is not an option. Just writing this down for the future – if there is one – is not enough.

I heard on the radio that the Americans are having a tough time because Afghanistan is 'target poor' – very little to bomb left, whereas America is 'target rich' -in grand buildings, wonderful museums, military institutions and sacred sites, in which Washington in particular abounds. In the weird new logic emerging, Afghanistan is at an advantage. It might win because there is nothing to bomb and its people can hide in caves deep in pitiless mountains in the winter.

TUESDAY

This farce of trying to write. Maybe I'll take a month off and throw myself into the hard slog of mobilising support for the refugees. The war and the refugees are obscenely interlinked. Will Howard still turn back those who are fleeing the regime he's vowed to help the US destroy? Very likely.

I'm sick to death of doing so little. You may not see me, my computer , for some time.

~

MONDAY MARCH 4, 2002

I haven't written anything for over five months. Thrown myself instead into probably the most intensive 'activist' time of my life. We started "Rural Australians for Refugees" and have worked so hard at it that I have not written a word apart from newsletters, press releases, ten point plans, fact sheets, or material for websites.

I'm going mad, not writing – not consciously, but losing the judgement that with me only comes from the deeper place that is real writing.

But it has felt as if there is no choice. The swing in Australia towards xenophobia, racism, callousness, repression has been so dramatic, that the fight against it is both essential and selfish. Selfish because I can't passively watch the deterioration in morality and civic values that is turning this country into a place I do not want to live in.

George Molnar is not someone from the faraway past. He died just two years ago. For a year or more when I was young and scared, he was my lover. Intermittently, we were friends. Because of him for many years I thought that the only attribute worth having was a well-trained, logical mind, and felt a failure.

MARCH 6

What has happened since early October? I turned 58. The Liberals won the election, and their win was strongly influenced by their use of the Tampa and 'children overboard.' canard. The war in Afghanistan is still going on, sporadically. Bin Laden has not been found. There are now prisoners treated like caged beasts in Guantanamo Bay. The boat people have stopped coming in the last few months, but no-one knows if it's because of the monsoon season or because Australia is now internationally infamous for being 'tough' on asylum seekers. The chorus of protest against the Government's policies and the Opposition's spineless acquiescence has grown into a roar, and still the majority of Australians remain unmoved. Still they back Howard, despite the self harm the detainees daily inflict upon themselves, the demonstrations at the detention centres, the horrors of the conditions revealed in them.

And that is what truly shocks me – facing what I have long suspected but haven't wanted to really confront – that this country's myth about itself as racially tolerant, easy-going, is just that, a myth at best and a great big lie at worst. There are no excuses, nowhere left to hide.

Kassak went to prison, then into exile. My father was in a concentration camp and lost his wife, two boys, mother, father and most of his brothers and sisters. Rosika was forced into exile. She died alone in New York. The child George nearly starved in Budapest and was saved by Wallenberg.

I have suddenly become an Australian. Till now I have never been really sure of that. I've lived here since I was five, speak with a broadish Australian accent, yet half my mind and heart have been elsewhere, feeling the Jewish and Hungarian parts of me lurking in the folds of consciousness.

But now, in the shame of these last few months, I can say I'm Australian. Because I identify with the worst in us – I understand even the shock jocks and the openly racist. I too have a skerrick of the fear and ignorance that drives them. I can identify with the middle Australians, the good hearted amongst us who now fear that the last vestiges of the old, decent certain Australia they grew up with will disappear if we don't 'control our borders.'

It's not that I don't understand the rest of Australia. I understand it all too well. I more fully understand its capacity for good and its capacity for evil.

After Kassak died he became more famous. There was a retrospective for him in Paris. Rosika sank into obscurity after her death. But someone in America is now writing her biography. George died of a heart attack aged sixty five on the steps of the Fisher Library. He had nearly finished his book on the mind.

My father died last week. This was one of his favourite jokes. A young couple marries. They are poor and are forced to go and live with the in-laws. The house is crowded, there is not much to eat, the in-laws quarrel constantly, there is no privacy. The young couple are miserable. They go and see the rabbi to pour out their complaints to him. He listens patiently then says,

"Go and buy a goat and take it home. It's to live in the house with you, not outside. Then come back and see me in a week's time"
The rabbi refuses to say any more. The young couple obediently buy the goat and take it home.

The week passes, oh so slowly. They return to the Rabbi, desperate.

"Oh rabbi", *they wail*, "how happy we were before the goat came to live with us!"

Marion M. Campbell

Hanging on his word

Extract from Tardis Envy, *novel in progress*

1.

Rose stands at the letterbox holding the envelope. It's like being realised in a memory that's been here all the time, waiting for her. She sees the she-oak shadow pulse violet, ginger; sees the magpie drilling for worms, head tilting the coppery eye to the dazzle. Then the stiletto beak resumes, stabbing the leaf litter up, down, like a sewing machine needle. The air is full of carolling now—the younger, greyer birds have dropped in to poke about.

She wouldn't have thought that the sight of Gregory's handwriting could give her this kick through her blood and this at her chest. Put the kettle on, cup of tea? Calm down. Savour, elongate this moment.

A cigarette? Gregory said it was only frustrated women who smoked, eyeing her Red Capstan packet as she reached for it. 'Besides,' he said, 'you can tell them a mile off, with the premature wrinkles around the lips. Tightening the purse strings,' he said, watching her mouth. He gave a short burst of that tenor laugh. She disliked him then and found herself avoiding the sun burst of chin and lip in the mirror on her next visit to the bathroom.

She sits down on the top step of the front porch. She doesn't want to open it in front of her mother—Stasia would siphon it out of her before she even had a chance to develop his message in her own head. She must try not to be like that with Joyce—poking about in her daughter's dark retreats to see what resentments fester, what passions strike.

The steps are snap-frozen in their molten spread downwards, a staggered series of curves. Another touch of deco boldness from

Stasia. Rose's taste has lagged back with her mother's old style, on the Puritan side, while, well into her sixties, Stasia has dared to change. But Rose has stayed put. Still, living in Stasia's house she hasn't really had the chance to find out what her own taste has become.

Back in Sydney Mink and Gregory teased her for her austerity, as they called it. As if she shunned decorative flourishes like decadence itself. She never suspected before that people read your taste, that they make you responsible for the cushion on the armchair, but it seems they do.

She tries to make out the postmark on the letter. In any case, there's a little blue Elizabeth II. Could that be that Basingstoke? Gregory often said he wouldn't mind taking advantage of the GP shortage over there and the National Health System, give the family a spell in Berkshire or Surrey, one of the Home Counties. She can just see him zipping around London in one of those Mini Couper S's. The address is a dashed scrawl. The look of speed is probably contrived but over time its refinement has reached the threshold of disappearance—with all the elisions and breaks. His patients must find it infuriatingly cryptic—probably more mystification than a cautionary measure against forgery. You've got to wonder at the genius of these mail sorters and postmen. The letters are tilted forwards like cartoon animals, outrunning their speedlines. Acceleration. Velocity. Celerity. The Thesaurus thing is a kind of addiction too — the paucity, parsimony of her pleasures these days—crosswords and endless cups of tea. Oh and the smoking.

If they could see her now, they'd say it's all ersatz. What's the word they used? She should really try to spend some more time in the sun; her shins are bluish in the light, vein-marbled. There's an operation for varicose veins. Was it Gregory who'd suggested that?

It's like they drew her into a new dimension. Almost literally in that devouring light, that day down at Berowa Waters. It was oil painting at the time, barely figurative landscapes he was doing, although heaven knows why the excursions were necessary for the paintings—the impasto slabs Gregory made with the palette knife turned river to table top and white gum to fish bone.

'Is that what you're doing Gregory; is that what you're after, turning everything into a sort of still life?'

'Of course, of course!'

Why this will to reduce, to strip away all detail? Who's being the puritan now, she'd wanted to say. As if all the detail, the little things in foliage and rocks had been nibbled away. As if some God had pick-pick-picked at it until it was all gone. Then she said, 'You could call it "After the meal".'

'Wha-at?'

'Well, all you've left is like the b-bones of the landscape. You'd wonder what greedy god has eaten there. The whole thing consumed right d-d-down to the b-bone.'

Blurting it out she saw it was transparent silliness—hardly knew where it'd come from. It was the wine.

Then his laughter boomed. It was worth risking his irritation. Now he flushed her with delight—sometimes he liked to be challenged. 'Ah, yes! I like it; I like it! Down to the bone. Pruned and pared. Stripped of all the anecdotal fuss. That's what I'm about, Rose. Spatial relations! Scale, Rose. Scale.'

She did think, I bet in his portraits we'd all end up as skulls.

As his look darted across her skin, though, it came to life; mapping her veins, an irrigation so intense she can bring it back even now. She need not imagine his touch, because it was there in his look—no it's not his touch she craves, and of course there is Mink and there has always been Mink, and perhaps it's always been to do with Mink. They basked in something together, in this having Gregory there, between them, an outrageous child whose tantrums and excesses they indulged. His dimples, his own neat skull, his quicksilver glances, his ripping laughter. Because. Oh yes *le monstre sacré*. Mink always had to be there, come to think of it, for it to work between them. There was something unnerving about him on his own.

Odd that time when he came in, supposedly to check on Joyce's asthma and he said, 'I'll just nip into your bathroom.' Minutes later she was aware of the jumping of the water pipes, of the clunk and throb of adjusted volume. Sure enough, there was steam coming from under the bathroom door. Then he was calling her, 'Rose, could you pass me a towel, please. Rose, Rosie!' He was practically singing. She didn't know what to say. She opened the door a couple of inches and dropped though the blue towel with the thick pile. Had he wanted her to see him? Oh, probably a lot of men are like that. You just have to ignore it.

And what is he trying to reawaken in her now?

The concrete is getting cold; the shadows are lengthening.

Standing up, she feels giddy, as if the vacuum is yawning there, right before her. She must try to remember to eat; once she has made Joyce and David's sandwiches and watched Stasia haltingly spoon out her soft-boiled egg or her thin soup and nibble triangles of dry toast, as if eating what Rose has prepared is a Trial She Must Undergo, she feels replete herself. And she knows she hovers over them, impatient to see them finish, her Wettex on the ready when they drop crumbs on clean Laminex surfaces and on her waxed linoleum.

There'll be words in Gregory's letter that will take days to decipher. That's a large part of the pleasure. The script is more like Arabic, really. It's extravagant . . . in its reductions. Like his painting. Extravagant reduction is exactly the sort of paradox he goes in for. You can practise thinking like that. Gregory makes everything seem paradoxical. The script is the merest trace of speed, like the racing shadow of a flying object, the vowels needing to be called back between the strokes of the consonants. Isn't Hebrew script like that too, marking through their absence the breath of the sacred in the vowels? She'll have to relax into the spaces of this ghostly writing and over days dream its materialisation. It's one way of creating suspense all right.

Of course Gregory and Mink tried to rescue her from herself, as they said, get her out of her little habits of sadness and self-denial. They asked if she weren't using duty as an excuse, if she weren't clinging to her grief over William, to give herself an alibi for not living, to punish herself because she couldn't punish him. How could she punish him? How ridiculous, she'd wanted to say. How ridiculous, when William was dead. Accidentally. Not through his own fault, was it?

But Gregory, 'Do you really believe there's such a thing as an accident, Rose?' And then, in her dreams . . . she did sometimes catch herself at it. Blaming him. It was all very well, taking off like that. They said, 'No, it's anger you won't direct at him, because you do feel it as an abandonment.' Sometimes she'd wanted to say: Surely, you've got better things to think about than whatever motivates me . . . She'd wondered why they couldn't look at themselves a bit more instead of always trying to fossick about in her hidden spaces.

But they had her thinking again about the way William delivered all that shopping. He could have fitted a few affairs into that time. And he was always too jovial for words when he came home. Like he was after early morning sex. Sex made him happy. Anything was forgiven after sex. Perhaps her not knowing he was having affairs made him very grateful too? Perhaps she was entirely in the dark? Or was this suspicion something they'd planted in her, a toxic seed taken root? This gnawing doubt? Is melancholy anger? How ridiculous. She almost got locked into their paradoxes. Surely melancholy isn't anger. Oh it's enough to drive anyone to distraction, this systematic cynicism, all this warped reading of motives. They could be smug; they really could.

The way they Gregory and Mink looked at one another, smiling over her, too. She was too young to let grief freeze her, they said, and she might well retreat into duty to spite fate but it was her kids who'd suffer finally. The dead certainly don't gain from grief and the living don't gain from acts performed for the sake of duty. It might have been Mink who said that.

Those long sessions over scotch or wine had made her feel diminished, voiceless. And yet they were trying to get her to speak up for herself. What was it then? Everything was dragged from under her feet. What was there to speak up for? The self that glowed earlier on with their attentions? Was that any more real than this, this returning mother's daughter? They were warming to it, like tennis. They were alight with one another's cleverness; it was nothing to do with her, really. She disappeared, except as a ghostly excuse for their talk. At these moments she saw they were no good for her. She should leave them. She felt marooned, bereft. Wasn't it Mourning becoming Electra, the play they took her to see in Sydney? She'd sunk into her velvet seat and felt the chill of realisation—they had set it up as a kind of parable.

That was four years ago! Has she fulfilled their prediction, then? Has she let mourning become her? Oh they do care. Beautiful Mink, with the deep cerulean eyes, violet towards the pupil and slightly slanted, her round fruity cheeks, her rosebud lips, her sparkling teeth, her dimples, her contralto laugh. As pretty as Jean Simmonds. It's fitting that they've gone there, to England, to Basingstoke.

Now Rose will have to revise the geography of Britain with the kids, so that they can see where their friends live. Mink said Gregory needed a whole team to service him, not just a wife. Sometimes she said she wished she could just do one or two shifts a week. He was insatiable for the energy of others; he's got his jump leads in all our batteries, she said. Oh, and applause, he had to have applause. Still, the Lancasters had fun; they never saw fun as a waste of time, as Rose had been brought up to do. 'Thought we'd go up to Sydney for the weekend, get in a housekeeper for the kids. Have dinner at the Hotel Australia. What about it?' Their looks challenged her.

Mink said she didn't generally trust women but knew she could confide in Rose; at least Rose saw what she had to deal with, daily. Gregory had undeniable magnetism, cleverness, yes, perhaps even something more than clever, more dangerous as well, an unpredictable something that could turn without apparent provocation. Maybe those romance writers are right; maybe we all thrill to a bit of the beast that can turn on us.

To tame the beast, each woman thinking she can. That we have the beast purring, lips closed over the canines for the moment, snout pushing with its moist, hot breath into our palm! See, he doesn't bite if he sees he can trust you! The risk of Gregory could be heady, if you didn't have to share its domestic space, if you didn't have to manage it, massage it, inflate it, placate it, Mink said.

But they mocked her softly for asking so little of life. It is a humble dream: just to look after her children well, to have some quiet for her thoughts, a reasonably rewarding job, cataloguing kids' books and advising readers—'There's another Georgette Heyer in for you, Miranda.'—time for a last cigarette over a sherry at night, and for no one to lord it over her. But of course, there is Stasia.

Sometimes she thought she glimpsed a touch of fanaticism in Gregory's eyes too, with their translucent aqua and pin-prick pupils but then his laughter made her dismiss that as mere fancy. And he was right actually; she's reduced her expectations to almost nothing. Still it's hardly as if she's chosen comfort.

At least there she isn't at fault. Even William, who very rarely criticised, who wouldn't have hurt a fly, said Rose's family out-spartaned the Spartans, said they were drilled in the Barbed Wire and Bindi School. Until William, she hadn't really questioned the way they'd been in her family. You don't question what you grow up with—bindis and barbed wire or the cotton wool crib—until you're jolted by an outside observation like that. It's true that they took a fierce pride in gritting the teeth and making stony forbearance the first rule for the children.

The purpose of cooking, for instance, was to discipline and punish the lust for food. The potatoes and carrots were relentlessly boiled until they relinquished their potatohood and carrothood in watery oblivion. The meat, which Stasia bought succulent and tender, was tortured on the grill into leather so carbonised it would clatter as it hit the plate, so twisted, that to cut it alongside the neighbouring, desiccated peas, you had to exercise extreme caution, a control verging on genius. If peas weren't squashed by the knife blade onto the inverted fork or impaled by the fork prong before their flight to plate-rim, there was instant banishment from the table.

Injuries were better not mentioned or Rose's father moved straight to surgery. He looked at the angry splinter lodged in the ball of her foot, took a knife from the drawer, sharpened it with quick flourishes of flashing metal, ran boiling water over the blade and sliced straight into her flesh. A whimper would have disgraced her: Stuarts didn't cry; Stuarts didn't faint.

Mink seemed to notice this; wondered why she didn't cuddle her daughter a little more. Well, Mink cuddled her children too much. No, coddling is the word; she coddled them, especially Brio. My Baby, she'd call him, taking the straw-haired, freckle-faced six year-old onto her lap, letting her kids stay home from school and watch westerns on television if they suffered so much as a cold.

It's when Joyce presents her emotions slug-naked that Rose pulls back. She used to feel uneasy rather than jealous when Joyce leaned into Mink for a hug or a casual caress, her eyes narrowing in bliss. It still makes her shiver to recall that look; needy needy Joyce, smarting for love. David has always been different; she enjoyed cuddling him when he was younger. Perhaps it was because he resisted where Joyce yielded, wanting, wanting always more. Even as a baby, David kept self-contained, secure in his contours, anchored in space. His muscular maleness has always been a kind of resistance; he's never seemed hungry for Rose. It's been Joyce's hunger that has almost repelled her, she has to admit.

And what is her own hunger now; it's as if Rose wants too much from the envelope, as if her own quickening heart might be nestled there. She will open it with Stasia's ivory paper knife, with the fretwork depicting elephants in a chain, tail-to-trunk. Fancy celebrating the elephant on the ivory it's killed for! Stasia doesn't seem to consider things like that. She has her ivory and her fox stole, its clasp contrived by locking jaws over the limp paws—as if the fox, having captured itself, is alone responsible for its parlous state! That's something Gregory would laugh at. She does miss the booming approval of his laughter. Something in that that set her free.

She will save for later the luxury of deciphering Gregory's writing; she'll retreat into that warm, magical sphere, once she's given Stasia her last pill for the day and she has disinfected the commode, rinsed and put out the milk bottles; once she's locked the doors; when David and Joyce are asleep; when the last clue is solved in the cryptic crossword; when her nylon stockings are draped to dry over the towel rack. She'll pour herself a big sherry and bring out the letter under the fluorescent tube in the kitchen, where the freshly bleached dish mop hangs still as a sculpture over the gleaming stainless steel draining board.

2.

Gregory Lancaster writes: Something something squire something virtue of the 6 bedroom something we've something something something over in . . . something something practice now, got a number of other something . . . Renovation going well plus something. Volusomething . . . Do the odd something and something article for New Something. Orangerie something. Why not something something something? If you and your something . . . kids. National Health: something heaps. If you want to contribute something, you know, what about just a bit of something. Catch up something etc. Know the British something curriculum? Make a something, do yourself a something something why not take a something—risk for something—once—Rose supposes.

3.

Sometimes Gregory doesn't know where the rage comes from. Its force unnerves him. And shuddering in its wake, yes he feels shame slinking in. Yes he sees it as a dog, as Maurice more precisely, his eyes averted, the amber of alert before the red. Pelvis pulled down and tail hooked low between the hind legs, the dog's cringing enough to recall the last surge of rage, bellowing through him even now, slamming doors shut, room after room. And then the kids' sudden silences, the intent focus on petty tasks when he burst in . . .

The judgement is there in Mink's mute concentration on the children, the nervous ripple across her forehead, then the compensatory, backward crawl of the skin around the brow, the quick blinking of the eyes while she feeds fabric to the sewing machine. Later, she says it quietly. 'This anger of yours, I think . . . You have to look for the source of anger in yourself, Greg. '

These flashes from the past, more frequent now. There are water ripples on the ceiling. There's the curve of Woody's beautiful little arse in the slatted light as he strips and turns slowly towards him in the changeroom at Manly. Woody's eyes soft on Gregory as he takes his hard prick in his hand. Woody is fumbling for him too and oh their gathering fury—he could weep for the surge and the savage intensity of it.

Sometimes he's felt an edge of horror to this need for women and their endlessness. The way Mink goes on and on, never, never enough. Oh her arching body and her breasts spilling back and her operatic moaning as she comes. Sometimes he wants to shut her up. To stop it all. To stuff a singlet into it. Less now. She will curl up, faking sleep breathing. But he hasn't; he hasn't hit her. He came close when she snarled about buying the Morgan on the second mortgage. Couldn't he stop being a playboy even for his own kids? And it's not her but It, the It that eats him, the It that pulls him back into ordinariness, that makes small talk over the paper, the It that discusses what is for lunch over breakfast, that wonders humbly, quietly, placating even before he's shown any irritation, about getting the kids home in time for a decent sleep. 'Kids need some predictability, darling; you'd be the first to concede that,' Mink says, the nerves rippling across her forehead. Predictabilty becomes sclerotic pattern, becomes deadening routine. He notes her all too predictable jerk of the neck to release the tension he's caused. She no longer dares venture any opinions point blank. It's all irony or sheepishness. That sheepishness sometimes makes him want to push her face in. To grasp its folds, soft as pastry dough and squash it in. She's become removed of late, holding herself in reserve. They both need something to relieve the claustrophobia, something to break the mortally predictable climate. She actually suggested Rose, anyhow. As if she'd even tolerate, or perhaps encourage an intimacy there, with Rose. Rose won't be so addicted to routines. He needs Rose's eyes on this work, which he is planning. Not the Medical Practice. There are millions just as suited to general practice as he is. Mink says it's charisma; that his practice runs on charisma. Mink distrusts charisma, of course.

He can't win Rose with charisma. Which is well and good. Has to try harder with her. He will let her understand that she can help him make some sort of a breakthrough. People laugh at the idea of muses now but she'll see that for him it isn't bound up with that sort of romantic stuff. Rose won't be mocking like Mink has become. Her quiet, fucking irony. That infinitesimal raising of the eyebrow. He will be able to move forward in that climate of disinterested clarity, that soft . . . attentiveness. He doesn't need libidinous careering about any more. In any case there'll be breaks he can take in London. Mink and the kids are always relieved if he does. Well and good, he will still take them. But at home he needs steadfast belief. Who doesn't?

Mink's sense of him is roiled now, to a degree by his behaviour, sure, but it's behaviour she brings on by dragging him down into mediocrity, by the edge of critique creeping into her voice, with her *Sorry to bother you with something so mundane but . . . .* Her safe little curtailed harbour of fucking expectations. Her deference, her slavish politeness to his patients, because their flow into his surgery maintains the flow of money, to feed the flow of bills. He's moored here, in this safe little harbour, his chain rusted into his anchor.

He needs a catalyst to change; everyone does, for Christ's sake. Things will get unlodged with Rose; they'll tear up the moorings all right. It'll be a pull each way; but Rose will want him to set the terms, the tone, the direction. Rose is like that. Changing is everything—it's being alive. He'll show Rose and Mink both what he can do with the house, for instance. Disrupt, create, renovate. Renovate is the word.

At least Mink is all for his turning his talent to the domestic, and not just cooking. She's quite happy for him to modernise the heavy-jowled Victorian mediocrity of this house. Of course. Well, he'll show her domestic becoming a little wild. He'll show what cunning winds can blow into that safe harbour of expectations. He'll show these English trapped in tradition and routine what a fucking so-called colonial can do with these spaces and in the process Rose will be his quiet collaborator. It's not a passive witness he wants; he'll let her into his thinking. He'll help her reinvent herself, help her open out her own spaces. If he lets her think she's half-invented it herself, she'll begin to trust his vision for the re-design. A woman like Rose is definitely not like Mink. Mink's obsessed with things he's abandoned, with his unfinished business. She maintains the ledger of failure, of incompletion for those puncturing ironies. She mocks each phase with its passing, as if it isn't all an evolution. As if he hasn't given her stuff to show for it.

Rose will understand catalyst. Rose will challenge him to go beyond himself. Rose knows that he wants to be teased into extensions, that the pleasure is always in going beyond. Well? He wants her to say, but why stop there, Gregory? She'll be allied, perhaps lagging just a little, his gaze blazing the trail, so to speak, so that she might see what it devours in one fell swoop, and always, in its insatiability, how it can conjures up something more fantastic at the next turn: Follow me, follow me, Eurydice, don't retreat into the zone of your own morbidity!

Because that's where he can help. Sever the bonds with the dead. That William has her in a time lag. In return he can launch her as the new style of beauty. The hairless, glowing face. Eyebrowless, virtually. All in structure. Glowing in the virtue of pure functionality, like a piece of Shaker furniture. Her small-breasted frame. Thin, almost boy-like in profile, she'll cut such a figure in a pencil line skirts and flowing top coat cut on the bias. A broad-brimmed hat. He could sell that line, that face. Fashion might be the way to go, after the renovations. All just spatial really. Bit of bottle tan on those lily legs. A photo essay of the renovations with Rose coming down the stairs. Rose in new nylon swimsuit stepping into the pool. The smoking will have to go, of course.

4.

Each elevation, each lobby, each passageway, each unfolding from room to room, each volumetric vision, is of course an essay in seduction, a theory of seduction. Rose will be the perfect recruit here. He'll tell her his gothic line: to induce to stray is the thing, to lose from sight all guidelines, if she's to see anew. To offer no direct routes— ah yes, through indirection to find directions out. There'll be no point of purview or surveillance—visitors will slip from all sure readings. Like neophytes, like new recruits to love, they'll be once again uncertain boys and girls, just drafted in, tentative in line, their blood coursing as if for the first time. Each breath an experiment, they'll approach in broken routes. Together they'll stutter from space to space and she'll feel she's fluked the journey by blind instinct; this might never be quite the same again. It will have to seem aleatory, a risky improvisation. She'll think herself straying while she's being played and he'll choreograph the drift from plane to plane, from volume to volume.

Take, for instance, he can hear himself saying, his neat scalp aglow, his dimples deepening, his eyes crystal-bright, take this entrance whose inner perspex wall offers what seems at first the merest flaw, the slightest warp; but then, fixed into it like a nascent pearl inside the oyster, an opalescent bubble—it's a convex mirror inverting the surprise on the her face! She'll find herself taken in before she's entered the real interior; the known lineaments will stream away into dissolution; she'll be trying to recompose her face before she sees her host –

Oh the last arrangements at St. Peter's gate! Host will take on new meanings here. She'll be the somnambulist reaching for the retreating shape of dream—then she'll see her new emergence in his eyes. And she'll be drawn to him! Literally—drawn to him, scripted to him by this slow, sure, ineluctably cursive flow. Already, just as she thinks she's presenting herself for the first time after such long separation, she'll be quite changed.

His talk will come in such mellifluousness, a sonic sphere to buoy her, all insidious gradation; there'll be no chance for her to catch her bearings, no space, until she's unfurling in that interior, to fetch an answer, and then it will be too late, a dialogue in which she, the visitor, is always retardataire, just like the mock retro-exterior.

Yes! He'll convince her that she is the muse of this vision, its primary participant. His ambition has to look like modesty. Rose'll appreciate the irony of inverted hubris. This beats painting. To have the viewer ambulant, caught in his volumes, threaded through his blind turns: to perplex and tease, that's the thing. In this house, a perambulatory tease will unfold. Perambulatory, Rose will like that. Front elevation: perhaps, why not? Clean lines, neo-classically sure of its rhetoric. Sober Palladian?

There must be a disjunction, between the formal rhetoric of façade and the interior. The wit, the surprise element depends on this. Not isomorphic . . . but what is it? The prefix cata maybe . . . Cata—yes. Catamorphic, why not. He'll sit up with Rose and Mink, spell out this vision. Mink will roll her eyes then wink at Rose. Too late—Rose will already be away with him.

Oh, the children. That rather sheepish, secretive, what's her name, again? Oh dear, Joyce. That's an irony for you, not much joy in that one. She's a strange shadowy girl. And David, the boyo Rose dotes upon. Bright enough. Well-enough made. He almost wanted to kiss that little prick when she was towelling him dry.

Catamorphic—now that's authority if you can skew a word towards new meanings and govern its deviation in the minds of others— between expectations raised by the facade and the unfolding of interiors; what he aims at is an involution. The catamorphic relation . . . performs a revolution of expectations. A façade is just like a title, really. A horizon of expectations always subject to revisions, subtle or radical, that's the adventure. Every building has to tell a story and in doing so, convert the visitor's expectations into something else in tune with the designer's purpose. Does he have a purpose? Is seduction an end?

Seduction is an approach, of course, an approach, only. Is this then how it is, what it is for him, with incompletion? Why he cannot ever finish? Why it so distresses him to finish things off? To see all desires reduced to convergence in a mere point, a puncture through which all expectation leaks? The waste of it. The uselessness, finally.

Ah, that he'll only know afterwards; retrospectively, once he's already changed. There must be no easy relation between outsides and insides. And like a façade, the face, the human face—the face that would be a window, well, there's something obscene about that! All faces—mobile, contractile, tensile, subject to spasms, stretched in smiles, rarely without malice, or contorted baroquely in grief, tears for the self, tears for the self, faces in surrender, rending themselves inside-out, are, when you start to think about them, all disgusting display boards, whose areas of opacity and transparency, soft systems of opening and shutting, beguile you into believing they're expressive of what they mask. Oh, and all that mucous lubricating the system!

'But,' he says, as he watches his Glenlivit carve its dark amber swirls, and the ice making branching crack diagrams, he sees that this has always been so; the catamorphic is an old law. As if the facade ever had a necessary relation to the spaces within ... That has always been his delight. The pure lines of Rose's face, the pellucid green eyes, the strange lack of indentation in the upper lip, the becalmed sadness of it in repose: no sign there of a turbulence he might harness into passion.

And as the catamorphic in space, so the disjunction in time, the anachronism. So the impact of the always anachronistic Christ, always about to come, always having come, or—his gaze wanders to the television the kids have abandoned—it's Dr Who, for that matter. Anachronistic in his public school courtesy, his Edwardian foppishness, and yet somehow very current. Through the amber light of scotch he sees Dr Who, the question travelling through time, the long coat flapping, scarf lifting to the cosmic draft, stepping into Her Majesty's red Telephone Booth, into a world impossibly vast beyond the imperial rectangular prism.

But so is consciousness itself, the Who behind each face; the roving consciousness. Always, with others, you have to deal with the Tardis Effect.

The only way to have others in your sway is to convince them you can read the catamorphic as simply as the isomorphic relation, that you can see where they travel in the private little Tardis of their consciousness. Again, take Rose's expression, when he and Mink were engaged in banter: he could read in the sheen of her moss green eyes and the pressure of her square-tipped fingers to her mouth not wonder, not *fancy that*, but rather something like: the banter and intimacy this couple displays excludes me and I'm thrown back ... He knows how to catch her at it, throw a spanner in the mechanism of that flight of reminiscence, Look at you now, Rose, tut-tut! There's no going back; the only way is forward; beware, your face will say, not: She has lived, but: She has decayed from inside-out not by living, but by not living, by living in involuntary reminiscence. Over-inhabitation of memory atrophies that space, he can tell her, use shrinks it.

Now when he goes back, it's with a purpose to fetch from afar, to be far-fetched, and to forward his thought; it's always a mission to bring back in order to up-date, to transform, not to take refuge from the possibilities of now! From that gesture of her fingers he can read so easily: blocked kiss, cancelled kiss and maybe memory of kiss and then he'll tease her about her oral compensations. Oh dear, the smoking!

Windows . . . No-nonsense—he'll go for crisp fenestration. Neo-classical massive? For articulation . . . perhaps, rather than over-modest Palladian sobriety, something more folksily assuring like Victorian vernacular: the outside of my house observes cosmetic accommodation, rustic kitsch, you could call it. Why not? Especially these Australians with no sense of history; they'll be reassured. How did the Hansel and Gretel witch get the children in? A house of candy! Nibble nibble like a mouse! Who is nibbling at my house?

Yes! Disguise is seduction, always. He'll also show a certain time-travel; why not? It might be amusing to illustrate here the movement through the stages of structural thought itself, from the depressile, to the compressile into the luminous zones of the tensile—isn't that how Garbett's treatise marks the stages? He is, of course, quite happy to have them call him dilettante for these incursions into different disciplines.

One day Mink will see the extent of his talent in pulling off new conjunctions—his syncratic propensity. It's through its interruptions that his talent masquerades as something *smaller* than it is. She'll see how this phase, the architectural, extends his experiments with scale in painting. Rose will make the connection!

He can see himself on BBC2 telling Kenneth Clarke that he's for a luminous revisitation of the gothic but through levity, fun, also, through a celebration of the new materials: industrial, aerial, defining space balletically through transparencies laid over transparencies—transparencies which would ensnare in their very promise of clarification. He'll do with transparencies what others have done with opacity in the maze. The future will always be underscored by the past, just as the futuristic looks in time retarded and stares back into the present with bulging, shocked eyes, but charming in its anachronistic confusion to the snobs of kitsch.

Gregory will instigate a witty dialogue between these conversants, past and present, by a projection of the future perfect, in the Tardis Effect. By the time you've walked through my spaces, your modernity will have become passé. He knows from Escher, he knows from Piranesi, just what he wants. Yes, Piranesi's imaginary prisons in which, starting from Roman ruins, he fantasised and influenced the future—Gregory can recognise a brother there, in what these vistas of entrapment portray. Yes, every dreamer of dimension is fascistic, but he can't try that out on Mink, let alone Rose. Piranesi developed from his brutal demolition of the past the most fantastic dungeons: menace is cast downwards in gigantic shadows from the immense arcades, or arced upwards like a merciless god in staircases leading to heights out-doing the most Sisyphean fatigue and despair. Just to contemplate their treachery makes the viewer cower: galleries from which one imagines a shocking purview but which lead nowhere whatsoever, because the balconies of these gaolers afford no egress.

No he doesn't want cowering docility, nor abjection in his visitors. Of course not; rather something like active tractability, ductility. Ah to renovate Rose. To enliven her; hardly a sinister ambition. Well, she's married to a dead man. Being dead, he's stretched into some god-like elevation. Perhaps she has clung to him so as not to love another; so as to preserve the idea that she can love a man, when in fact she might not even desire men? He'll see. And Mink can be relied on here: of course Rose might well crave some sort of intensity, some sort of intimacy with a woman. He'll let them have that space, needs be. The invitation will come wholeheartedly from both of them. To the whole family. As far as the Williamectomy is concerned, he'll work it slowly. In the end she might see him as simply that, the withered puppet of her nostalgia and just like sloughing off an old habit, will insidiously but surely leave behind all remnants of his pitiful mediocrity.

Yes! Paramnesiac: to lead her to that kind of recognition; to have her believe that her perception of these events, even as she's going through them, is as disturbed as her hagiographic memory of William. Oh what a tiny shrine her interior will become! Some renovation: atrophy back to zero! Then her memory will enlarge as Gregory's own inhabitation.

The thing with women, even quite intelligent ones like Rose, is that they are habituées of doubt. The first thing, of course, is to induce her into a regime of confession. What you do is get them to spill their past. Oh the relief of honesty and total acceptance, that's what's so seductive in the confessional wager: *now I've told you all my secrets and you still love me*? He'll suggest to her that too many visitations rub away the reliquary. Too many pilgrimages wear out the pathway to the saint. Ha, too many kisses and the shroud is shredded. Too many hauntings and the ghost wears thin. Oh he enjoys himself in this epigrammatic mode. He'll have Rose laughing again.

He'll see the effect of his first lesson when she gapes at his Orangerie roof, vaulting through his optical tricks higher than the Crystal Palace, higher than the Quai d'Orsay. He'll make her see, A far cry from William Macdonald's little cottage planted on the flat cement roof, eh? This is what the volumetric imagination, unfettered by puritan platitudes can do! She'll look downcast as a pilgrim before a desecrated shrine where nothing but dog turds remain! In bed later, he'll turn to Mink whose eyes will be smarting, their blue fierce: Cruel to be kind, remember. She needs to get rid of that god, to free herself from necrobloodyphilic worship. She needs to see that there was an ordinary, perhaps even boring, and certainly limited, nice man. What was his virtue, after all? A bit of charity, a bit of hail-fellow-well-met, I bet, a bit of whirling the kids about till they got giddy, but a lot so he could congratulate himself on being something bigger than *p'tit bourgeois* domestic, just to jump off the *p'tit train train quotidien*? Well if it's derailments she's looking for. Yes, he can lead Rose back to cut new routes, help her shift the signs. And there, what is it really she calls the Past, that massive corpse blocking new ways, that immoveable mass of memory she calls William, he'll help her eviscerate that dead beast once and for all, and exposing its parasitic inhabitants to the bacteria of the present, they'll kill them off, once and for all.

Like one of the masters of the rogue gothic he'll submit spaces that seem reasonable to his own brand of volumetric violence—oh his riddling interiors. Days like this he knows he can engage with any discipline, look at its problems and, uncluttered by old habits and prejudice, unfettered by the ruling codes, he can renovate their thinking. There'll be no end to surprise; one long tease in the approach to understanding: he'll be the Great Procrastinator. This is what rapture is about; no such thing as the *last* wave. Rapture is suspension over the gap of understanding. There's no end to your inventiveness, Gregory, what will you come up with next?

And suspended there, over that gap, Rose'll be literally hanging on his word—

End note

The pseudo-architectural rave of Gregory Lancaster owes much to J. Mordaunt Crook in his *The Dilemma of Style: Architectural Ideas from the Picturesque to the Post-Modern*. Chicago: University of Chicago Press, 1987.

Kate Lamont

Delicious

Tying shoelaces dripping ice-cream listening silently cricket on the radio in bed in the dark bitterness of burnt caramel lingering sensuousness of chocolate don't suck let it melt

flavors of lanolin in unsalted butter abundant roses crumbly yet moist cinnamon tea cake short black warm afternoons just one more piece

warmth familiarity moons of lemon rind to pick out with the quills crunching on the pistachios in smooth chalky risotto stonefruit chardonnay charry oak linen serviettes laughter fondness brimming over

chopping wood lots of chips bbq citronella wafts of onion burning meat ripe beefy tomatoes ripped basil can't sleep for the heat icy pawpaw lots of lime foaming vb slapping mosquitoes cranky children hot foreheads

spilt juice haste vegemite clinging on dripping butter slides from toast blowdrying hair toothpaste greasestain keys traffic lights stalling engines anxious colleagues nervous start find your feet relief sculling cool water smiling

play nicely hand shaking faces touching egg nog delighted shrieks paper hats trifle wrapping paper succulent turkey bad jokes cold cranberry cashews fizzy drinks what is the magic word take it easy now buttery shortbreads scalding tea heated words quick departures never again

gritty strawberries peaches mascarpone sambucca botrytis sparkling bowls gooey lemon curd perfumed honey velvety parfait crochet doileys
fragile friands sip sauterne cooing voices back stroking

roast lamb under tinfoil little bits torn no one will notice rosemary peas trembling jelly tannic shiraz bring it on pangs from other eras football foggy ovals sweatsoaked jerseys

rice in the ricecooker water up to which joint on which finger soy bitter home brew puckery lips salty peanuts pungency of spices in the dank evening Northbridge chilli snow crab slippery noodles

voices louder just one more haven't you had enough fruit cake jewel like peel

club sandwiches room service flags no smoking tiny screw caps crumbs on sheets cnn heavy drapes poor tucks sign here

adjusting sheets on your sleeping partner aromas of frying butter for breakfast eggs juicy pink grapefruit runny yolk crunchy toast macchiato latte soy decaf

passionfruit mango dripping over the sink spitting watermelon seeds across the road you are useless.

Nancy Berg

Camp Ellis Beach

The postcard shows a typical nineteen sixties beach scene – small figures on the sand, blue water, blue skies and fair weather clouds. The ocean line curves into the shore, two white spots are either delinquent waves or small boats. The figures closest to the camera are two men, one in a white t shirt and dark shorts sitting on his heels, hand to mouth, probably smoking, looking toward the water, the other propped up on an elbow. Looking more carefully I see that he too is wearing a shirt, a bulky watchband on his left wrist. The cluster to their right is more familiar, one woman in a two piece bathing suit, another basking in a low to ground chair, kerchief keeping her hair from blowing in the breeze, a man crouched over the blanket, another beach chair to his back. Small items littered around them. The beach is strewn with bathers and their items, tufts of weeds, big black trash cans as punctuation. A mother and child lean over at the shore's edge, looking for seashells. The masts of a sailboat far off. I tell myself I recognize the exact spot; we are just off-camera past the bottom right hand corner.

I look at it and am flooded by remembering. Eating overripe fruit on dark scratchy woollen blankets, the color of the peaches' flesh improbably vivid, the sticky juice dribbling down to my bent elbow, the gritty sand mixed in no matter how careful I am. My sister and I are brown as berries, splashing in the cold salty water, between the estuary of the Saco River and where the fishermen unload their lobsters.

Every morning we wake when the sun lights up the green shades on the windows. The beds are higher than usual, iron frames, flat feather pillows and thin woven cotton bedspreads in faded pink. Our feet run across the bare floor, some of yesterday's sand between our toes, we are quick to put on a dry bathing suit and get to the beach.

The cottage is on a choice lot – in the morning one gets the breeze off the ocean on the back porch, in the afternoon it's time to move to the front porch for the river breeze. It is on the corner, crab grass in the sandy yards, the front yard big enough to park a car and homemade trailer. The local fire station, maintained by an all-volunteer force, is on the other side. One night we hear the alarm and run out with everyone else. Either we got there too late, or the fire wasn't much to begin with, a pathetic flame on the sand. For years it is what I imagine when someone talks about house fires. My sister says I'm lucky, my pajamas have feet and I won't have to wash my feet again when we get back.

My grandmother is the rarest of creatures here, a summer person who has become part of the landscape. She spent nearly every summer of her adult life at the cottage once she owned it. Yet we never saw her on the beach. She would stand on the back porch in her sleeveless housedress and call us in for lunch. Bessie is famous for her lobster sauce and potato pancakes, always cooking full meals even in the heat of the summer. Lunch has a side of salad: iceberg lettuce, thickly sliced cucumbers and tomatoes with her favorite Catalina dressing, sweet, glutinous and orange. We sit in the kitchen, still in bathing suits and sand-covered, sticking to the dark red vinyl of the booths. After lunch we are free to return to splashing in the waves and lounging on the blanket. My sister chases me with wide ribbons of seaweed. At low tide we wander the sandbanks for starfish and other treasures, bringing them back to the cottage to save. We rarely get to keep them; they start to stink as they dry out. When the tide comes in we move our blanket back up toward the rocks just in case. We run into the water with an inner tube hauled up from Boston and take turns floating.

Dinner is more of a production. Clutching a few dollars we walk down the street toward the pier to Huot's, the place that set the standard for onion rings for all time to come. The menu was typical seaside take-out; clam cakes were their best selling item. My sister and I would fight over who got to keep the wooden fork that anchored the onion rings. The soda machine on the side of the clam shack dispensed small bottles of grape and orange soda. There may have been other flavors, but none I would have chosen.

There was a sit down restaurant around the corner. I don't remember ever eating there until I was in college, visiting my grandmother on my own. The rhythm was different then. Every morning I would walk a block or so in the opposite direction from the pier to the corner store for Bessie's daily ration of newspapers. I think my mother was friendly with the woman who owns it when they were both teenagers. Huot's was now shabby. The soda machine was gone, and they didn't even put the wooden fork in an order of onion rings which now looked much smaller. But the rings were still perfect – golden and crispy batter, sweet juicy onions inside. Few people know I am Bessie's granddaughter; I masquerade as one of the summer renters, or even a day tripper.

The house that partially blocked the ocean view was gone, taken out in a winter storm a few years back; the road between the cottage and the beach was no longer there. The firehouse is blocked up; any emergencies are attended to by the larger Saco station. There is a gift shop near the restaurant selling souvenirs and such. The woman who owns it is too friendly, tries too hard. I try to avoid getting caught there. It's next to the new ice cream parlor. The water is cold, too cold to swim. Some years later – my last trip to the beach – I wade into the water only so as not to be embarrassed in front of my brother-in-law and niece.

The cottage has two floors. When we were little, the second floor was usually rented out. A woman who looked and laughed like Phyllis Diller brought her Boston terrier Queenie with her. I don't know if she rented the place because she was friends with my grandmother, or whether they became friends once she began renting. Upstairs had a second kitchen, a bathroom with a claw foot tub and a shower that leaked, two bedrooms and a sitting room. When there were no renters we could stay upstairs. Otherwise we stayed in one of the two bedrooms downstairs, the one with the staircase to the second floor, or the one with the wood stove and improvised shower. The cottage was white, with trim painted in a dark shade I came to think of as Camp Ellis green. Latticework hung from the bottom of the house, stapled to the stilts. Sand, cats and more crabgrass fill the space where we thought a basement should be.

The one-way road that ran by the back and the side was all that separated the yard from the beach. At night the constant crashing of the waves was punctuated by the whoosh of an occasional car driving by, from the pier or the restaurant. Sometimes we heard snatches of music or laughter from the car with its windows rolled-down.

My grandfather came up for the summer once he was retired. All those years he had rarely spent even a weekend, too quick to return to his tire shop in the city once he drove his wife. Often she would just take the bus.

In no time at all Dave became a fixture at the pier. Hanging with the fishermen and their families, he was warmly welcomed in this most insular village. He bought a motor scooter and would zip around, offering rides to some of the children. Bessie would stand at the porch door, worried that he would hurt himself, concerned that he was making a spectacle, perhaps even wishing to join in. She was famous in her own way – accompanying her early in her widowhood from the social security office to the fish store in Roslindale, she was greeted and offered condolences by everyone from the fish monger to the government clerk. "Bessie for mayor" said one, in tribute to her political insight and her sharp tongue.

Of all the visitors to our dead-end street back at home, my grandfather was the most popular. While my grandmother would hasten to the front door, he would just be opening the door of his very old black Cadillac, and would sit half way out offering big bunches of grapes to the neighborhood kids.

Years after he died, Bessie continued to spend her summers up at the cottage. It was the rhythm of her year. She would stretch out the season, staying through the Jewish holidays if they came early enough, praying at the modest synagogue the next town over. She would have arranged for someone to drive her there and back weeks before.

At least a month before her annual migration she would be packing for the summer, and for at least a month after her return she would still be moving back in. She tried to do the same thing with her winters, purchasing an inexpensive condominium in Florida, and spending several months packing in anticipation. It never took. Too many old people, too many snowbirds, too few memories.

After she died we sold the cottage. Too often one of us would have to drive up to check on it after a bout of severe weather. One year we were sure we saw its gray roof floating out to sea on the television news. The burden of ownership seemed to outweigh the pleasures. Now in memory, I can forget the long rainy days, the inevitable family squabbles, the certain boredom, and instead bask in the warm sun, tasting the dried ocean salt on my skin.

Rosslyn Prosser

Writing + Memory = Memory Writing

> The difference between the detective's abduction and the philosopher's induction and deduction is that the detective reasons with memory rather than argument.
> Gregory L. Ulmer. *Heuretics: the Logic of Invention*

Memory.
Something happens. An event. A physical rupture that turns onto internal membranes, deposits of blood, left for trace.
In a clean and Catholic hospital ward, with a crucified Jesus hanging over the bed, a man dies.
He dies with the bolus of morphine surging into his body, the noise of the automatic syringe, electronic and
straightforward, a comfort and a fright.
White sheets and no visible blood.
As part of the souveniring of this death, locks of hair are cut from the father's head and given to his children.
There is an opening made with death.
An unexpected excitement, elevated emotions.
An adrenalin rush of living.
We go on with the everyday, punctured with the knowledge of the potential for death.
This death happens in the beef city of Rockhampton in Queensland, where two large cement bulls grace the highway entrances from Brisbane in the South and Townsville in the North. The bulls' cement testicles are regularly souvenired.
Into this opening after death a possibility is produced for telling, for talk, the revealing of secrets.

Secrets become lodged in memory. Memory is never pure in the sense that in the re-telling, in the recovery, it is made through versions, through editing, through selection.

To handle the secret and its attendant investigation I imagine myself a detective, with the carefree allure of a Marlowe and the commitment of a Mary Wings protagonist.

My character will be made of tough stuff, cool and well cut .

My skin is melanoma prone.
White, fair even.
In this country with its 'wide brown land for me' and seering sun escape is almost impossible.
White must protect itself from the sun and white often runs from this and from its past. White will not wear hats.
"Where's your hat?"
White sweeps under the carpet.
The condition of 'coming to terms' with a past is productive of all kinds of stories, denials and acceptances.
White burns in the midday sun.
White turns out for events that memorialise itself.
The individual, personal story can be read for its belonging to a time, for its connection to ideologies and discourses.
White is not a primary colour.
It means something to be white.
Black makes white visible.

I am guilt.
I am shame.
Guilt and shame and fear.
I am the dog, the blue heeler, out of the dingo, cowering under the tank stand, the half tank, the dust road, the gate, 'shut the bloody thing', thrown a bone.
Chained and cursed. Leaping uselessly in the air at strangers.
Blue heeler.
Blue who is really red.

I will be re-cycled, dispersed and felt in your generations.
I am.
I will be your operating principle, your modus operandi.

Your bottom line, your end of the day.
Your striped shirt in all of the photographs of all the stock exchange workers the world over.
I will be your new age look in the mirror, your personal growth book.
Trust me.
I will inhabit your hours before dawn, your spoken words.
Will attach myself like unspoken grief,
leeches in the wet forest creek.
Salt will not ease, nor staunch the flow
Your blood will flow like feathers on the wind.
Your wasteland, your toxic spill.
Inescapable corruption and deceit,
find me here,
find me there.
I will work to invade your every thought
Your dress will be read in this way.
You will not leave,
this space is let to you.

Your troubling eczema, your balding spot, your knee problems.
Guilt, your shame, your fear.
You will go white before grey.
Denial, your sporting achievements, keep busy, busy, very busy.
Your lizard's tail falling off will not distract me.
I know you are still alive.
It's stoicism.
Stand by, stand by everything.
You are still alive, I know where you are hiding.
Your institutional blindness will not deter.
Formalin, formaldehyde and storage cabinets may keep your artefacts intact and isolated
but the stench of mastery will soon cloud their beauty.

Guilt, shame, and fear lead you to forget or to remember in certain ways.
A melanoma style of remembrance
long in the making
made in the soft skin of childhood
the evidence is everywhere strewn about.

Thick with marks of life
you may dress to conceal.
Throughout we knew something
about the fence, the barbed wire concealment, the dingo length of
your world
things leak out.
Calici like, jumping fences.
The stranger in the wide brimmed hat, the night train to the coast,
the kangaroo down under the front wheels of the car.
My waist size.
the cost of a sewing machine.
The black and white photograph, 'family group on verandah',
shuffled away under other photographs.
A blind woman on a sugar cane farm, smell of the sea.
Family will prevail.
Blood flows on hospital tiles.
Fingermarks on mirrors.
I will be your little girl dancer, tutu-ed and shy.
Bogey man outside under the street light, with toads.
Chopped into a thousand pieces and fed to the puppy dogs.
A black man with a sugar bag, you slip the lid open a little.

Bible stories reduced to small sentences
"Be not afraid" Mark 6:50
Little stories in the dark.
Mother is white Australia.
Colonising with shame, guilt and fear.
Unspoken detail and distorted memory.
Mother is singing with Hank Williams, Rolf Harris and
Slim Dusty
Australia is mother.
Leaving it all cowed, quaking, quivering.
A slide guitar opening.

Hide in the desert.
Red desert. Red desert, giant sky.
Exposed by the skin of our teeth, could be gone troppo.
The sign says – 'Parking Aria'
Core shifts. And shifts again.

All cliches for open rush into my mouth.
Better to stay gob-smacked.
And here I am.
Fate of birth, accident of placement.
We come out here at the same time but your verse is different.
Synchronous but inflected against some other system.
European wasp like you invade my drinking cup.
Listless in your wake
I cannot find breath in this heat.

Mother is desert.
This harsh, nothing there landscape.
But filled with secrets to the other eye.
A life sustaining barrenness.
An uncomfortable place to live.
Constant gaps allow the history of someone else to seep to the surface, salinity like, to bother the crust.
Skin scrapings reveal stories and factions.

We live in history and memory and the oldest house we might live in – white house – might be a lot less than two hundred years old. There is always a sense in the Australian landscape of something coming before, of footsteps walking or leaving clear, of animals free wheeling without fences. I brake on the freeway as an echidna trundles over the bitumen. I drag a giant wombat off the road on a Sunday morning. Saturday night carnage. Erasure is impossible. These little pieces of geography that have whole lives embedded in them. These places that stimulate the memory against forgetting. That document marking birth and signalling the beginning of a new story, connected to stories of the past. How does space inscribe memory?

Event becomes memory.
Remembered in current detail.
The way you tell the event to yourself,
over and over, turning it in your hands, over, over.
"and then, and then . . . "
When memory is passed onto you, onto me it becomes my memory of you telling me, not the event itself.

It moves from membraneous, felt in your body, impacted on your skin, your brow – memory.
To my current embellishments, as I heard it, as you told it, memory shifts, like film scenery, I capture my own mise-en-scene, your dialogue re-interpreted.
I see your memory, your emotional re-telling on your skin,
but only for me on paper.

If there is an echo in me
is it an echo of story?
It travels, it is sound, it is expected.
We establish echoes in certain sites and return to them, knowing they will be there.
Echo Point: where we call and call, echo returning
a memory of voice.
Where are the best echoes?
Visiting Victoria Falls where the echo is drowned by the bellow of the water falling over the edge.
Is there in echo in here?
I hear my own voice returning to me with fear of the past.
I have said I thought I knew, wherever, whenever I go.

A detective echo
is an echo of astounding meaning
each line of sound
tested beyond it's strength.
Rubber band like
returning in the pull, in the repair
you can't repair it, it's too late.
You mightily changed the course of lives
struck out any other possibilities
finalised the story before the ending
ensured the strength of your own capital to hold sway.
No other voices to be heard, a long masculine drone
reaches me where I am lying in the creek bed
waiting to see a leaf fall
how it falls
and is lifted on the wind
blown lightly, a path in the air twisting

how a leaf falls
rapidly to decay and become soil.
That was you then
lift leaf into mulch
body into soil
a patience for life
little point in fighting.
You might think you know something
Then after your death there will be an absence in the landscape.

The maps stand in between the site mapped and the cartographer. Cartographers like all text makers are culture, history, society and gender bound. What map I might make here is the same. The memory I might attribute to each artefact is also bound.
The personal museum sees each artefact embedded with memory, each artefact speaks of these memories, but each artefact is only partially rendered 'readable'.
Imagine the house as a site of memory.
She walks through the house of memory. In each of the rooms, in each corner of each room, in each and every object, embedded stories and evidence.
Some of these will be known and told, repeated and altered, shared and judged but with her sit the meanings.
In these she invests the pleasure of looking, of touching, of nostalgia and of ownership.
She sets them out, positions and places them in sections, in invisible orders and categories, in groups, in similarities or differences.
They are in glass fronted cabinets and on shelves, on dressing and bedside tables.
They sit on embroidered and crocheted doilies, she makes them herself, each stitch perfect, each hook placed according to a predesignated pattern.
There is an order and a knowledge, a technique of performing and it is here that she excels..
"Do you put egg in the stuffing of a chicken to be baked?"
These knowledges are covered in her daily existence.

I write the words that are visible in public places and stated on days of memory.

"Lest We Forget".

Throughout Australia these words appear as little poems of memory. United in knowing what these words mean, some long ago war, "not that long ago", she said, a strange national unity made out of the re-stimulation of ceremony, Anzac Day, Remembrance Day, don't forget mother's day.

We were there, that war we saw from our verandahs and while it ran, another war, a war of family, a war of masculinity versus femininity, a war of sexualities, a war with consequences and casualties but no memorials.

I read into already existent memorials my own space.

That soldier, that horse.

Memory is something worth travelling for, worth staking a claim for, little acts of memory-making accumulate and become a history of desiring subjects. It is the memory I want to return to, the living out is filled with dissatisfaction, the memory, however I look at it, is available at unpredictable times, surprising in its intensity, triggered by unexpected connectors and then I hear you telling me stories of memory.

In your heart, heart of hearts, heart of Phar Lap, museum piece and ordinary, a horse's heart for heaven's sake.

More for the horses perhaps than for the racing, a heart a memory of a horse's heart.

In the womb already beating, mate.

Memory is uninhabited by grace
but laid over by ideology
and the cost, the cost of life
the cost of framing memories.

Is the landscape implicated in her death?
The sound of currawongs on a clear blue, frost free morning.
Bead yellow eyes seeking fledglings, pierce sounds.
The gum tree as witness, invader, story in its rings, how old, how old are you really, boat tree, canoe tree?
Forget that, fibre glass lasts longer.
Around the canoe tree scar meanings coalesce,

a bitumen road going by, one hundred kilometres per hour, top speed.

A ghost in the space between barbed wire and white lines I follow and stay on the right side of the road.

A memorial of something completely misunderstood, memorialised in guilt and yet, living, branches out with new growth, how old, how old did you say?

Insert the measuring stick, that is a particular kind of truth, formalised in a measurement.

This tree is the canoe tree.

Horizon

Take good note of the horizon. It's your mark and your measure out that way always trying to get to it, out this way receding from it, a small thing stuck on the rear vision mirror each time I look.

Take note of the horizon, each step in your hip style of walking – keep an eye on the distant line.

It's differently organised in different places that horizon. For some it is simply not there, for others, the mark of being.

That is the horizon of your life, your expectation ever expanding outwards, a taken for granted mark.

It appears to cut through the frame of your drawing, your writing. You need the horizon.

The horizon in a city – Sydney, is a horizon forever changing. Somewhere there is a spot where you can stand and look at the horizon but it is always filled with a "Significant Landmark", so that it's not really the horizon you look at. Onwards, forever forward. But look in closer. The horizon is always the future.

Endo's canoe in the Art Gallery of South Australia has the water on the inside and is a clear, still water reflecting the observer. It is lined with tar, the blackened wood a seal and a reminder/a memory of burning.

"Love many, trust few, always paddle your own canoe".

The boat of memory brings with it empty space. The artefacts encrusted in the gaps between the timbers, They are no more than this, pieces of paper with names and instructions on them. Lists and lists of detail of how things work, some photographs and some diagrams. And this is all it is. No large piece, no cannon, no anchor, no hull, only the fragment of a story, filtered out into the archive. No trophies, no jewels, they left nothing, no heirlooms, working class leaves only scars and kitsch. It is all paper in the end.

You give me your memory
it does not appear as a gift or a fine thing
but a blurting out
an unpicked hem, dragging behind you.
A lost story.
Your memory is pushed through onto your life clouding, clouded actions.
Your action in the world always tempered, always cautious.
Memory spilling out into your everyday.
Memory accused.
Memory confessed.
I have this life filled to the brim with the cautions of memory.
That is how you pass it on.
It doesn't need statement, story, explanation, explication, summary, forever told, out in the open.
It's always there
the soft skin of your belly, memory makes your illnesses, headaches, fears.
Parlous dog watching for your fall devours you limb by limb.
The brain, memory brain, delicate so easily injured.
Memory from out of place, out of race.

With collage the partial can be fulfilled.
The problem of memory is in filling the gaps, in the need to manufacture, to fictionalise, where the lack of evidence leaves me wondering.

The artist Rosalie Gascoigne used the detritus of the tip, the rubbish dump, the abandoned farmhouse, the incidental tip in the Australian bush to build collages that unmistakably speak Australia. Parts of cars and machinery, broken bottles, thick green and blue grass, bed springs and anything that has not broken down, now lying in dust and dirt. Everywhere in Australia it is possible to find these impromptu dumps, where any hole in the ground, any open space is a possible dump for the no longer required. These objects provide an appropriate backdrop for thinking about the colonisation of space, the culture of disposal and the cluttering of the bush. Here, representative objects of culture lie, possibly never to break down into any other material. In the future these will be the treasures of the archaeologist. It is to these informal tips and rubbish heaps, throwaway lines and artefacts that the detective returns, again and again, searching for the crushed metal, the shattered glass, the found object. I tell you this because it feels just like that, a search, in the first place for the tip, the place of the discard, and the search within for the clue, the small piece of evidence that can illuminate this story and the borders around it. I tell you this because it is rusty and unidentifiable. I recognise the tip, the heap of rubbish through years of noticing this in the landscape, but the source of it, the night time furtive dumper, the ute loaded up and driven quietly through the bush, there you go you see, you know what I'm trying to tell. Now it is the black plastic bag filled with waste, not as good as the waste of the past. It is more telling of the kind of dumper found in the modern, where weeds escape from the holes of the plastic and invade the bush.

It's too late now for the manifesto of love, except between the lovers, ensconced in each other's breath, a surface layer impenetrable. They are the looked upon, her eyes are blue, her face held in two hands, and what I am really investigating, turn away turn away, is how you exist, what choices you make, what lines you delete from your tale. You say you can never know me or is it the choice of hand covering skin against, and only ever knotting together, two ideas.
In fetid water I will be memory for you.
Line my pockets with shards of meaning
of English made crockery, lying in shallow creeks.
In particular, lesbian memory.
Australian lesbian memory.
A wide-ranging and varied state with one singularly uniting principle.
With a beach, a city, landscape, and foreign inflections.
Her body on the beach, walking, is there a lesbian walk?
What about when you stopped being lesbian?
Now queer, now bi-sexual. What is your walk like?

Your washing hangs damp in the winter
a moment caught in another place
frozen for remembrance
but that's not all
that cause and effect
is longer, not easily cured or read
she said, "where is the body?"
Return.
As representative it can tell, will tell, has told
hold on, it's a fine day here, looking back at other fine days
A poet sees.
It's a fading time for mixed emotions
they fall, they fall.

Things that belong in the past, memory triggered, the smell of her hair, the disarray she left behind, a permanent mark of sadness. You think you might clear it up, what stories you tell yourself and others that might track down and release you from that past.
The country returns your love, some squeamish, cannot see it, but attempt to cover it with the built and the idea, but there it is, country.

Mother makes gardens that become memorials, each place she leaves, she leaves gardens and a re-constructed site. The texts of her memory are those gardens, each one planted to keep away memory, to keep busy, to immerse in activity, she keeps busy, busy. When she sells houses she sells gardens, the house itself is unimportant. She gives away work and labour and closes the door on memory. She keeps plants, some for forty years, she rescues the neglected plants on sale in the supermarket, over or under watered, carelessly placed in windy spots, victims of air-conditioning, she makes incoherent gardens according to all of the gardening texts, she doesn't read them, she is an untrained gardener, she has a green thumb.

Negotiating the everyday with the memory of the body in water, floating, now there's a thing, making stories that work to create a swoon. In one sentence she creates that. You wish for it. Writing that invests the everyday with body memory. Pages that speak like lips against skin. We watched our moon shadows in the still water, moon lit night. Calling back, dragging the moon back into it's phases, imagining that we had something to do with it, appropriating as many myths as we could for our own understanding, seeing ourselves as intellectual owners of 'global' knowledges, understood intellectually but dispirited that we could never quite enter the embodied space where dust, blood and ritual inhabited the occasion, where the myths existed to explain the world. Now I explain the world through all of those stories and past meanings, as if, as if I have the right to assemble them in that way, to take a portion of explanation and reconstruct them into my own. The everyday is often a place of uncertainty and trepidation. It feels at times as though I am constructed out if iron filings with a magnet underneath controlling movement and creating chaos.

On becoming a detective and refusing to be the feminine, the pretty, a detective must be hardened and diamond like, placing nurturing into something where memory resides, not in living, the life form, the everyday, the detective must balance deception with knowing. And in return? In return she will know that the clues that she has been pursuing, seeking everywhere in every distant place, every place filled with the scent of history, an embroidered pillow case where your head had been secure in sleep until reminiscence catches you and throws you out into the sea of angst and negativity.

The detective you see is positive, ah yes, positive she will find the answer, struggling with the worldliness of simply staying in the material, needs to look beyond, find the answers in some strange mixture of walking through the sites, reducing everything to it's possible meaning, lifting the veil and the skin and the lid and finding all before ruin. Detection is ultimately about return. Of remains, of meaning, of clues, of lost body parts, of a range of ideas that will lead to a solution.

The boat must eventually come to shore, bringing the end of the story, the resolution, the results of the investigations. They will tip them out onto the deck, emptying – books of their words, leaving questions unanswered and forces not responded to. If it was only that simple, if it really was possible to simply empty out onto the deck, the story, the meaning. She waits on the shore-line, anticipating the contents, even as the sun sets and she sees the last of the light go down into the horizon sea. Yes, it is true, the detective is a fall back onto some kind of archetypal character, seeking out the lines in the story, withholding any indication of knowing exactly what has happened.

Echo Kiss

Echo is a memory of sound
Echo kiss a memory of kisses past
returning across the tyranny of distance
held up momentarily by the Goyder line
some kisses like that chocolate with proverbs
wrapped around it
easily summarised from some famous dead
philosopher
Baci
Echo kiss not so easily surrounded
some smacking in the air,
the South Australian air of a red dust storm filled with top soil
A western desert kiss looking close to Sturt's pea
eaten by the dog in jealousy

your face in the echo kiss
in the north light, throughout the rain forest wet

Echo kiss in the mouth opening shout across a valley, across a gorge

Echo kiss will return
memory of mouth, voice, lip, skin

locked to the back of the train as you leave
light as down
soft like this
echo will remind you of, will remember itself
in the dark night
2 am lying in wait for your return

will bruise with teeth marks on lips
share lip balm secrets and watch for blisters

lysine in the bag
will wash your clothes
search your pockets before you put your lipstick on let me kiss you
the coffee cup stained red lips

draws my hand
across the air trail left as you go
through dust on the books unopened
since you left
outside you wait
and speak something lost to the traffic

hair across my pillow
on my clothes in the machine
lost to life washed to identification
dna positive
echo of the living

she said kiss me too late
shot out from a nocturnal rest
to find the kitchen empty
the cupboard bare of nourishment
yet filled with smell
of closed doors
it's a Nick Cave day at last
mourning
echoic left overs.

Memory is a complex process of stories without end, coincidences and fatal landings. Memory is made new in different remembrances. Versions of events and stories that could be true, could be false. They all contribute to something and become a way of thinking about events. They are all versions.
Think about boats and trees, how they are differently thought. Embedded in previous stories about boats were all of the arrival stories, or and as a good example of discourse matters depending on speaker positions – invasion discourses. We are all of us arriving or being arrived at. On the way to Victor Harbor in South Australia, the aboriginal canoe tree is wrapped in a black shroud to protect it from

vandalism. Boats were once made from trees, great swathes of timber bent and manipulated, or boats were made to carry trees, great river red gums felled and carted down the Murray River, the other side of the invention. Producing a land stripped.

Memorialising the thylacine.
Science wants to clone a memory.
The Sydney Museum is a storehouse of memory. These memories have the potential for restoration. Memory in this instance is made real by the possession of a preserved thylacine pup. The pup, behind glass, is made a specimen by the use of scientific methods. The representation we are most familiar with is aided by the constant use of images of the last thylacine in a cage in a zoo in Tasmania.
The animal paces and walks around the cage.
Each time the thylacine cloning is discussed the memory is represented by the pup preserved and the last of the tribe in the cage in the zoo.

The day after the announcements are made about the successful cloning of a lamb and a calf- two species introduced to Australia by white settlers, one of which, sheep, enabled the extinction of the thylacine with a bounty placed on it to stop the destruction of sheep in Tasmania, the Sydney Museum follows up an earlier announcement about the desire to clone the thylacine with an announcement of the successful retrieval of DNA from the preserved organs of the thylacine pup.
The Sydney museum representative jokes about picking up DNA from the scientist who originally placed the pup in the alcohol.
Much of the Australian landscape is embedded in memory, lost through farm clearance, development, the stories remain. There are before and after photos, firstly fat with nature and diverse ecology and then thin with land scraped bare and built on. Many things are irreversible.
Loss comes down into your consciousness after you've made the cut, after you've taken apart the machine or the battery operated toy to see what is inside. Filled with regret and shame, reversing the act is impossible.
Is that what torture forgets? Bodies pasted onto nothingness to not allow memory.

Memory cannot be cloned. Skin may be, flesh maybe, bone maybe. You can clone a favourite dog or horse but will their memory of you be intact. You will have to invest all of that effort over again. What is it you are cloning? You think you will be keeping the thing itself out of memory and alive in the present. You cannot clone memory.

The grave is a site of memory and the museum is a kind of grave. What makes some things available for museum inclusion?
They gather around, hands clasped behind their backs, never showing except in the clench of lips, the close-up there please, don't show weeping, cursing, what are they mourning? I watch in some kind of quietude, is death a new thing, because for a while we have been protected from its stories.
The institutional grave, the protected space, ensconced inside sandstone walls, a museum to an idea.
The labels describing the exhibition have been written in the smallest print. the time it takes to read them sees a passing of viewers and audience.

There is a body, a body that has many things said over it.
Where do you come from?
What is your name?
Once I knew your body
body history
body memory
bodies collide
body value.

Text can become a kind of memorial, words placed on paper, making sense in particular ways, words that look back at events or stories and compile them.
Text can make sense of but never know.

Kate Hislop

Re-membering: A Line of Thought Reviewing the Colonial

For nearly a century, Australia's architectural psyche has been haunted by the 'Myth of the Colonial'. Championed since the 1890s by those of Nationalist and/or Modernist persuasion, terms such as 'primitive', 'crude', 'utilitarian', 'simple' and 'honest' effectively absolved colonial architecture of artifice. My purpose is to retrieve it from such limits by means of a different explanation, another *line of thought*. Suggestive of a position, reasoning or *view*, this phrase conjures associations with memory and with writing, and can extend to include those marks made in the act of drawing. These are some of the avenues that will be explored: another is the proposition of 're-view', meaning to look again, revise and, as well, in regard to looking (at something) – especially 'in regard to *the view*', the title commonly given in the nineteenth century to landscape or architectural sketches. As key protagonist in Australian architectural history, the Colonial is the subject not only of such sketches or view(s) but also our *re-view*, the focus of our *re-membering*.

My argument is developed in relation to the neo-Georgian or Colonial Revival tradition in Australian architecture that authorised the myth in the opening decades of the twentieth century. I am interested in the historiographical method used in these accounts, especially from the 1920s by Hardy Wilson, who effectively deployed the sketch as a form of historical narrative. His skilful renderings of exemplary late Eighteenth and early Nineteenth Century colonial buildings reflected the value judgments and tastes of subsequent generations of architects and historians, by whom the myth was confirmed and perpetuated. Gloriously illuminated were their present and future by what were already memories of a faded past. Historical representation and production of architecture became closely linked: not least in Wilson's own neo-Colonial house designs, such as Eryldene (1913) or Purulia (1916), this phenomenon is evident in the writings and buildings of Robin Boyd, for example.

Used as architectural historical mode and as ideological tool (by Wilson, Morton Herman and Boyd), the sketch has helped shape the perception, reception and production of Australian architecture. My intention here is to review and *re-member* colonial architecture according to a line of thought that I am calling the 'outline methodology', explored through examples of Nineteenth Century Australian sketches, and in particular an 1890 sketchbook, containing drawings of houses, by architect, builder, surveyor and artist, Thomas Turner. This approach can be used to interpret colonial architecture not, as has been customary, by evaluation within our present frame of reference, but rather in light of the late Eighteenth/early Nineteenth Century ideologies embodied within the acts of sketching and, arguably, of building. This other line of thought might also invite a revision of the orthodox historical narratives and their modes of production (not to mention on-going consumption, interpretation and eventual built translation). It is possible to locate the work of Wilson, Herman and Boyd, for instance, as episodes marking the line of thought that is 'Outlining'. This path is one that engages primarily with the construction of antipodean architecture and its history through the practices of sketching and, as well, moving or travelling, processes that have been paired with architectural implications since at least the Seventeenth Century European Grand Tour.

Within the 'travel-sketch' tradition, numerous Australian examples can be seen to precede Wilson.[1] However, unlike Wilson's, the majority of earlier work is not concerned with exalting age-value, nor prescribing architecture's future and neither with creating architectural history. Instead, many Nineteenth Century sketches both describe and *perform* the intentions, actions and outcomes of colonialism. They image, record and elevate the various colonial imperatives, many of which were associated with creating settings and building settlements for individuals and communities. They played an integral role in the colonialist mission to civilise and contributed to what Paul Carter has interpreted as the appropriative travelling of colonialism, where the need to travel equalled the desires to know and acquire.[2] And it has been well documented that in Australia the sketch was indeed employed as both topographical representational instrument and as acquisitive device.[3]

But the antipodean sketch was also more than just conspirator to British imperial expansion, as can be seen in examples other than those depicting Sydney. Too often a euphemism for 'Australia', New South Wales has typically been used to define the experience of the nation as a whole. However, like Adelaide and Melbourne after it, the Swan River Colony was established using private funds, with a population and for purposes quite different to those accompanying Sydney's founding. And sketches of Perth are also distinctive. Where Sydney was commonly portrayed as a classically powerful imperial centre, majestically commanding dramatic panoramas, Perth was rendered as a village – or even a country town: small scale, spread-out and suburban.[4] A comparison of Charles Wittenoom's 1839 sketches of Perth and Fremantle with those of Sydney by John Eyre (1809) and D D Mann (1811) is illustrative of the distinction. Sydney's images display a grandeur approaching monumentality never possessed by (nor perhaps desired for) those of Perth.

Whether by private colonists or government officials, many Swan River sketches utilise Romantic techniques and rhetoric: contour outline (sometimes with watercolour wash), roughness and irregularity, loose pen/brushwork, simplicity and provisionality. Most serve both descriptive and creative functions, combining topographic mimetic purpose with design intent. And this is arguably the difference between the sketch (and historiographical) practices of Romantic England and colonial Australia. In the case of the former, the sketch is primarily a vehicle supporting Romantic History's new interest in discovering, representing and viewing the predominantly medieval past.[5] In the latter, however, it is a form at once negotiating, firstly, the *relocation* of the knowledge of that rediscovered past to a paradoxically new yet ancient and exotic land and, secondly, the *outlining* of a brand new present and future (and, eventually, past) on ground mistakenly believed to be void of History (and civilisation).

If the question of *relocation* is concerned with the antipodean transformation of the Romantic notion of 'the Past', the issue of *outlining* addresses the ways in which the relocated awareness of the past negotiates with the processes by which settlement in individual and collective instances is imagined, imaged and constructed on 'new' ground. Outlining embraces a range of constructive practices (including sketching, narrating, writing, surveying and building) and broadly serves artistic, historical and architectural purpose. An outline is at once a type of drawing, an overview or abstract, a delineation of boundaries, and a preliminary or provisional plan. Each mode is characterised by openness, incompleteness, roughness, changefulness, provisionality, the display of simplicity and the *apparent* absence of rhetoric: qualities all definitive of Romantic sketch and historiographical practices. Traits such as these, as well as the negotiation between the issues of relocation and outlining, are evident in Thomas Turner's 'series of views' of houses: a mixed-form historical series that is effectively a colonial settlement narrative.

Outlining as occupation

In 1890 Turner reproduced in sketchbook format, from his earlier original drawings, a series of small ink line and watercolour sketches, prefaced: 'Within is a series of views; houses that have been my home at various times; in all thirty, during a period of seventy seven years'.[6] Throughout his life he moved and settled, quite remarkably, within two continents, three Australian states, and several towns. By profession a surveyor, Turner was in the business of casting lines, fixing boundaries and delineating (delimiting yet inevitably extending) settlement(s). His was a job that entailed moving around the country to obtain work. For Turner, the constancy of mobility was advantageous: moving had personal-philosophical as well as professional motivations, and his sketchbook is almost a kind of philosophy of history-as-process speculating upon the benefits to individuals and society of movement and change. Further, as a builder and, later in Victoria, a practising architect, he was involved in imaging and constructing, upon measured ground, places of residence and worship.

But not by profession alone was Turner involved in 'outlining'. By vocation (having received no formal art training[7]) he was also an artist whose multiple occupations resulted in two distinct modes of representation. While not the subject of this discussion, most noted has been his topographic landscape (of which there are examples in the Art Gallery of Western Australia and Sydney's Mitchell Library collections). The other entirely unacknowledged (because more private) form in his sketchbook is effectively an architectural-historical topography. In chronicling colonial settlement, the sketchbook's outline method combines his diverse skills and experiences as surveyor, builder, architect and artist with his interests as colonist (and even historian). For surveying, designing, planning, writing and sketching are all *comprised* of and, in turn, *create* the outlines that are effective agents in the settling of ground (the processes of colonisation) as well as of time (the processes of memory as well as the interpretation and representation of history).

The outline technique and approach

Insofar as Turner's sketches are literally *comprised* of lines, his technique combines professional as well as general Romantic traits: his images temper technical precision with an element of roughness. His can be described as a form of 'map-making', not only for obvious reasons. For, by virtue of his technique and choice of subject matter, as a topographical artist the mantle of 'map-maker' is perhaps equally applicable, although historically this had pejorative connotations. In 1805, for instance, then-Professor of Painting at the Royal Academy, Fuseli, disparaged work that depicted the accidental, the momentary and the empirical, in place of the substantial, the general and the abstract:

> To portrait painting ... we subjoin, as the last branch of uninteresting subjects, that kind of landscape which is entirely occupied with the tame delineation of a given spot; an enumeration of hill and dale, clumps of trees, shrubs, water, meadows, cottages and houses, *what is commonly called views* ... The landscape of Titian, of Mola, of Salvator, of the Poussins, Claude, Rubens, Elzheimer, Rembrandt ... spurns all relation with this kind of *mapwork* [my italics].[8]

Prejudice aside, Turner's indeed *is* mapwork by Fuseli's definition, and not least because he prefaced his sketchbook with the phrase, 'a series of views'. But also because, with respect to theme and technique, his sketches conform to the general principles of Nineteenth Century topographical representation.

Thematically, Turner's sketchbook consists of thirty-one views of which all, bar one, are residences and all feature trees, shrubs and other elements of mapwork. And because the series illustrates houses in various landscape settings, it also fits the definition of 'occluded landscape', distinguished from the more extensive 'panoramic prospect' (favoured in the late eighteenth century as a 'microcosm of the world' and the predominant representation of Sydney) by a characteristic image of a cottage seen usually from a low vantage point. Imbued with meanings of seclusion, privacy, domesticity and sensuality, the occluded landscape typically displays objects in terms of their consumption and possession.[9] And, in these terms, Turner's are clearly occluded cottage landscapes, having no expansive public vista nor any great depth, no sublime scenery and no classically composed subjects of historical or religious importance. These are, at one level, portraits of buildings of his private creation and inhabitation.

Technically, the sketchbook exhibits a number of distinctly Romantic characteristics, including emphasis on process and the achievement of provisionality; the assertion of sincerity, immediacy and originality; and themes of simplicity and naturalness. For instance, evident within individual frames as well as in the integrated narrative is his commitment to process: qualities of openness, roughness, incompleteness, provisionality and mobility are favoured over signs of labour, finish, perfection, monumentality and fixity. Moreover, Turner's sketches adhere to the theme of simplicity, in terms of both subject and technique. The theme of simplicity, however, is paradoxically complex. For while simplicity is a primary requisite of the Romantic (sketch) aesthetic, the ideological rhetoric of 'denied rhetoricity' that promotes the *appearance* of simplicity is ultimately sophisticated. And this is a crucial point for, as Richard C Sha explains in *The Visual and Verbal Sketch in British Romanticism*, the rhetoric (ensuring the appearance of simplicity) of the Romantic sketch has been so successful as to significantly undermine its subsequent critical interpretation and evaluation.[10] This is arguably one of the major reasons for Turner and other topographical artists achieving little notoriety. It may also explain the impoverished critical interpretation of Australian Colonial and later Nineteenth Century sketch practices. A consequence of the latter has been a misreading, in architectural historical terms, of sketches depicting buildings and settlement: the rhetoric of denied rhetoricity is never unveiled, drawings are read at face value and colonial architecture seen as (and believed) innocent of artifice.

In advancing simplicity and opposing monumentality, Turner's medium is pen outline filled with flat patches of watercolour; his linear style at once schematic (in depiction of form) and texturally rough. Almost without exception, buildings and fences draw clean straight lines, especially in urban views, whether English or Australian. But considerable emphasis is also given to more densely depicting the materiality of building surface and evoking textural roughness. His use of linear devices recalls Thomas Girtin's method of pattern-making, in which a network of horizontal and diagonal lines 'quarter' or map a landscape. Although this technique generally works to better advantage in larger and deeper views, Turner nonetheless sets the houses in relation to lines inscribed by fences, paths, roads, stands of trees, building skylines and even the horizon, such that the views are intimately contained. Simultaneously, however, the images are open, their very enclosing lines being extended in every case outside the limits of the cropped frames.

To a large extent, Turner's sketchbook embodies Romantic qualities and interests, yet, in its mode of production, it also signals a departure from this precedent. For, while the Romantic sketch was concerned with the *display* of immediacy – the spontaneity of on-the-spot observation – Turner's sketchbook cannot sustain this appearance. And, though it is now understood that drawing from observation and memory involve processes that are, in fact, very similar (each involving mental manipulation), the critical factor for the Romantics was the *appearance*, rather than the actuality, of immediacy.[11] Turner's appear neither immediate nor spontaneous, the sketches being reproduced when compiled to construct the 'series of views'. They were most likely redrawn, in 1890, as a group formatted four per page in what might best be described as a two-and-a-half dimensional outline codifying a three-dimensional reality.[12]

In its two-and-a-half dimensions, and being a *re-membering*, the sketchbook has a schematic quality that depicts objects and landscapes less as their 'realistic' likeness than their more diagrammatic equivalence. For example (Image 2), the urban background in silhouette in the second English view is little more than a metaphor: hardly 'naturalistic', it nonetheless symbolises the urban setting we are told is Camden Town. Less than the specificity of each house or place, this kind of analogous or schematic approach is interested in chronicling the general and reiterative colonial processes of moving, building and settling. This is reinforced through the format of the sketchbook, which has a collective and comparative effect in place of the singularity of individual artistic plates that feature in Wilson's *Old Colonial Architecture in New South Wales and Tasmania*.[13] Turner's concern is not merely aesthetic but also cultural and historical, and his sketches not just marking (and made of) lines but also about forming an outline: a memory but also a speculation.

The series as outline(s): a colonial settlement history

Insofar as it implies an overview, a plan, a summary – even, in itself, a 'sketch' – Turner's sketchbook is an outline operating concurrently at a number of levels. Firstly, the series broadly outlines the processes and outcomes of imperialism. Turner's individual experiences highlight the larger patterns of movement and settlement: when amplified, the singular stands to reveal the enormous cultural, environmental and architectural impacts of the full reach of colonial occupation. His example makes apparent the extent to which occupation (understood as invasion and settlement by a dominant power of subordinated peoples and lands) often was achieved and became indelible through nothing so much as the ever-expanding spread of domiciles. Core to colonialism's institution of the domestic was the right to legal and monetary ownership of a patch of ground, perhaps imperialism's most effective tool in both displacing indigenous peoples and implanting alien ones. Erasing signs of Aboriginal inhabitation, felling trees and clearing ground, naming sites and mapping boundaries, making fences and erecting buildings all advanced the proclamation of a plot in an indefinitely repeating process inscribed in word and image (as well as in practice) by Turner. While graphic evidence of the erasure pre-requisite to house building features in his early Swan River Colony views, the aftermath of settlement colours most of the Australian scenes: houses rest on bare, roughly cleared ground, offset by a bounding curtain of bush cut back hard. In his multiple accounts of moves and periods of settled pause, Turner exemplifies the reiterative acts and subsequent impacts of colonisation.

Secondly, the series outlines empire-colony relations, drawing a visual essay of distinction between English and Australian domestic environments in regard to their respective architectures, landscapes and living patterns. Buildings, nonetheless similar in form, are flatter, smoother and more vertical in the English scenes that open the sketchbook than those of Turner's first Australian abodes. The latter are rather given greater textural roughness and appear more laterally spread, by virtue of window and door openings of broader proportions, facades horizontally attenuated and roof pitches less steeply inclined. Where the first four views of established English conurbations feature iron fence railings, roads, driveways and footpaths, manicured lawns and, most especially, stylised urban skylines, subsequent Australian images show tents, houses, sheds and a church set upon rough terrain in the colonial 'bush' setting. Yet even in Australia's urban situations, the buildings retain (un-English) textured surfaces and more prostrate form. Further, from Old to New World, there is a sense of spatial expansion. This is conveyed in some instances by the introduction to the Australian views of blue sky and the horizon, now with sufficient room to appear after the confinement of England. Others depict an altered figure-ground relationship: the diminished scale of buildings relative to ground and/or sky accentuates the perception of Australia's spatial openness.

At a third level, Turner's series is descriptive of the literal and metaphorical outlining of Nineteenth Century Australia in geographical, architectural, social and historical terms. Insofar as Australia's cultural landscape exists, actually and poetically, as a network of lines, the sketchbook exemplifies this layered phenomenon. On a large scale, Turner's movements map a convoluted weave across the continent's southern half. As explained by A J Rose, lines such as these replace the 'delicate tracery of Aboriginal lineaments on the land' with a settlement pattern dominated by lines (in the form of transport routes) connected to England and, within Australia, tying regional outposts to the knotted nodes that are the coastal capitals. The cultural landscape is delineated also at a smaller scale, and it is

Turner's settlements that represent what Rose refers to as 'Cottage Australia', characterised literally by a 'low profile'. The cottage begets the loose networks constituting Australia's towns that in turn accommodate self-contained suburban living. And, in preserving the definition of this small-in-bigness (or big-smallness), in Rose's mind and Turner's view(s), Cottage Australia is a function at once of enclosure and emptiness, 'an amalgam of the small scale and the large scale', an utter inversion of the cultural landscape of the old world.[14]

When traced with an eye to urban-, architectural- and socio-historical detail, Turner's movement-settlement pattern illustrates Twentieth Century work in urban, cultural and architectural history. Firstly, in moving between states and towns as well as in and out of cities, his movements compare with the paths generally beaten by Australians throughout the nineteenth century, reflected nowhere more clearly than in his first cross-country move to Victoria. As with his travels around Western Australia's southwest, this intracontinental shift confirms J M Freeland's observation that settlers followed explorers in opening up the country. After leaving WA, Turner arrived at the Castlemaine goldfields in 1853 amidst the 'full swing' of Victoria's building boom and lived (with some hundred thousand-plus others into the late 1850s) in huts or tents.[15] From then he began a thirty-year period of constant mobility. His moves map such profoundly shaping moments as the introduction of railways (from the mid-1850s in Victoria)[16]; the increasing density of towns and the move from single storey to terrace houses; the creation of suburbs and the onset of sprawl; and the blurring of urban and rural Australia in suburbia's liminal zone. But Turner's movements, though closely corresponding to dates and trends given by Graeme Davison, Freeland, Boyd and others, are rather laterally fluid than linearly progressive. His sketchbook does demonstrate the general rural to urban to suburban drift but not especially as a chronological sequence. Instead, Turner depicts a series of coexisting paths, shifts and lifestyles.

The domestic alternatives outlined by Turner are, moreover, of various architectural types and styles. So, secondly, not as movements but as settlements, Turner's views are virtually a taxonomy of Nineteenth Century Australian housing, preceding (and closely matching) Boyd's 'Major Steps of Stylism' in *Australia's Home*. In the following passage, Boyd might well be describing Turner's houses:

Most houses [of the 1850s] were of timber walls and iron roofs. Only one house in seven (as against every second Victorian house by 1900) was of brick or stone. Gradually the gold-fields quietened. Ballarat and Bendigo and various smaller towns paved their streets and settled down into everyday urban life. Building thereafter developed rapidly on the Melbourne pattern, and by 1871 the number of people in tents had dropped to 45,757.[17]

Over this same period, Turner's residences included (after the tent at Castlemaine) a group of tents and timber sheds on his Taradale farm; then, in town, a small timber cottage followed by a more substantial timber building; and, finally, a series of single-storey urban terrace houses, complete with paved streets and iron railings. The first two terraces, of timber and probably iron – one with striped bullnose verandah – were in Ballarat (1868–70); the third, possibly of brick, and also with a verandah, in Emerald Hill, Melbourne (1870). In the 1880s, he occupied two-storey terrace houses in Paddington and then St Leonards, Sydney, perhaps exemplifying the kinds of houses built, claimed Boyd, as rental investments. Several of Turner's urban terraces in both Melbourne and Sydney feature cast-iron lacework, a material locally produced in quantity from the 1880s, which, for Boyd, had the consistency of an 'afternoon tea d'oyley' in patterns 'intricate to the point of obscurity'.[18] And it is at this point that Turner's chronicle challenges Boyd's narrative. Where Boyd ultimately caricatures architectural styles, whose progression reflects Australians' growing fascination with Featurism, Turner documents a similar range of (Nineteenth Century) building types and architectural styles as an inclusive collection, a variety of options rather than a linear progression (or, for Boyd, decline) from Colonial to Victorian.

Interesting in this context is Turner's concluding view (Image 31) of the house he built in 1885 at Digby in Victoria's Western District. This house can be seen to represent what Boyd termed 'Hardy Wilson style' which, owing to the wide circulation of Wilson's books first drawing (attention to) Australia's Old Colonial architecture, became euphemistic for buildings associated with the colonial period generally.[19] Clearly resembling the Colonial architecture of the Myth, this house brings us full circle, for it is with this last view that Turner's series at once precedes and challenges the neo-Georgian or Colonial Revival tradition. On the one hand, Turner's design places him at the moment when, circa 1890, Australian identity was a major concern in most cultural fields, and not least in architecture. The notion of an Australian architecture had been touted as early as 1892[20], though in terms of a contemporary Romanesque form, so while there was no shared preferred style, the nationalist drive nonetheless shaped the milieu eventually nourishing Wilson's early Twentieth Century Colonial Revival. In creating his series of views at this time (1890), perhaps Turner, too, was remembering preceding decades through the glass of nationalism, outlining a version of Australianness. And, certainly, with its low slung iron roof extending into wide verandahs sheltering a symmetrically-fronted weatherboard 'homestead', the last is probably the most stereotypically 'Australian' building in his series, if we interpret both house and sketchbook as precedent to the Myth.

But there is another way to understand Turner's sketchbook, and this is as alternative to the Wilsonian tradition. We have already acknowledged that the series chronicles colonial settlement history not as a closed linear progression (of ways of living or styles of architecture) but as an open-ended collection of concurrent social, spatial, geographic and architectural possibilities. In this context, the final sketch is not so much a culmination but rather another instance in Turner's repetitive process of movement and settlement. The sketchbook is, in fact, rather *in*conclusive and in place of the absent thirty-second sketch is a speculative verse:

And now for number thirty-two
My next move: in prospective view
I can't forecast. I'm in a fix
Next move may be across the Styx.[21]

Fundamental for Turner, and in accord with Romantic precedent, is the notion of process as theme and method, a commitment that is as much ideological (or philosophical) as aesthetic, requiring interpretation in terms more broadly cultural and historical than just architectural. In respectively outlining imperialism, empire-colony relations and Australian Colonial and Nineteenth Century development, Turner's series is descriptive of both universal civilisation and regional cultures, where 'the first is pledged to appropriative expansion, the second to cultural difference'.[22] His narrative is not evolutionary but episodic and, insofar as we can discuss Turner's sketchbook both *as* an outline and in terms of its (out)line techniques, it is both descriptive (provides context) and figurative (is text): his sketches slide between empirical topographical representation and artistic expression, between memory and drawing-writing, occupying at once background and foreground.[23]

End notes

[1] Wilson belongs to this 'travel-sketch' tradition by virtue of his making sketches of buildings 'discovered' by him on his extensive walking tours of New South Wales and Tasmania.

[2] Paul Carter, 'Second Sight: Looking Back as Colonial Vision', *Australian Journal of Art*, 13 (1996): 9-35.

[3] Paul Carter, and see, for example, Bernard Smith, *European Vision and the South Pacific*, 2nd edn, New Haven: Yale University Press, 1985.

[4] This comment applies equally to sketches of other Western Australian settlements, such as Fremantle or King George Sound (Albany).

[5] Stephen Bann, *The Inventions of History: essays on the representation of the past*, Manchester, UK; New York, NY: Manchester University Press, 1990.

[6] 'Thomas Turner's Sketchbook 1813-1885', Manuscript Collection, Battye Library, WA. MN746 Acc 2835 A/1-35.

[7] Chapman, 'Thomas Turner', p. 377.

[8] Fuseli quoted in Sam Smiles, 'Turner in the West Country: From topography to idealisation', in J C Eade (ed.), *Projecting the Landscape*, Canberra: Humanities Research Centre, ANU, p. 39. [Note that Smiles is writing of the more famous J M W Turner.]

[9] John Barrell, 'The Public Prospect and the Private View: the politics of taste in Eighteenth Century Britain', in Eade, p. 17.

[10] Richard C Sha, *The Visual and Verbal Sketch in British Romanticism*, Philadelphia, PA: University of Pennsylvania Press, 1998.

[11] Jonathon Fish and Stephen Scrivener, 'Amplifying the Mind's Eye: Sketching and Visual Cognition', *Leonardo*, 23, 1 (1990): 117-26, argue that the sketch combines information from the eyes and images from memory. Moreover, quick recognition of line drawings (as in sketches) is aided by highly processed mental representation.

[12] Fish and Scrivener, 'Amplifying the Mind's Eye', explain that this fractional dimension actually approximates the early stages of human vision, which produces this kind of representation by extracting and amplifying contours, the distance, and the slant and colour of surfaces.

[13] W Hardy Wilson, *Old Colonial Architecture in New South Wales and Tasmania*, Sydney: Union House, 1924.

[14] A J Rose, 'Australia as a Cultural Landscape', in Amos Rapoport (ed.), *Australia as Human Setting*, Sydney: Angus & Robertson, 1972, pp. 61-70.

[15] Robin Boyd, *Australia's Home: Its Origins, Builders and Occupiers*, Melbourne: Melbourne University Press, 1952, p. 31.

[16] Turner's moves along railway lines parallel Graeme Davison's observations of Melbourne's Nineteenth Century urban development. See Davison, *The Rise and Fall of Marvellous Melbourne*, Carlton, Vic: Melbourne University Press, 1978.

[17] Boyd, *Australia's Home*, p. 31.

[18] Boyd, *Australia's Home*, p. 45.

[19] Boyd, *Australia's Home*, p. 112.

[20] E Wilson Dobbs introduced the notion of a contemporary Romanesque architecture suitable for Australia in 1892.

[21] Turner's Sketchbook, closing page.

[22] Hal Foster, after Kenneth Frampton, 'Architecture, Development, Memory', in K Michael Hays & Carol Burns (eds), *Thinking the Present: Recent American Architecture*, New York: Princeton Architectural Press, 1990, p. 116.

Tanya Ring

Control and Release

1.

The words are few and far between: economic, frugal. They bridge with a certain ease and clarity that schism between minds into which most words, perfunctory lemmings, fall in a throw-away heap. He is speaking them with a detectable sense of calculation and she is wondering of ulterior motives. What lies behind, what must be simmering beneath the shell of self-sculpture.

2.

High noon, high summer. Freeway driving: car-noise and speed, window down and radio up and sun and sky all blaring, all is constant full blast, bare and white-hot, flat sheets of energy stinging the air. Charging his mind. Fuelling his pursuit.
  Of what?

And what is he? Part recorder, collector, distorter, inventor. An assimilator of small significances. A writer.

3.

Click and taps and nothing and *tap-tap-tap* and quiet *click click* and nothing and rapid-fire wordkill: delete-delete-delete-delete.
  These sounds annoy her, they divide the silence unevenly, load it uncomfortably, it is him at the word processor, again. But these words aren't being *processed*, she thinks, oh no it's far messier than that, this birth and death of words played out all over the screen. This fractured rhythm of stop and start, clicks and taps, inscribing its urgent code onto the blank night.

From the bed she glances outside through the window, sees a figure walk past down below, watches the cold edge of his street-light shadow slide over the pavement. Gone. The night clear, quiet, still. The figureless scene poised, silver lit and outside of time, it strikes her for an instant. Photo-real.

The black pixels of his words, they are mere absences of light. She thinks he is writing his own shadow.

4.
And what is she? Part recorder, collector, distorter, inventor. A stockpiler of semblances. A photographer.

Photography: drawing with light.

Click and hold that – no – towards me a bit. Just a bit. Great. Hold on. Quiet *tic-tic-tic* of instrument adjustment, delicate *tic-tic*. Tic. Right. Silence. *Click*. Great. Tic-tic. *Click*. Hang on. Silence. *Click*. *Click*. Right. The staccato, mechanic, of her own work.

And it's mostly advertising and recipe books, really, for the money anyway. Food. Oh she knows how to make an image good enough to eat. Once, for an exhibition, (she exhibited, occasionally, her own personal work) she had taken photos of some of these photos arranged on a plate, glistening sumptuously. Consuming the image and all that. She then took a photo of *these* photos, and continued the process over and over, photos of photos of photos, until the Veal Cutlets Modena Style and Profiteroles filled with Praline Cream were lost in an endless game of artifice.

5.
She says, stop playing games, let's talk.

HE: All conversations are a game. For me to stop playing games I would have to remain silent.

She says, you're doing it again.

HE: It's all a game. Strategic. Winners and losers, good moves and bad moves and we all place our personal bets, and go home richer or poorer, and wonder how we can get better at the game.

She says, old clichés, your metaphors.

HE: Or better at cheating. Ourselves.

She says, worn and full of holes.

HE: Instant replays played over and over in our minds.

She says, you bore me.

HE: It's all in the editing.

She says, hold that, I'll get my camera.

6.
And again, here he is driving, again.
   Subservient geometries of car and road soothe. Slow, rhythmic scrolling of sulphurous street-lights like film credits across the windscreen hints at warm lullabies, distant. Radio on. He changes lanes. Sounds sixties and squealing:

> *I stand up next to a mountain*
> *And chop it down with the edge of my hand.*

The night is still, warm. In wait. A car speeds past, excess Hendrix spilling out a wound-down window, messy trail of rifts and rhythms eddying behind. That car sure is moving; any faster and the blues will soon be red-shifting, blistering with distortions.

7.
Keyboard clicks and taps:

From a fixed viewpoint, the whole thing can never be seen. Without you moving, something always remains hidden. Attempts to compose the messy shebang of all three-hundred-and-sixty-degrees into a fixed, seamless two-dimensional image, a single picture, a single story, able to be absorbed in a single glance, a single sitting, from a single viewpoint, will always distort or leave gaping holes. Shutter-click. We say that we have 'captured' something, but we what we've left out often weighs more.

1569. Gerhardus Mercator wins lasting fame for his transcription of the entire planet onto a flat sheet. Into a single glance. The distortions at the extremes were shadowed by the eminent practicality of the device. Is my image of you stretched and pulled for easier circumnavigation? I want the jagged edges, the extremes as they are. Beyond the image.

Distorted, or leaving gaping holes. A collage of photos showing the entire thing. Front, back, above, below, left, right. They never meet at the edges. Something slips out. Or enters. But all is seen, is it not? This, the hyper-reality of the fragment.

This is where he's headed: the spaces in between.
Slips out, escapes.

Annette Trevitt

Myra

I waited with my mother for my father to pick me up. I was going to his house for lunch; the last place in the world I wanted to go but Janice, his second wife, had insisted. Janice and my mother used to be friends but not any more.

My mother, still in her dressing gown, sat at the kitchen table. The newspaper was open and her eyes followed the lines but I knew she wasn't taking it in. She was preoccupied with the forecast of heavy rain that she had heard earlier on the radio.

A car sounded its horn and I got up.

"See you mum."

"Yeah," and waited a moment before she looked up, "see you love."

It wasn't easy for her, I knew that, but still something about her eyes annoyed me. I let the front screen door bang shut behind me and walked down the steps onto the path. I heard a chair scrape on the lino and knew she had got up to pour another drink and to check the weather. She couldn't help herself. She was obsessed.

I waved to my father; he waved back. His new car sat low on the ground and he sat even lower in it. All I could see of him was his head. He had already turned the car around and was waiting on the other side of the road with the engine running. I walked around the front of the car and felt the heat come off the bonnet. He was still staring at the house when I got in. I had no idea what he was thinking and he never said anything. It was different when I was 13; we used to talk and he would call me, his little angel. But now I was 15 and it felt different and I didn't know why.

The wheels spun in the gravel. I pretended not to notice. Instead I looked out at greenish grey clouds gathering in the distance. The same clouds my mother would be watching. I pictured her at the window; squinting out at the horizon and not liking what she saw in the same way Clint Eastwood did.

My father only slowed down once we got to his caravans, his new, shiny white caravans. They were lined up in long neat rows from the biggest to the smallest. I was wondering whose idea that arrangement was when we swung into the drive and came to a sudden stop. Janice was out the front lingering only feet away from their neighbour who was sweeping pine needles off the grass. She didn't seem to be doing anything until she saw us. Then she waved, straightened up a stake, crossed the lawn and turned on a sprinkler.

Before I knew it; I was on a kitchen stool, holding a glass of lemonade, while my father stood over a plate of barbequed meat that he had marinated and Janice was getting changed in the bedroom. They were going to have a game of tennis, before lunch, on their new court. It was my father's idea. He had stayed up watching Wimbledon until three in the morning and got fired up, convincing himself that he knew how it was done.
  "It's like chess," he said, "you have to be at least five moves ahead." chess? He had never played chess. The only indoor game I remembered him playing was Monopoly once which ended when he stormed off owing thousands to Park Lane and Mayfair. I looked at him as he bent over the meat, probing it with a fork, while dressed in his tennis whites. I didn't recognise him like that: all clean, white and so sure of winning.

It was clear that I was to watch the game. I wanted to go back inside and watch TV but I felt I couldn't. Instead I sat at a perfectly set picnic table and felt reminded that it wasn't my place any more. It used to be until my father got caught in a caravan with another woman – a woman from out of town – by a group of boys who had gone into the yard to have a smoke. By the time school had ended that afternoon, nothing was going to be the same for me again.
  My mother and I moved to a small weatherboard house on the flood plains but it was only after her friend, Janice, moved in with my father that she lost the plot. She would stand at the window and stare out at the swampy paddocks for long stretches of time and then she would open a bottle of wine and pour herself a drink, nearly

always in her slippers. She told me that she would rather drink herself to death than drown. Something that she really believed was a possibility living there.

When Janice moved in with my father, she sold her house. She drew up a rough plan of what she wanted, hired a builder and before long, she and my father owned the only two-storey house in town. The caravan business which my father had inherited from his parents, and had barely kept afloat with my mother, thrived. And now they also owned the only private tennis court in town.

"I turned his life around," Janice said to me once. Even now I felt angry thinking about the look on her face when she said it. And I thought of the word, bygone, that she had used in the same conversation, and of what a stupid word it was.

A ball flew out of the court and into the neighbour's back yard.

"Out" Janice cried with her hands on her hips. They looked at each other and then Janice lost interest and looked down at her racquet. She plucked at the strings in the same way that the players did on TV.

I didn't know what was going on but something was up. Something that made the game particularly hard to watch. Janice and my father pelted shots at each other. The shots piled up on top of each other like storm clouds; each one darker, heavier and more important than the last.

My mother said that she had heard things weren't good between them; 'things were rocky in paradise,' were her words. Despite knowing that my mother heard what she wanted to hear, and nothing else, it did seem true.

Janice walked off the court, a winner, and plonked herself down next to me and then, without really looking at me, asked,

"Where'd you get your hair done?"

I went red. She knew. She fucken well knew my mother cut it. My mother always did. She had trained as a hairdresser before she had me. I knew it looked funny but I couldn't let any one else cut it. My mother loved doing it. And besides the times when she did, were some of the only times that she seemed all right. Janice flattened down loose tape on her racquet's grip with her fingertips and started to say something about the new upstairs bathroom but I didn't listen. I was trying to step outside of myself and then look back at myself and particularly at my hair. I couldn't remember what I looked like. I couldn't remember at all. I didn't know but Janice did and it made me sick.

My father came to the table looking like he was in the early stage of a heart attack. He pulled out a hankie and wiped his face. Of course he lost; he always lost. Why did he think it would be any different? Janice had played since she was six; she was a strong and fast player. My father had come to the game late, overweight and with no natural ability whatsoever. He sat down and continued to wipe his face. Janice looked over at him, putting up her hand to cut the glare. Her eyes rested on the top of his head and stayed there. I wondered how he stood it; he was very delicate about hair loss. Even knowing that I couldn't help but throw a quick glance up there as well.

"Ray, you look dreadful, go and have a shower," she said.

He stood up, without a word, crossed the backyard and went inside.

Janice reached for a cigarette packet under a tea cloth and I grabbed the nut bowl. All that were left were inedible, unsalted peanuts. I picked one out and remembered that Janice didn't eat nuts. Or butter. Or chocolate.

A door opened and banged shut and Janice's neighbour walked out carrying a huge basket, piled with washing, to the clothes' line. She put it down and spun the line around while looking up at clouds that were moving across from the east.

"Do you know her name yet?" I asked knowing that Janice didn't.

"Who cares what it is. I haven't time to worry about people like that... Shirley, Cheryl, it'd be some sort of name like that, Melissa." I didn't know what those names meant to her but clearly they were names that she didn't go for. I knew that she had never had a conversation with the neighbour. The neighbour was new to town and kept to herself. She had no interest in chatting with or getting to know Janice at all and Janice hated it.

"She's a drinker," Janice said and pulled back sharply on a cigarette as if it was a full stop.

"How do you know that?" I asked.

"You can tell, no one visits, she never leaves the house or makes any effort whatsoever. She's a miserable person."

I looked at her; she didn't look miserable, she didn't look miserable at all. Then I thought of my mother and got angry. She was miserable; she was bloody miserable. Everyone knew it. Janice knew it and I hated her for it. I hated her for knowing anything about my mother. I hated her for what she had done and I hated my mother for being like she was. I pictured her at the window staring out and trying to convince herself that the storm will pass; everything will pass. Her only solace was a clear blue sky. I sat and watched clouds as they gathered over the caravan roofs and realised it had become mine too.

A flock of white cockatoos flew overhead and landed in gum trees behind the tennis court. There seemed to be hundreds of them. I watched them and thought of when Cathy and Kim said, in Geography, that they wished things would happen. I didn't; I wished things would stop.

I looked at Janice, out of the corner of my eye, as she stubbed out her cigarette and watched the neighbour go back inside. The zipper on her tennis dress wasn't done up all the way to the top. She continued to stare at the back door as if waiting for something to reveal itself. After a long time, she sighed, turned back and looked at the butt in the ashtray.

"Who cares what her bloody name is."

You do, I thought, you do, more than anything. She hated not knowing. She hated not knowing anything. I looked at her hand wrapped around the ash tray and realised that her voice had sounded the same as it did the last time she phoned my mother.

"Is your mother there, Melissa?" she had asked.

"No," I lied. My mother told me to say that if it was Janice.

"Well if that's the way she wants it, that's the bloody way she can have it. I don't care," Janice said and hung up. But what did she expect?

My father crossed the lawn. He had showered, put on cream trousers and a beige shirt and smoothed down his hair. It was obvious who bought his clothes now. He put down an esky, pulled out a can of beer and handed Janice her racquet.

"Aren't you going to change?" he snapped. She glared at him and stood up.

"Of course I am," she said, taking a swipe at an imaginary ball, "the meat's over there," and pointed to the plate under a tea towel with her racquet.

I watched her disappear inside. Christ, it'll never end. My father picked up the plate and walked over to the new electric barbecue and turned it on. I looked at my watch with the same feeling I had once, on a train, when I was only three hours into a twelve-hour trip. I just wanted it to end so I could be home.

The cockatoos weren't so white any more. They had been dulled by the clouds. I stared at them and the trees for so long that eventually everything blurred and hurt my eyes. I closed them and remembered the esky. It was full of UDL cans, and cans of beer. I looked at my father. He was flipping over steaks on the hot plate with his back to me. I looked over at the kitchen window but it was too dark to see inside. I waited a bit longer for any movement and then pulled out a can of Southern Comfort and coke. It tasted sweet. I had another sip, looked at the label, and put the can down beside me. It felt good and cold and full and secret in my hand.

My mother was right. The house was a charmless red-brick eye-sore. Something that she loved to say to who ever was around to listen and that was usually me. But I didn't mind hearing it; I liked the way my mother used the word, charmless.

My father continued to flip over the steaks, flattening them each time, then he pushed some aside and came over to the table. He picked up a plate and as he did, he knocked over another and, before he could catch it, it fell to the ground and smashed. He stood and stared at the mess he had made. We both did. Then all of a sudden, out of nowhere, Janice appeared and knelt down and carefully picked up the broken china. I looked at her neck and at the way the dress cut into her back and I felt sad. I continued to watch her and then it dawned on me that my father never picked up the pieces. He didn't even try.

The cockatoos screeched as they rose out of the trees. My father looked up at them and then glanced down the driveway. He looked startled and grabbed for his can of beer.

"Hello Myra," he said.

I turned around and saw a woman walking across the drive towards us.

It was mum, still in her dressing gown and wearing no shoes.

ANNE BREWSTER AND HAZEL SMITH

ProseThetic Memories

Lost in Thought

Today, at last, I had some time for reading. I sifted through all sorts of bits and pieces, everything from Levinas to de Certeau.

In the mid-afternoon I forced myself to take a break and do the shopping. Driving to the supermarket and wandering among the aisles I didn't feel quite adequate to the task at hand. I wasn't thinking of anything in particular; I was simply suspended, lost in thought.

De Certeau says: *like those birds that lay their eggs only in other species' nests, memory produces in a place that does not belong to it . . . It derives its interventionary force from its very capacity to be altered – unmoored, mobile, lacking any fixed position.*

～

what I know now must change
what I lost then. what you have
never owned you recreate.

                        the present coughs into the faces of the past
                        knocks pictures sideways on the wall.

so memory digs up birds have flown away
are laying eggs in foreign beds

∽

To remember is to evoke loss, the *disjecta membra* – the *scattered limbs* – of the thinking body.

Memory is a narrative cue. To remember is to create instantly the trajectory of a story. What remembered image does not trail a narrative in its wake? Can you recall a face without the narrative figuring of your connection with that person?

Memory, then, is a practice of ethics in that it is embodied and intersubjective. To remember is to realise our connection with those we have historically considered "other". Sometimes it's difficult to acknowledge the mutual imbrication of our histories and the way the effects of the past live on in the present, at least in the "other's" memory: we, on the other hand, claim for ourselves the right to forget. I guess this explains how the John Howards of Anglo-Australia, in disavowing the continuity of the past, have been able not to say "sorry".

∽

"memory" is not a generic term of analysis, but itself an object appropriated and politicized. Or, equally, nationalized, medicalized, aestheticised, gendered, bought and sold.

MATSUDA

∽

Fellow-consumers—visit our web-site! Download any of our 10 million virtual apologies! Listen to a stereo byte or two in the voice of your choice. Wipe out all those guilt feelings! Cleanse the past! Choose any phrasing you like, or let our resident writers pick the most soothing words. The essence of all our apologies is that they don't have to be what they mean, *or think what they say*. We have every kind of apology you could desire: beginner and advanced, family and national, racist and multi-cultural, new age, site-specific, low-fat, easy-care, quick fix, superglue and slow-release. All with state of the art graphics and available on instant demand.

Remember: our apologies can be made-to-mood—also cut-price sets available if you buy now, complete with automatic renewals.

Staff choice and bargain of the month: an apology to indigenous people, carefully worded to avoid any real expression of regret.

If we haven't got the right style for you in stock, all we can do is say how terribly sorry we are, and advise you next time to place your order several altercations in advance.

And please do business with us again.

∽

white night

the sky is as busy as television; clouds hurrying by, morphing from one shape to another, fluent in an arcane language. behind them it was all happening; the once-in-a-century eclipse. same planet but with a different face, lit obliquely. a secret moon, a blind spot. the eclipse, occulted but happening: a story we're drawn into by virtue of not seeing, then suddenly seeing. so the memory of terror is drawn into history. and we see what we did not see: the huge night of (our) otherness; the illusion of forgetting.

∽

    Somebody has given me a dolls' house, I've always wanted one and I'm very excited by it. It's Victorian, and there are people puffed up in fancy clothes, others dressed down as servants. I adore the tiny figures and the furniture: the chaise longue, and the large china basin for washing in. It's more elaborate than the usual doll's house: all the rooms open out into other rooms as if it had endless depth. I'm excited by the wooden doors, I like to open them and peep into the rooms without being inside. I can move the dolls around in any way I like: I make up stories, pushing them into new lives. But there is one door I can't open; it seems to be stuck and there is no key. I look through the keyhole and, before I have a chance to see anything, it opens effortlessly. I'm no longer outside looking in: the room is all around me, huge and windowless, and I'm shaking and afraid. The floor is covered with ripped out pages of books which ripple as if there were a breeze. On one wall, painted in swirling letters, is the word 'Nachträglichkeit', on another, 'amnesia'. But the room is crammed with heavy oak chests, pushed against each other at every angle. The drawers are gaping, and in them are hundreds of black dolls, grief-eyed, squashed together: a few heads, arms and legs dangle out. I don't know whether I feel fear or pity but I have to act. So I pull one of the dolls from the drawer, put my mouth to hers in a way which is half kiss, half resuscitation. I'm breathing into her mouth and I blow harder and harder, until my mouth becomes all breath. But as I blow the doll breaks up, its head rolls off, and its arms and legs fall to the floor. I stare at the scraps, I am no longer thinking, and time seems to leave me behind. Then I find I'm outside the doll's house looking in, the house is tiny again, and the dolls are pale and still.

Note

Nachträglichkeit: a term used by Freud which has been translated as "afterwardsness". It implies that the present continuously transforms our conception of what has been.

∼

When I was a child my aunt and uncle lived in an old house in Epping that had been a hospital. It was so large that several wings had been converted into small flats. Once when we were visiting one Christmas holidays, a distant cousin and his family, who I had never met and who kept to themselves, were living in one of the flats. There was a long dark corridor which took several right-angled turns before it came to the door that led into their flat. I was exploring one day when a young child turned the corner in front of me; I thought it must be one of my first-cousins-once-removed and composed myself to greet this familial stranger, an awkward task as the child seemed reserved, regarding me with a taciturn curiosity. When I was almost upon the child I realised with a start that it was my own reflection. Looking up I saw a huge dusty old mirror in an elaborate gilded frame propped up against the wall.

~

in a fluid suspension of time and place
a lens flattens suspense till it's senseless
this faltering landscape builds the new sentence

museums dress warm for digital winters
whose endless forgetting is cyber revival
virtual breath, volatile bodies

dislodge the space the cool house settles
a guest's absence ghosts into filling
antique glass: holographic revisions

~

Dear Anne,

You asked what I've been reading! Have been thumbing through an essay by Alison Landsberg called 'Prosthetic Memory'. She argues that prosthetic memory is the way we acquire, and treat as our own, memories which do not belong to us. She talks about the contemporary urge to turn collective history into personal memories through 'experiential museums' or historical reenactments. It resonated with me because I enjoy immersing myself in historical disasters and often question my motivation. This desire to tap into the misfortunes of others for emotional release is something Landsberg doesn't really confront.

Landsberg sees the appropriation of memories as a form of prosthesis, and argues that it could be the basis for a new kind of politics which is not based on natural or essential identities. Instead individuals might form alliances by adopting positions or identities which do not fully belong to them.

But isn't the word prosthesis a gift, with its shadows of prose and thetic, and thesis? I suppose we might talk sometime about the balance in our piece between exposition of ideas and the fictional and poetic? And also the degree to which our styles are merging in the collaboration. I'm anxious that when we edit each other's work

I could find myself trying to rewrite yours so it would be more like my own.

Hazel

~

Stein, Sturken and Thoreau : a collage

hysterics suffer mainly from reminiscences. naturally I would then begin again. he is blessed over all mortals who loses no moment of the passing life in remembering the past. I did not begin again I just began. the object has not perhaps actually died, but has been lost as an object of love. then I said to myself this time it will be different and I began. above all we cannot afford not to live in the present. in the case of women's recovered memories, the question of belief is crucially tied to the history of disbelief. then I said to myself this time it will be different and I began. he is blessed over all mortals. the victor can afford to forget. and after that what changes what changes after that. can we have a theory of experience that allows for the suggestibility of memory, but which does not label women as hysterics? there was an inevitable beginning of beginning. preserving the love or idealization of the object. I went on and on to almost a thousand pages of it. naturally one does not know how it happened until it is well over beginning. this trackless initial forgetting.

~

in the middle of the story

in the middle of the night, time seems to stop and you're marooned. into this beguiling hiatus, one could inveigle any history. how to invite continuance, movement, to this stalled moment? to start again to keep going, inevitably to admit the impossibility of ending, which is, after all, only the pause between events. even this story must go on, eventually, and not necessarily tirelessly. there is more to come, nudging the newly opened space, neither wholly predictable nor unpredictable. you are at once reluctant, compelled; for a moment you've imagined narrativelessness, inoperable freedom. then the cat steps onto the bed, brushing the surface of your attention and you are in the world again; alive for one more day.

∼

Mark Poster suggests that the internet has brought about an explosion of narrativity: email and bulletin boards proliferate cyber-tales, often told between strangers.

He made me think about the way stories consort in cyberspace: you click and are suddenly in the middle of someone else's life watching them steal sweets; you click again and another transient friend is losing his virginity. But push another button and the computer is suddenly a black hole: it remembers absolutely nothing.

Poster thinks that "little stories" appear on the internet as an antidote to the grand narratives of progress and authority. I'm fascinated by those determined diminutives, their steely half-lives! The man who sits next to me at the theatre and then abruptly leaves; the couple on the train clearly relishing betrayal. In hypertext I squeeze each tiny tale onto its own screen. And the little stories endlessly dodge round each other, passing balls, sharing jokes and throwing shadows.

∼

When my aunt died all my memories about her had to be reassessed. As a child I adored her, but as I grew older I became more critical of her: I identified her with my father's values which she also heeded. I grew distant from her but she, in turn, felt intimidated by my education, independence and alienation from my Jewish background. That was the central issue in my family: where you stood in relation to your Jewishness. As a young adult I reacted heavily against this circumscription of my identity, and the adherence to tradition. That is why remembering her has to be a process of reconciliation: between those memories of her which are everything I want them to be, and those I am willing to put to rest.

∼

Diary

Things I wanted to tell her when she wasn't there:

That I had wanted something different for us, and had tried, but perhaps it wasn't possible. I didn't know quite how to talk about this: whether I would be caught unawares staging the moment as tragic, elegiac, blackly comic or bathetic. I didn't want any of these. High art or soap opera: it's the same thing. Closure is so uncompromising. It reduces something palpably chaotic to the banality of genre. When someone has died, remembering may be a process of reconciliation. But when the loved one is estranged we are buried alive: consigned to rehearsing a repertoire of readings of a "past" which refuses to be past but animates a proliferation of possible futures. We live out the vexed impossibility of the binary past/present – the terms of which indeed fail to be held apart as oppositions.

Today the mist has drawn the horizon in and the sea and the sky are almost the same colour. Once you walked up to the lighthouse after an argument. The lighthouse is the colour of the sea which is the colour of the sky this afternoon. Every day the light and the texture are different. Every walk is every day.

When you're not here I invent you. I memorialise you. To memorialise is to be in a dual relationship to the lost one: neither to disavow connection nor to refuse disconnection, difference, loss.

It's hard to resist looking at the news but it's always about the olympics.

The good thing about a catalogue is that you can just keep adding.

Disclaimer
all further connections with other moments in this text are purely fictitious; their relationship to living persons or intentions is purely arbitrary.

Images of something that has not yet happened and that may in fact never happen are no different in nature from the images you hold of something that has already happened. They constitute the memory of a possible future rather than of the past that was.

DAMASIO

Isn't it odd that when you part ways with someone – an estranged lover, a friend or neighbour – that you mourn not only the rupture in the continuation of a shared past, but also the abandonment of the future possibilities that you had dreamed of?

Maybe this sentiment is co-extensive with growing older and for the first time in your life realising that certain options will never again be available to you.

∼

Sometimes she had a nightmare and did not know whether it was a dream or real. It often contained unforgivable acts of which she was the perpetrator or the victim. With dreams like these she could never feel relaxed.

Frequently she seemed to be the space for other people's recollections. They would cross over her as if she didn't exist, and enter her as if she was a ghost. But they took up residence inside her as if she was a habitation.

Occasionally she wanted to remember the future but she found she couldn't because it was already lost, more memorialised than memory.

Many times she wished that all the acts of which she was ashamed would exit with the garbage. But generally it was OK as long as nobody kicked the lid.

Often she perceived that other people's blueprints were defective.

Usually collective truths were difficult to round up.

Repeatedly she rebuilt but the structure fell apart.
Always she knew that memory could outwit her death, historical facts, the sickly pride of nations.

∼

Marx's suggestion that the past is continuously obliterated to serve the logic of competition and markets is discussed by Matt Matsuda. He argues that there develops *an ever increasing technical capacity to investigate, record, and generate references* to the apparent disappearance of the past. The *crisis* of nineteenth-century memory was that there was *simultaneously too little and too much*. Matsuda refers to Walter Benjamin's figuring of the modern city where the constant consumerist search for the ever-new immediately transforms the new into the old, the discarded. The superceded, divested of the aura of newness, becomes *the prehistory of an eternally changing present*. Modernity, he concludes, is deeply prehistoric; memory persists as *the record of things strangely familiar for being so quickly gone, only half-forgotten*.

∼

Psychoanalysis is a therapeutic practice in which memory is considered restorative. Forgetting, on the other hand, is seen as counterproductive, causing the subject to deliquesce.

∼

Analysis

At one time all my friends were getting divorced
Now they are in analysis.

                They talk and I like to listen.

Tell me your story.
I only need glimpses
an arm will do
I don't need to see the genitals.

      I never knew he thought he was the most intelligent
      person in the world or that she thought she was the least

when we meet again they
speak about other things
as if nothing had been undressed

            and I'm not sure that the past explains
            the present or
            designs the future

     but I gather
     sort
     and mix

           Re-member

∼

She is a creature in limbo, removed from the present with her blank stare. Difficult to imagine this haunted creature animated by intimacy; previously an inseparable companion. As an adult it's hard to trust her. She is a compelling emblem of memory, charged with aura. She embodies loss in all its impossibility and necessity – the fact that we are so definitively estranged from our childhood, the traces of which are nonetheless indelibly and invisibly present in our psychological life. But the doll itself doesn't look childlike, you realise with a shock. Its knowing gaze is devoid of innocence or curiosity.

As an adult you cannot possess her as you did when a child. She is preoccupied, immersed in her own memories, unavailable. But she seems to own something of you, something you can't quite recall; she is witness to the child you were. What kind of child were you? Beneath the gaze of the doll you feel uneasy in this void of memorylessness. She is vacant and luminous. You too are replete and bereft, living and lifeless, forgetful and returning.

∾

Bergson defines memory as a bodily manifestation. It is sensory and motor. It is the *virtual state* of the organism, the accumulated past which acts on us and which makes us act. For Bergson, memory is not a passive faculty of storage and retrieval – it is that which is bodily *enacted*. Memory is the instantaneous materialisation of the senses, reflexes and perceptions. The past, through memory becomes, bodily, *a present, active state.*

∾

Do you remember the story about the man with Alzheimers who had forgotten where he had parked his car but was able to find his way home by walking, his body remembering the route although he could not recall the address?

∾

This is what separates the living from the dead: the dead no longer remember anything.

The personal is only the political if it falls out that way. History will mark it as the day the Berlin Wall came down. For her it will always be the day her father died.

The night before had seemed like his last. She couldn't sleep so she wrote a poem. But in the morning he was still there, clinging to his comatised life. He couldn't talk now, and the irony was that for the first time in her life she could have found the right words. Then she left the room and when she returned his eyes were rolling out of control. He has died now the nurse said and no, you weren't out of the room, you were with him.

That night she turned on the TV. The wall was crumbling and they were climbing through in their thousands. I'll have to rethink everything she thought, as the blocks came tumbling down. He'll never know about the wall. He'll always belong to a bygone era of history.

Afterwards, during TV replays, she longed to bask belatedly in the mass jubilation. But she had missed the emotional moment, or turned it to other uses.

The reruns were always jagged and incomplete

a balkanised mess of bits and pieces

Works cited

Bergson, Henri. *Matter and Memory* (1890), tr. Nancy Margaret Paul and W. Scott Palmer, New York: Zone Books, 1988.

Damasio, Antonio R. "Descartes' Error and the Future of Human Life", in James McConkey (ed) *The Anatomy of Memory*, New York: OUP, 1996, pp. 60–3.

De Certeau, Michel. *The Practice of Everyday Life*, tr, Steven Rendall, Berkley: University of California Press, 1988.

Landsberg, Alison. "Prosthetic Memory: *Total Recall* and *Blade Runner* in Mike Featherstone and Roger Burrows (eds.) *Cyberspace/Cyberbodies/Cyberpunk*, London: Sage Publications, 1995, pp. 175–190.

Matsuda, Matt L. *The Memory of the Modern*, New York: OUP, 1996.

Poster, Mark. "Postmodern Virtualities", in Mike Featherstone and Roger Burrows (eds.) *Cyberspace/Cyberbodies/Cyberpunk*, London: Sage Publications, 1995, pp. 79–96.

Stein, Gertrude. "Composition as Explanation", in C. van Vechten (ed) *Gertrude Stein*, New York: Random House, Vintage Books, 1935, pp. 165–206.

Sturken, Marita. "The Remembering of Forgetting", *Social Text*, Vol. 47 (4), Winter 1998, pp. 103–26.

Thoreau, Henry David. "Walking", in James McConkey (ed) *The Anatomy of Memory*, New York: OUP, 1996, pp. 67–81.

Maria Robinson

Ethan's Angel

Ethan's Angel is inspired by the memory of my precious cat, Ethan. Ethan, not only my faithful companion but also my child substitute, was euthanased in January 1998 after a lengthy battle with a feline illness. He was entwined intimately throughout all of the areas of my life in the three short years I had the privilege of his company. Ethan's angel is made of ceramic and painted gold. It was purchased for two dollars at a budget store during Ethan's illness to watch over him. It symbolises for me memories of Ethan and is by far the most precious item in my household.

I am a 46 year old divorced woman who has tried desperately to have a child through a fertility clinic. My story in a nutshell is about my struggle with my empty womb and the events and issues which surround these incredibly fragile years.

I was married in 1982 and was deeply in love with my husband John. We had known each other since I was nineteen. Our romance was a mixture of pleasure and pain, break-ups and erotic make-ups. It was an intense liaison and one, despite all of the heartache, I have not come to regret. During the first two years of our marriage we lived in a small house on a few acres of land. I fell in love with the house and the freedom of the bush. It was as though I was in another world. After two years we decided to start our own business. This meant selling our little house and moving further up the coast. John went ahead of me as I stayed to sell the house. The day he drove up our gravel road loaded with equipment for our business was to become the beginning of the end of our marriage. The sale of the house took twelve months to finalise. There was tremendous strain put on us, both emotionally and financially. John was only able to come home every few months. The business did not fare well. We hadn't anticipated most of the issues that arose: problems hiring reliable staff, our profit dependent upon the weather, the list was endless.

The situation had deteriorated so badly after the house sale that I went to live in Perth. I was only to stay a few months and then travel up the coast, but months turned into years. We were not able to afford to live together in our own rental place. I found work with my former employer and sent most of my wages to John for the business. The time we spent together became less frequent as time went on. We eventually sold the business and John and I moved into a flat in Maylands. By this time the effect of the past few years had taken its toll on both of us. We tried on a number of occasions to make the marriage work.

We had given up our lovely country house and secure employment for what turned out to be a living nightmare. We divorced in 1993. I never wanted the divorce but the marriage had broken down irretrievably. I moved into a small unit in the suburbs which wasn't too far from work. I spent most of the time on my own in an office. Hence began the cycle of social isolation that to a much lesser degree still affects me today. Working alone and living alone can be a dangerous combination for anyone unless they enjoy a full social life or have regular visitors to their home.

It was around this time that I started waking up during the night panicking about the prospect of not ever having a child. I would have go to an open window and deep breathe. There were times when I thought I was going mad. While these panic attacks were happening I was terrified that they would not stop. I still wanted John and spent many years waiting for him to get his life together. I imagined us remarrying and living happily ever after. I met one lovely man who often took me out to dinner and brought me flowers. We tried very hard to make the relationship work. We were together for about three months. My thoughts were still with John and I was forever comparing other men to him.

When I was thirty five I decided that if I hadn't met a suitable partner by the time I was 40 I would consider asking a friend if he would father my child on a donor basis. I had been intimate with him a few years before. He had never married or had children, although he had been in long-term relationships, but I was nevertheless reluctant about asking him. There were so many issues to consider. He was really flattered that I had asked him and greatly excited at first. He insisted on going for a medical check-up to make sure he was in good health. In the end, however, we mutually decided against it. I began to see that a donor from a sperm bank had many advantages and far less complications than a known donor. The semen is thoroughly screened in order to test for blood-borne viruses including HIV and Hepatitis. The donor's family medical history is also readily available. On a social scale there is also the advantage of complete anonymity.

Thoughts of financial insecurity and the daunting task of single parenthood were issues I needed to deal with before commencing treatment at a fertility clinic. I decided that a tertiary education would seal my fate in a positive way for our financial future. I passed the special tertiary admissions test and I was accepted into the faculty of Social Sciences at Edith Cowan University. I qualified for support as a full time student and my income was supplemented by my employer.

I moved into a rental house with a lovely garden and spacious back yard. It was very peaceful and just the right place for me to settle into my studies. I found my entry into University to be mixed with feelings of both fear and excitement. I was never a brilliant student at secondary school and passed my Junior Examination with average marks. The difference now was that I had chosen to embrace an education and had set clear goals. As I walked around campus on my first day I wondered how on earth I had even dared to dream of such achievement.

In the first few weeks of University, however, my nightly panic attacks started again. They were associated with the fear of not having children and the breakdown of my marriage. I asked my General Practitioner if he would write a certificate for me to withdraw from University. He said he would do so if I wanted to but he asked if I would consider seeing a therapist rather than withdrawing. I agreed to this and he went to great lengths to find just the right person for me to see. I attended sessions with the therapist for three years. In that time and with her support I managed to deal with the panic attacks, and they were gone within a few months and have never recurred. She made such a positive difference to the way I deal with life I will be forever grateful to her.

I decided to get a cat for company. I went to the Cat Haven intent on adopting a ginger kitten but I arrived home with a four-year-old silver grey tabby whom I named Ethan. Ethan was intrigued by the seemingly endless time I spent at my computer. He was never very far from me and we spent a great deal of time together.

After enquiries regarding access to fertility services by single women I found that I was able to participate in the sperm donor programme. I was however refused access to IVF as it is deemed illegal for single women to access this service in Western Australia. I was put in touch with another single woman named Louise via a donor insemination support group. Louise was to play a very important and supportive role throughout my journey and far beyond.

The following are excerpts from my diary that I had written for my unborn child.

Sunday 6th July 1997

This is the beginning of my correspondence to my unborn child. I want you very much and have completed a University degree so that I can support us both in a reasonable manner. Over the past few years I have gathered a lot of baby clothes and other necessities. Financial issues are a major factor and my ability to support us both generates a great deal of fear.

Monday 7th July 1997

When I was undergoing tests in January to establish my fertility it was discovered that both fallopian tubes were blocked. Last Thursday I had a procedure to find out the extent of the blockages. It was found that I have one patent tube and I am not sure if the other one will be blocked. My obstetrician will let me know in a fortnight what the score is. I am able to participate in the donor programme regardless.

Tuesday 8th July 1997

I don't really want to write tonight as I am feeling very emotional and teary-eyed. The path ahead seems even more daunting and I missed out on a very good job opportunity today. I may have to go away to earn some decent money. I need to make a move soon as my final semester starts soon and I really don't feel up to tackling post graduate studies at this point in time. Everything is just a bit too much but I am seeing my counsellor tomorrow. I love you and want you so very much and will end on this note for tonight.

Tuesday 30th September 1997

I had my first donor insemination procedure at a fertility clinic last Wednesday and I am not pregnant. I am lacking in a hormone called Progesterone. However this will be addressed in the next cycle which will start again tomorrow. I have learned to inject myself with hormones to stimulate my ovarian production. I will be honest in saying that I was not entirely unhappy about not being pregnant the first time round as I am experiencing some unexpected job insecurity. I am trying to address this by volunteering to do some work with women with alcohol and drug problems. I may find a job at the end of it and an agency is very keen to put me through a counsellor training course. However I am also very sad about not being pregnant at the same time. I love you very much and hope to feel you inside of me very soon.

Tuesday 30th September (middle of the night)

I can't sleep tonight as with last night so I have decided to write some more. I am very concerned about my financial state although I feel hopeful about the training course. I know this is a difficult time, but one day soon I will look back and see it as simply the process by which I find a job that I feel passionate about for the first time in my life.

Sunday October 5th 1997

I am feeling tired and my financial situation has deteriorated further. In spite of this I have become more hopeful of my ability to earn money as a writer in the near future. I begin a week's holiday starting tomorrow and I will try and land myself something more secure. The problem is that although insecure my working hours leave me with most mornings free if I need to attend the clinic. To take on a new job and then ask for time off work may leave me choosing between you and a job. To have you is my heartfelt choice.

I will take the opportunity to attend a meeting at a writing society on Tuesday. I feel passionate about writing for a living. I need to further develop my skills and network. The training course fell through and I am sure that I am being led in the right direction. Louise called me during the week and we had a good positive talk. I am on my second cycle at the moment and need to have blood tests in the morning to determine my ovulation status.

Monday 17 November 1997

I have just finished my third cycle without success. I have my period at the moment and I feel disappointed and disheartened at the prospect of facing Christmas without you inside of me. Anyway my obstetrician is attempting to unblock my right fallopian tube on November 28. I love you so much and can't wait to hold you.

Monday December 1st 1997

I had some terrible news today about Ethan. He has pneumonia, caused by an illness that has affected his immune system. He may not be able to recover, depending on how advanced it is. Ethan is on very strong antibiotics. I am feeling really sad.

Sunday 21st December 1997

Ethan has been backwards and forwards to the vet for weeks. He has had a few bouts of pneumonia. I took him to a vet this morning who also specialises in alternate therapies for a second opinion. Ethan really connected with her. We came home with all sorts of alternate therapies to boost his immune system and I feel more hopeful about a recovery.

Saturday 3rd January 1998

I took Ethan to the vet this morning. I decided to have him put to sleep. I am feeling devastated. The emotional pain is so intense that I can also feel it physically. A friend came to the vet with me. I stayed with Ethan during the procedure. I placed my hand on his head until it was over and there was a sense of relief as I didn't want him to suffer any more. The vet was really understanding and wrapped Ethan up very carefully. Jo and I came back here to the house and we buried him in the back yard.

I remember a dream I had about Ethan about one month before he was diagnosed with his illness. I dreamed that Ethan had fallen asleep in the garden outside my bedroom window. He was curled up under a bush and had died in his sleep. When I awoke in the morning I was really haunted by the dream. Ethan occasionally slept outside my bedroom window. Soon after I awoke he jumped up on the window ledge outside my bedroom. He was meowing to come inside, and I was relieved and let him in. I went back to bed and Ethan followed. He curled up in the foetal position and snuggled into my belly. We both curled up together until we fell asleep. It was an act of incredible love. In hindsight I think that Ethan knew what was to follow. It was probably his way of saying goodbye. The memory of this unique experience will stay with me always.

Monday 27th April 1998

Although I am still tired I want you to know that I am sitting the Public Service Recruitment Exam this Wednesday so that we may have a secure future and a home. I am very lonely at the moment. I graduate from University on May 5th. There is great excitement in the family as no one in our family has previously attended University. Nanna and my sister Anne and brother-in-law Jack are coming from the country for the ceremony. I am having second thoughts about having you as I am not sure that I can support us both without living below the poverty line. I am also concerned that my biological time clock has expired. I still love you but we may never meet.

I am still grieving Ethan's death which has devastated me more than I had realised. I was given leave without pay from work to take up a temporary position in the country. It turned out to be a disaster and I returned to Perth after two weeks. I had given up my rental house when I went away. I am living in a tiny flat in the suburbs. I will return to my job soon. My therapist has moved to Europe to practise and I said goodbye to her on April 4th. She gave me a beautiful rose quartz stone to remember her by. I miss her terribly but have been referred to a colleague of hers who I like very much. I will be seeing her tomorrow.

Thursday 30th April 1998

I am feeling more confident about my ability to support us both after seeing my counsellor on Tuesday. We had a long talk about it. I need to be careful not to make a decision I may regret simply on the grounds of how I am feeling at the moment. Louise phoned last night. We support each other very well and help each other to remain positive. It has made such a difference and I am so very grateful for this. I have seen Mike, my GP, this morning to have a pap smear. I feel some pre-menstrual tension coming on and I am looking forward to my next cycle at the clinic in the hope that you will be conceived. It's a beautiful sunny day and there is a cat named Misty lying on the lounge. She belongs to one of the tenants at these flats and takes turns at visiting the neighbours. She has helped me so much in the light of Ethan passing on.

I wasn't very happy with the Public Service exam yesterday. I don't think there will be a job for me. Not to worry. At least I sat the exam for better or for worse. I really have nothing to lose. I don't feel passionate about their type of job. It was just the security I was after. I need to concentrate on my writing ability. Although I am still physically tired I feel hopeful about the future.

I can picture myself in our house. It is nice and bright. There are rays of soft sunlight coming through the window. I am painting a room in a pastel colour. There is a security screen on the window. I look very happy. I will continue to see myself in this wonderful house and work towards making it a reality. Goodbye for today.

Monday 4th May 1999

It's the night before my graduation ceremony. Nanna is staying for the ceremony. Jack can't attend but Anne is coming down. I collected my academic regalia at Churchlands Campus this afternoon and the excitement and reality has set in. Just walking through the campus was enough to make me want to do another degree. Anyway, enough of that. I may study for a professional writing degree either part-time or by correspondence.

I have some period pain at the moment and it looks as if things will be happening very soon. I am feeling very hopeful about this cycle. Bye for now.

Tuesday 5th May 1999

My graduation ceremony is held tonight at Challenge Stadium. I am writing at 11am as Nanna has gone to town. I am reflecting on the time when I commenced my degree in 1994. I am also sitting here with Misty who is curled up on the lounge. I am grateful for the gift of her company, which I feel is very symbolic. I know that it is not a coincidence that I have been graced with her company.
I hope to meet with you soon. Period hasn't arrived yet.

Saturday 9th May 1999

My graduation went well on Tuesday evening. It was awesome. The whole thing was so emotional and I am so grateful that I didn't miss it. The academic procession was really something to see. I felt overwhelmed with emotion. I sat with the other course Majors and there was a real feeling of comradeship and achievement. It became clear to me while there that I want to do further studies. I started my period on Thursday and started my hormone injections at the fertility clinic on Friday morning. I have given myself an injection at home this morning. I hope to conceive you this month. Misty has been in for a few hours. I love her so much. I think I am becoming too attached to her.

I still haven't lost sight of the chance to buy us a house. I am joining the writing group very soon and hope to at least make a start on writing for a living.

Wednesday 13th May 1998

I am writing to you this evening although I am very tired and a bit irritable. I went to visit my friend Jayne today in her new old house in Victoria Park. There is a lovely atmosphere there and I was taken with the smell of paint and the creative energy inside the house. We sat for a while in the lounge room, painted in a lovely shade of green. The daylight coming through the window helped create the energy and I photographed it in my mind as an inspirational and healing time in my life. I am on day six of my cycle and will have blood tests on Thursday morning. I am a little confused about the future and financial issues are on the agenda again. Jayne says that I simply need to write instead of studying further in order to gain some more writing skills. The reason I am so taken up with her view is that at a deep level I know it to be the truth. It was a good day overall. I don't really want to go to bed even though I am so tired. Hoping to feel you inside of me soon.

Friday 15th May 1998

I am on day nine of my cycle. Yesterday I had a blood test that showed my hormone level to be 500. Tomorrow I have another blood test and an ultrasound. I may therefore have an insemination within the next few days. I hope to conceive you this month. I haven't made mention of your father at all in this correspondence. I have a document from the clinic that records his details. Although I intend to show it to you when you are able to read I feel the need to tell you how I feel about him. Although I don't know who he is I still feel not only a deep connection but also a tremendous sense of gratitude towards him. Whenever I have had an insemination I feel a closeness with him and wonder where he is at the time of the procedure and what sort of a person he is. I feel sure that you will meet him when you reach adulthood. I think the current laws will have changed dramatically by the time you grow up. I had some very good news today about a home of our own. A Building Society has approved a loan for a house. I will however need to get back to work to pay for it. It will probably take a while for me to choose a home. Maybe it won't. Anyway I am thinking positive about this news.

I am intending to writing to the women's co-ordinator at an institute concerning some work as soon as possible. Frank Sinatra died in the United States today. I am feeling good tonight. I will sign off now sending all my love.

Saturday 16th May 1998

Hello again. I didn't have much sleep last night out of a mixture of fear and excitement about the house and my ultrasound at the clinic. The blood test shows my hormone levels to be 850. The ultrasound shows three eggs on my right ovary. I hope that you are one of those eggs. I have a very warm maternal feeling as I am writing this journal. I can't wait to hold you. I need to have another ultrasound next Tuesday to decide on the insemination time. I am also praying for prosperity so that the supply of "large sums of money come to me quickly from God, under grace, in perfect ways." I have faith in this way of thinking. It comes from a book I am reading called *The Game of Life and How to Play it*[1] written by Florence Scovel Shinn in 1925.

Monday 18th May 1998

Well I'm not feeling very positive today. In fact I feel very much in turmoil. I am starting to feel as though I should return to work in mid June. I am starting to feel apart from other people in the work force. I feel as though I should phone work and arrange a time to start. Another part of me wants to bide my time and apply for jobs that pay more money. I feel the need to phone Louise but I spoke with her last night.

Something is brewing inside of me. Although it appears to be negative it isn't. As I am writing this journal I am becoming clear that I need to pursue a writing career rather than running away from it. I also need to be employed very soon in order for the housing loan to become official. Tomorrow I will phone a writers' society again for some information.

I will have an ultrasound at the clinic tomorrow to see if I am ready for an insemination the next day. I really hope we meet this month so I can get along with my life as I would like. Louise is having an insemination with the help of a friend this week. She has travelled to Queensland as this is where he lives. We may be having them at the same time in different parts of the country. It would be incredible if we were both to be pregnant on or around the same time.

Friday 22nd May 1998

Well, today at 4.30pm I will be having an insemination so that I may conceive you. Yesterday an ultrasound showed that there are two eggs on my right ovary. I then had an injection to make me ovulate, and I will have another insemination on Saturday morning to give me a better chance of conceiving you. Louise is undergoing an insemination at the same time as me this week. It has made me feel more confident and happy about the chances of success. CONTINUED THIS DAY. I am writing at 2.25 just before having a shower and making my way to the clinic. I have welcomed your spirit into my womb and prayed to God for a successful cycle. I have also lit a candle in front of Ethan's photo and his angel and reflected on my successes in life and all the paths I have travelled in order to make them happen. I have recited this saying "Thy will be done this day! Today is a day of completion; I give thanks for this perfect day, miracle shall follow miracle and wonders shall never cease."[2]

Saturday 23rd May 1998

I am having another insemination at 10am today. It is now 8.30 and I have finished breakfast. I have said my affirmation and will now have a shower.

Sunday 24th May 1998

The insemination yesterday made me feel more confident about this cycle and the chances of conceiving you this month. I may have already conceived you within the last 48 hours or so. Louise comes back from Queensland today. I am eager to talk to her about both our experiences. The nurse who carried out the procedure reminded me that I would become pregnant through persevering with the cycles.

She said that couples trying to conceive often had to persist for a long time before they achieved a pregnancy. The message was not to lose heart. I hope you are inside of me now. *I salute the divinity in you*[3] and welcome you to the warmth and comfort of my womb.

Monday 6th July 1998

I was supposed to have a pregnancy test today. My period arrived instead. I have felt period pain for five days or more. I feel very disheartened and upset. I want to conceive you. I am starting another cycle tomorrow.

Louise is pregnant. She was successful with her insemination in Queensland. I am really happy for her. I love you very much and won't give up.

Friday 21st August 1998

I haven't written to you for a long time because to do so was too painful. I have decided to conceive you at another clinic as I was not successful at the other one. I need to have an operation first. I am moving from this flat into our new home at the end of next week. I am packing here already and now back at work full-time.

Friday 16th April 1999

Well it has been a long time since I have written in this journal. It has been too painful to write again before now. I started my first cycle at the new clinic on Wednesday. I decided to talk to my supervisor at work about occasionally needing to start work later . I told her what I was doing and my connection with the clinic. She was really understanding and very supportive. I feel really relieved. Other women at the clinic have talked about the fear of speaking to their employer in case they lose their job. I hope to conceive you this month.

I moved into our house last August. It is a really lovely house painted in soft crisp various colours of cream. When the sun is shining in it looks and feels like a house of light. The gardens are also perfect in every way for me. Misty's owners decided to move to Europe. They asked if I would like to have her. They said that they knew I loved her and would take care of her. I was so excited about not having to leave her behind. She settled in here really well.

Saturday 24th April 1999

I have been to the clinic this morning for an insemination. The nurse informed me that I had eleven million sperm inserted into me. It was very different to the other clinic and I feel more confident of a positive result. I am a bit scared of what is to follow. I really want you but I seem to be dominated by fear of financial insecurity. If you are not going to be conceived then I can at last see myself living a full and reasonably happy life without feeling that I will go mad. However I want you so much and there is a light feeling about me as I write in this journal. I was sitting on the toilet about half an hour ago and it came to me that whatever happens I will manage very well financially. Then my degree came to the forefront and I realised that it was all part of a plan and that I needed to believe in myself. Self-efficacy I think is the correct term. Bye for now.

Sunday morning 25th April 1999

I am writing to you on the morning after the insemination. I am feeling a bit tired but very relaxed. I really hope it works this time as I am becoming weary of the tie to the clinic and the ongoing injections and so on.

It's Anzac day today and I started the morning reflecting on Dad and his war experiences and war in general. Misty has just come into the room and is wanting her breakfast.

Friday 7th May 1999

I am writing after work today. My pregnancy test is due on Monday and I have felt period pain for a few days. I am very confused and I don't think you will ever be born. In fact I am seriously considering not trying to conceive again and taking another direction in my life. However I haven't totally given up. It's not that I don't want you: it's that maybe this isn't meant to be.

Wednesday 12th May 1999

I did start my period on Monday. I had a pregnancy test to determine my levels. The nurse said that my oestrogen levels were low but on the other hand my follicle was fully formed. My obstetrician wants to do a laparoscopy. I don't want one. I have to see another doctor on Tuesday. I couldn't go to work today and I woke up crying at 5 this morning.

I can't go on in the job. I need some time off. My eyes are aching. I have a week off next week. I feel miserable.

Tuesday 11th April 2000

It has been a very long time since I have written to you. In fact almost a year has gone by. I have completed a cycle at the clinic, and have a pregnancy test on Thursday 13th in two days time. There was only one egg this time on the right side. My only patent fallopian tube is on the left side. They are hoping that the egg will find its way to the left side. I am however experiencing what feels like period pain. This could also be due to a drug called Pregnol that imitates a pregnancy. I am very down in the dumps. I don't know if you will be conceived at all in my womb. I am seriously considering an overseas adoption. You may be born into someone else's womb and this is how we may meet.

Saturday 6th May 2000

I wasn't pregnant in this cycle. I am not disappointed at all. On the contrary I was really relieved. The only reason being my immediate financial situation and my terrible feeling of helplessness to do anything about it. I am exhausted. There is some fear that my feeling of relief will be short-lived and I will have to deal with the grief of not conceiving you. I have always known that at some stage I may need to stop. You may come to me in another way.

Now, as I reflect on my story about my marriage, my attempt to conceive a child and my relationship with Ethan, I do so without regret. I am able to look back and see that time is a gentle healer.

End notes

[1] Florence Scovel Shinn *The Wisdom of Florence Scovel Shinn* .(New York: Simon and Schuster, 1989) p.90.

[2] Shinn. p.32-3

[3] Shinn p.53.

Carmen Lawrence

A Nation in Denial

> To transform the world, we must begin with ourselves. However small may be the world we live in, if we can transform ourselves, bring about a radically different point of view in our daily existence, then perhaps we shall affect the world at large, the extended relationship with others.
>
> Krishnamurti

I grew up on a wheat farm near Morawa in the Western Australian bush on land that was first taken for farming in the early 1900s. Like most kids in the post-war years, I knew nothing about the local Indigenous people or their culture. It was as if there was a conspiracy to deny their existence.

There were a few families living in the district working on farms and for the railways, but they remained almost invisible, except on the football field. They were clearly not encouraged to parade their aboriginality. It appeared to me, as a child, that being Indigenous was a handicap that had to be conquered if these families wanted to be part of the wider, white Australian society. And what else, we thought, could they want?

We were told that *our* Indigenous families were different, almost like us, not like the ones who lived in grinding poverty on the fringes of neighbouring towns in humpies huddled together on government reserves. We didn't know much about these people either, except what we heard the grown-ups say in passing: that they were unreliable workers, prone to disappear without explanation (to go "walkabout") and given to roaring bouts of binge drinking. These observations were accompanied by an air of resigned pity, at best, or angry disgust, at worst. No one apparently thought to ask why the

Indigenous people were living as they did or how they had lived before the farmers arrived.

The nuns at school sometimes asked us to raise money for the Indigenous kids at the missions at Beagle Bay or Tardun or Mt Margaret, but we really didn't find out much about these kids either, except that their mortal souls were in danger. We were taught nothing of their history or their culture or the effects on them of our arrival. We were urged to pray for them, as well as giving money, so that they would hear the word of God and become good Catholics worthy of entering the Kingdom of Heaven.

As objects of our charity, they appeared no different from kids in other missions in India or in Africa who were also on our prayer list. I cannot remember ever being told that the Indigenous people had any special claim on us because of what had been done to them by European settlers. Only later did I become aware that many of these children had been removed from their families "for their own good" and were part of the stolen generations.

On one occasion the local community revealed that, for some at least, the Indigenous people represented a potentially malevolent force which could explode at any time. A young Indigenous prisoner, Bobby Jones, was being taken from a remote part of the State to the capital city to be tried for the murder of one of his community. He jumped the train and escaped custody. For days, the local community was in a state of terror. The men headed out with the police and a tracker to hunt him down while the women and children huddled nervously, firearms beside them, fearing that he would murder again.

It was only much later in my life that I began to think about and to understand the monumental wrong that had been done to our Indigenous peoples, to appreciate the seismic shift in their lives wrought by the colonial invasion of their lands. I began to gain some insight into the horrors of dispossession and separation they had endured. And to know that all of this damage was made immeasurably worse by our easily assumed sense of superiority. That we rubbed salt into open wounds by our patronage, by our ignorance, our prejudice and our indifference. Why had we failed to see what was staring us in the face? Why had we failed to ask the obvious questions?

And worse, why, now, is there still such antipathy and prejudice toward Indigenous people? Why now, when Indigenous witnesses and academic research have shown us so much, when stories, long ignored, are finally told? Why now, after a decade of effort by the many involved in the journey toward Reconciliation are we still hearing the same hateful resistance to acknowledging what has happened?

Perhaps it is because this information provokes severe discomfort, even anxiety and fear. It challenges our view of ourselves as a generous and tolerant nation committed to fairness and justice for everybody. When confronted with such information so damaging to our view of ourselves, many of us respond by questioning the validity of the new information or by shutting it out altogether; we go into denial rather than facing our history and ourselves. We are angered that anyone would dare question our virtue and we turn on the messengers. Racism thrives on such denial.

When our political leaders encourage us and join in this denial we are in serious trouble. Our Prime Minister John Howard has made it clear that he hates 'the black armband' view of history. Howard wants to live – and wants us to live – in a "sun-drenched, guilt-free, amnesiac present", where the dispossession of Aborigines represents nothing more than a "blemish" which does not confer rights to land or merit an apology."

He appears to endorse the image of Australia as the land of the "Lotus Eaters", slipping into insensibility and living moment to moment in soporific detachment from reality. In the Odyssey, the Lotus Eaters fed the sailors the "honey-sweet fruit", not to kill them but so that "all memory of the journey home dissolved forever". Only resolute action by Ulysses saved them from oblivion – "I forced them, hauled them under the benches, lashed them fast and shouted out commands to my other steady comrades: "Quick, no time to lose, embark in the racing ships!"- so none could eat the lotus, forget the voyage home."[1]

There are some who prefer to live in a "relaxed and comfortable" state with the Lotus Eaters. They find it easier to live in the illusion of assumed superiority and insist that they have earned their place; that there is no need to puzzle over the obvious inequalities in our society, no need to confront the suffering of many indigenous people. They would be relieved of the need to inquire into the "journey" and to reach more complex understandings. They convince themselves, in any case, that the solutions do not lie with us – either that it is entirely a matter for the Indigenous people or that fate has predetermined the outcomes.

But we must not avoid facing the facts. Our nation's health depends on it. I know it is difficult for many Australians to stomach, but it *is* fair to say, as Dodson and Strelein have done that racism was a "founding value of Australian society"[2]. It was used to justify the "the wholesale denial of Indigenous peoples' rights to retain their social, economic and political structures, while denying their rights to participate in the polity that was under construction."

Upon federation, the nation incorporated the same values of racial superiority and exclusion. The "White Australia" policy *was* one of the founding principles of the commonwealth, encouraged by the newly formed Labor Party and enacted in legislation as the first act of the new Federal Parliament in 1901. It was feared, as R.D Lang thundered, that Chinese immigrants would "swamp the whole European community of these colonies" and "obliterate every trace of British progress and civilisation."

This "invasion anxiety" has always had racial overtones and is often expressed most forcefully by the same people – and governments – who deny that Indigenous Australians are entitled to recognition as the original owners of this country and recompense for what has been taken from them.

Beginning in the late 60s, progress was made in removing the racist underpinnings of both Aboriginal affairs and immigration policies – and there was bipartisan support for these shifts in direction.

Sadly, that momentum has now stalled, and even reversed. This is evident in the refusal by the Government to deal effectively with the Stolen Generations report, the chiseling away at Indigenous land rights, the imposition of a brutal detention regime on those people seeking asylum on our shores and changes to the assessment system for migrants which have resulted in a noticeable increase in those from white, English speaking nations.

Australians have been asked to close their eyes to our past, to deny the existence of racist attitudes and behaviour in our community and to resist the pull of our common humanity which might otherwise inform our relations with Indigenous people and migrants. Part of this shift has been propelled by political expediency and part by the peculiar obsessions of the current Prime Minister and his acolytes whose view of the nation encompasses only our virtues and none of our vices.

These retreats demand a response. We must, as Paul Keating said in 1993,

> "bring the dispossessed out of the shadows, to recognise that they are part of us, and that we cannot give indigenous Australians up without giving up many of our own most deeply held values, much of our own identity – and our own humanity."

We must understand that Indigenous Australians are daily subjected to personal disrespect and harassment and that it is the continuing, official tolerance of this disrespect that maintains racist attitudes in our community.

If we are to combat racism in our society, we need to acknowledge those prejudices and attitudes of racial superiority that shaped our nation and which still govern our behaviour. Denying the reality of our origins or the negative influences at work in our society will only prolong our discomfort. We should use that discomfort, that discordance, creatively, as a spur to action not as a reason to escape into denial.

It is time to face the fact that far from being an unusual and universally repudiated belief, racism – the belief that race is the primary determinant of human traits and capacities and that one race is superior to another – is still all too common in our society and around the world.

Racism is not just a belief system. It influences behaviour, producing discrimination and sometimes violence against groups believed to be inferior. It is also used to justify the domination of such groups and disrespect for them and their culture.

With the connivance of the present government, we are encouraged to believe that, unique among the peoples of the world we are incapable of racist behaviour and that those who attempt to shine a light on human rights abuses are somehow "unAustralian". On the contrary, those who seek to prevent such examination are condemning all of us to a blighted future.

We have, until recently, made some progress away from paternalism and denial, but we are now in the grip of what Guy Rundle calls "the triumph of reaction"[3]. This stance seeks to reduce the government's – and the community's – responsibilities to encompass only so-called "practical reconciliation", to replace the need to recognise and protect Indigenous rights with what should be their unquestioned rights to services enjoyed by all citizens. Both are essential.

The current government's approach to the history of the relationship between Australia's Indigenous people and European settlers is based on wilful denial and a refusal to acknowledge the reality of the experience of racism by Aboriginal and Torres Strait Islander people. They encourage other Australians to join them in this refusal, repudiating what they disparagingly call the "black armband" view of history and the" guilt industry".

This is the antithesis of what is required, which is "a serious working through of the past, the breaking of its spell through an act of clear consciousness. It suggests, rather, wishing to turn the page and, if possible, wiping it from memory. The attitude that it would be proper for everything to be forgiven and forgotten by those who were wronged is typically expressed by the party that committed the injustice.[4]"

A conscious act of empathic imagination is required. We need to imagine these things being done to us. We need to ask – how would I feel if this were done to me?

As former Prime Minister, Paul Keating, put it in his Redfern speech:

> As I said, it might help us if we non-Aboriginal Australians imagined ourselves dispossessed of land we have lived on for 50 000 years – and then imagined ourselves told that it had never been ours.
>
> Imagine if ours was the oldest culture in the world and we were told that it was worthless. Imagine if we had resisted this settlement, suffered and died in the defence of our land, and then were told in history books that we had given up without a fight. Imagine if non-Aboriginal Australians had served their country in peace and war and were then ignored in history books. Imagine if our feats on sporting fields had inspired admiration and patriotism and yet did nothing to diminish prejudice. Imagine if our spiritual life was denied and ridiculed.
>
> Imagine if we had suffered the injustice and then were blamed for it.

It seems to me that if we can imagine the injustice then we can imagine its opposite. And we can have justice.

Many, including the current Prime Minister, seek to reassure themselves by chanting the right wing mantra that "we are all one and we should all be treated equally" and the politicians' reliable platitude that "the things that unite us are greater than the things which divide us".

The Government is happy to exhort us that we should feel proud of our wonderful achievements while refusing to acknowledge and make reparation for our mistakes. This resembles the behaviour of a young child or an adolescent who may become defensive when criticised. There is a clear readiness to blame others rather than accept responsibility for our actions. A mature nation would be able to deal with its history and all the experiences, both admirable and shameful, which have shaped our attitudes and institutions. In refusing to acknowledge in any tangible way that mistakes have been made and that reparation is due, Howard infantilises the whole nation – in our own eyes and in the eyes of the world.

While saying and doing all these things, the Prime Minister has wanted to claim a mantle of decency and compassion and is angered when anyone accuses him of having another agenda. What he is saying, in code, to those who share his views: "There's no need for you to feel any pangs of conscience or to worry that all may not be well in the wider community's relations with our indigenous people – see I think these things and no one would dare criticise me."

He often asserts that he's a decent man and beyond reproach. It's a constant refrain in question time and on talkback radio. The behaviour, however, is not what we would expect of a leader of any party or of any era. No amount of protestation that his intentions are good will disguise the fact that his actions are not.

Surely we should all be brought to understand that for Indigenous people the experience of forced removal is still having profound effects – both on individuals and communities. This was carefully and convincingly documented in the report "Bringing Them Home" and in countless other stories now being told. It should now be clear to all is us that loss of identity and culture are devastating, particularly when coupled with continuing discrimination and disadvantage producing unprecedented social breakdown – alcoholism, substance abuse, depression and suicide, law breaking and violence, mainly of Indigenous people against one another.

Separation occurred not just in one generation but for generations on end, since European contact – under various guises, some more malignant than others: from the fatal impact of infectious disease to brutal murder, from assimilation to "welfare".

In my home state of Western Australia, Indigenous people were massacred as recently as the 20s in the Forrest River area of the Kimberley. Neville Green,[5] who researched these atrocities, reports one of the whites in the area explaining why it was better that "some things should be left alone".

In a statement which has an eerie and disturbing resonance with recent pronouncements by the Government he said:

> You must realise that times were different then, and police methods were not always carried out by the book.

His informant goes on to say:

> There were killings right across the Kimberley. When I was working the stock at Nookenbah along the Fitzroy River, a heavy flood uncovered a whole patch of skeletons, some with bullet holes in the skulls.

As Neville was to discover, the Forrest River massacres were not aberrations, but "almost the end of a trail of destruction that came to the Kimberley with the pearlers, the pastoralists, the prospectors and the police".

As he put it:

> Violence flourished in a climate where a group of people, armed and with the authority of the law, could regard themselves as worthy and see others as unworthy; where technological superiority was equated with intellectual superiority; where people were measured, not by their actions and values, but by the colour of their skin. Racism and genocide came as strangers to the Kimberley but were soon in familiar company.

Perhaps this is what our Prime Minister means by the "black armband" view of history.

Tatz[6] quotes the English novelist Anthony Trollope who visited Australia some 120 years ago. "There has been some rough work", he wrote:

> "We have taken away their land, have destroyed their food, made them subject to our laws, which are antagonistic to their habits and traditions, have endeavoured to make them subject to our tastes, which they hate, have massacred them when they defended themselves and their possessions after their own fashion, and have taught them by hard warfare to acknowledge us to be their master."

The effects are much the same regardless of the official explanations and excuses. There cannot be an Indigenous person in Australia unaffected by such practices and policies; that is why an official apology for these practices has such significance for our Indigenous people. Many of these practices are not in the remote past; they were happening when I was growing up and in the region where I lived. They are still happening. No amount of denial, of attack on those who refuse to be silent, will obliterate these experiences.

We can do better than this. If we forget and deny the past, we will not create a better future. The ideas and values which underpin our institutional and public policy need to be tested – and continually tested – for prejudicial and racist attitudes. Walking on tiptoe and calling them by other names, will not prevent us repeating these wrongs. Indeed, the legacy of denial is now being played out in the brutal treatment of refugees in remote, detention camps hidden, until recently, from our gaze. The same prejudices abound.

The task is to dismantle institutionalised racism and discrimination in the Australian state, to fully engage Indigenous people in our body politic and to build respect for Indigenous peoples, recognising their honoured place as the first peoples of this land.

This process should start with our Constitution and work outwards. It means continuing the tentative voyage we have begun in repudiating the insulting doctrine of "terra nullius" – the conceit that the land was empty of law, government, property rights and civilised society or culture.

It means insisting that the needs of indigenous people are accorded the same priority as they are in the rest of the community. Community safety is just as important in a remote Indigenous community as it is in suburban Sydney; treatment and rehabilitation for chronic drug and alcohol abuse as necessary in Palm Island as in North Ryde. In both communities it is obvious that such help will be of little use unless it is provided with respect and compassion, in a culturally appropriate manner by people who are trusted.

It requires the re-education of our community about our history and our current practices. It needs governments and community leaders to repudiate hateful and aggressive behaviour and as Freud described it "the mindlessness of the group mind" which gives people a false sense of superiority, specialness and omnipotence.

We must be alert to the way in which people can take actions as a group which would be unthinkable to them as individuals. Countering racial vilification and propaganda should be part of our responsibility as citizens. We should not fall for the propagandist's three-card trick, which as Aldous Huxley put it is to "make one set of people forget that certain other sets of people are human." [7]

We need to remind ourselves in framing our policies that luck, rather than virtue, is one of the great determinants of our lives. H.G. Wells and his socialist friends began their influential Declaration of Rights [8] with the observation that "since a man (sic) comes into the world through no fault of his own" ... and they might have added and with no choice over where and in what circumstances.

We must all take responsibility for our children and our young people so they can develop without the poisonous distortions of racism. We must all act from recognition of our common humanity.

The message should be that there is nothing to fear or to lose in the recognition of historical truth, or the extension of social justice, or the deepening of Australian social democracy to include indigenous Australians and a generous response to refugees.
There is everything to gain.

People like our Prime Minister have often resisted the argument that we bear responsibility for past: 'I do not accept the doctrine of hereditary guilt. I acknowledge that, in the past, wrongs were done to Aboriginals, but they weren't done by me. They weren't done by my parents. They weren't done by my generation ... I am strongly against dividing the country between black and white. I think that is a recipe for disaster.'

He is wrong on two counts – both about our moral responsibility and about the facts of the matter. Wrongs were done by his generation and that of his parents. Children were still being removed from their families as part of the assimilationist strategies well into the 60s. And wrong is still being done today.

No one is asking the Prime Minister to fall on his knees and assume full responsibility for all past wrongs. But if he really claims to be a national leader in more than name, he should face the facts and assist all of us to do the same. To drag us from the forgetfulness of lotus eating and back to the journey, painful and demanding as it may sometimes be, that will take us home.

Notes

[1] Homer. *The Odyssey*. Translated by Robert Fagles. London: Penguin, 1996, Book IX, 88–117.

[2] Dodson, Michael and Strelein, Lisa. *Australia's nation-building: Renegotiating the relationship between Indigenous peoples and the state*. UNSW Law Journal, Volume 24 (3), 2001, 826–839.

[3] Rundle, Guy. *The Opportunist: John Howard and the Triumph of Reaction*. Quarterly Essay, 3, 2001.

[4] Theodor Adorno

[5] Neville Green, *The Forrest River Massacres*, Fremantle Arts Centre Press, 1995, p 16–19.

[6] Colin Tatz, Genocide in Australia, *IATSIS Research Discussion Paper*, No. 8, p 8–9.

[7] Aldous Huxley. *The Olive Tree*, New York: Harper & Brothers, 1937, p 101.

[8] H.G Wells, *H.G.Wells on the Rights of Man*, Penguin, 1940.

Melissa Lucashenko

Memory and Survival

I am at a retreat for women writers in Washington State, enjoying myself immensely. The feathery green fir trees, the Amish-built timber cabins, the January cold: everything astounds, enchants, delights. I have brought familiar music to feed the Antipodean soul, and it is weird, though thrilling, to watch snow fall on the dark roiling waters of Puget Sound with Archie Roach and Deborah Conway murmuring in the background.

My fellow writers are a lively, engaging bunch. Andrea, a light-skinned black Canadian working on a memoir of her Montreal childhood, where accusations of 'Chinois' left her more bemused than scarred. A white Southern dyke, Kylie, who lives in a mobile home with her dying partner, and who brings to the surface the exquisite poetry of poor people's lives. Insomniac Elaine from St Louis ('inertia, plus its cheap') with her parent's Holocaust stories as well as her own evocative memories of the post-war Bronx. Anne, Chinese-American, labouring on a second novel which she releases only in cryptic soundbites: *Ohio, horses, drought.* Anne is untypically self-effacing for a New Yorker but the work she does share is subtle, devastating.

And my Aboriginal self, with a fourth wretched novel driving me mad all over again. We write each day in the solitude of our cabins then meet at six for loud, hilarious dinners in the farmhouse. In the more serious moments I encourage Elaine to read Lily Brett, and she teaches me to say (though not to really understand, since the Yiddish is essentially untranslatable) 'Ess ist schwer ztu zein ah yid'. *It is hard to be a Jew.* I describe the skin system of relatedness that links every Aboriginal person, and recall for her Charles Perkins' parable of Aboriginal childhood. Never say no to a white person, he was instructed. It doesn't matter what the question is, whether you understand their white words or not, you never say anything except yes. Just smile and agree. (We are great smilers, us blackfellas). Elaine – the first baby born in the Polish displaced persons camp after the war – nods knowingly, tells me of the time her father was pulled up in Manhattan by a traffic cop. Yes, officer. No, officer. When the cop had gone it was safe for the family to know that her father had fouled his pants at the sight of the approaching uniform. The war and the camp lived in him, and his memories were not merely subconscious, but visceral.

~

On my fourth evening we sit up into the small hours, yarning, telling jokes, playing games. We laugh a lot. Then sometime after two the talk turns for the first time to the terror attack of September eleven, which the Americans call nine-eleven, making me think of convenience stores. I was in Alice Springs for Yeperenye, I explain, the dry desolate centre of an arid continent, and watching it all unfold like everyone else on TV. Phone calls in the middle of the night roused us, then unreality ruled for two hours, before I had to scavenge some sleep and be on a plane that very morning. I explain what Pine Gap is, and where, describe the sight of American uniforms at the airport next morning and all the Australians wondering just who these people were and where they were being summonsed so quickly. How all of a sudden an American flag on an arm became a solemn, notable thing.

"Just paint an X on that forehead of yours," calls someone, laughing.

But I was on the other side of the world, I quickly add, my experience hardly relevant. I was an anxious voyeur, nothing more. Andrea, the Canadian, tells how the gamblers in the casino where her daughter works actually stopped betting for once. Even the early-morning pokie addicts couldn't drag themselves away from the television screens. Cheap thrills come in so many guises.

"The people in my mobile home park were like, panicking and loading their guns, some of them" Kylie reports in her I-can-survive-anything Texan twang, "But I never had any feeling like anything bad was going to happen to me. I don't know why. It just never affected me in that way."

We are nodding, musing abstractly on the individuality of response when Anne silences us.

"I saw it happen out of my apartment window."

She forces out a half-laugh. "You know - those panoramic city views . . . " She pauses, and then the words which come are precise, careful, clipped. "It was unbelievably worse to watch it happen in front of you, than when you watched it later on TV." Anne had gone into the bathroom to wash her face, and when she came back there was blue sky and smoke where the plane had hit. The second tower was still there as a reference point, and she, though horrified, was still thinking it was an accident. It struck her that that entire part of the building, all the offices, all the people, was simply *gone*. She was on the phone, frantically dialling, when she saw the plane fly into the second tower.

She had used to work on the fiftieth floor, doing the flowers in a restaurant. She wasn't at work. Her sister should have been there, but the restaurant hadn't liked the flowers Anne had done the day before – an all-green arrangement – and her sister had stayed away in order to fix them.

Her voice is very controlled as she explains how priorities instantly altered. "Any other day, if you were told your airborne loved ones were in, like, *Canada*, or *Argentina*, and no-one could tell you exactly where, you'd be totally outraged. But now it was like – so you're in Argentina, oh Thank God. The phone system melted down of course, so everyone spent all day picking up the phone to try and get through. When you finally got a dial tone you'd go 'You alright? Right.' then hang up and go on to the next call. It was all total function, no emotion until later."

She tells us of office girls streaming across the bridge, their high heeled shoes slung over their shoulders; of Mayor Guiliani, of the ongoing traumas and ironies. For days afterward, she could only get one TV channel, since all the satellite dishes had been on the WTC. "It was like living in this weird communist state with only one station ... and of course it *had* to be Dan Rather." She is laughing now, keeping it light, giving us permission to find unlikely humour here. I want to ask her about the people who jumped – those horribly plummeting figures - but dare not. She *must* have seen them, I think. You couldn't not have seen them from her vantage point, but they are entirely absent from her account.

Several days later, apropos of nothing much, Anne allows as how she thinks denial highly underrated as a survival mechanism.

∼

It came Elaine's turn to talk. She was on a meditation retreat – a silent ten days in West Virginia. The WTC attack came on the fifth day. Someone came into the meditation hall, a woman, and whispered to someone else. The group was told to assemble upstairs and wait for an announcement. Something was obviously wrong, Elaine says.

"My God, for what would they stop a *silent retreat*? But they did it well. They told us it wasn't the worst thing that could have happened – and we were by now all thinking nuclear war – but that it was very serious. Then they told us what had happened. I burst into tears on the spot. I became a child in a Polish camp again. Everything came back to me, everything."

Elaine's memories – the ones that stop her sleeping more than two consecutive hours – paralysed her before they became the gold standard of survival. When she regained herself it was comforting to her that grown people were crying. People who were *not* in New York, who had *not* lost loved ones, who were adults with their identities formed, their lives already half-lived, these people were traumatised by the terrible news. "It was very weird," she explains, "I'd already been through this as a child with nothing. *Nothing*. And now these adults were having a hard time dealing with it. And so in the midst of the terror I felt very strong."

Elaine knows how to survive war and was possessed by her knowledges. Shaking in the West Virginian wilderness, she wanted to teach the others, protect them – the vulnerable ones. She was periodically filled with utter rage at their stupidity, their naivete, that they didn't know what she knew. She ran straight to the medicine cupboard, began stockpiling pills. At meals, she wanted to scream at them at the top of her lungs. (The voice of the Jewish mother should be hilarious, but isn't). "Eat! Eat it all and eat till you can't eat another bite!" she wanted to yell at the ox-dumb Americans, the innocent Gentiles, "You don't know when you'll eat again . . . " There is an awful matter-of-factness in her voice as she recounts those first hours. War speaking. *Ess ist schwer ztu zein ah yid.*

We all stagger to bed around three, sober and sick of memories. I put Paul Kelly on the CD, and fall asleep to *Leaps and Bounds*, the white brother to Aboriginal Australia asserting, as though it is a good thing:

I remember . . .
I remember . . .
I remember . . .
I remember everything.

∼

Notes on Contributors

Nancy E. Berg is an associate professor of Hebrew and Comparative Literatures at Washington University. She lives far from the ocean in St. Louis, Missouri. Author of Exile From Exile: Israeli Writers from Iraq (SUNY Press) she has just completed a book on the politics of literary reception. Currently Nancy is working on the motif of fathers and daughters in Israeli literature.

Tony Birch is a writer who lives in Brunswick, Victoria. He teaches Creative Writing in the English Department at the University of Melbourne.

Anne Brewster teaches at University of NSW. She has recently co-edited with Angeline O'Neill and Rosemary van den Berg an anthology of Aboriginal writing, Those who remain will always remember (Fremantle Arts Centre Press, 2000).

Hazel Smith works in the areas of poetry, experimental writing, performance, multi-media work and hypertext, and her web page is at www.australysis.com. Her latest print volume is Keys Round Her Tongue: short prose, poems and performance texts, Soma Publications, 2000. She has made two CDs of her performance work, is a member of the multi-media group austraLYSIS, and co-author of a number of multi-media and hypermedia works. Hazel is Senior Research Fellow in the School of Creative Communication, University of Canberra, and Deputy Director of the Canberra Centre for Writing. She is co-author with Roger Dean of Improvisation, Hypermedia And The Arts Since 1945, Harwood Academic, 1997, and author of Hyperscapes in the Poetry of Frank O'Hara: difference, homosexuality, topography, Liverpool University Press, 2000.

SCOTT BROOK writes across a variety of genres and locations, a far from unusual situation discussed in his essay "Does anybody know what happened to Ficto(-)criticism?" (The UTS Review, forthcoming). An occasional tutor at the University of Melbourne, he lives in Footscray (Melbourne) where he is conspiring with Footscray Community Arts Centre on a multimedia anthology of local writing called "West of the West: A Glocality Guide".

DANIEL BROWN is the author of Hopkins' Idealism: Philosophy, Physics, Poetry (Oxford: Clarendon Press, 1997), contributions to Hilary Fraser, English Prose of the Nineteenth Century (London: Longmans, 1997) and Joe Bristow (ed) Cambridge Companion to Victorian Poetry (Cambridge: CUP, 2000). He is currently writing the Hopkins title for the British Council's new Writers and their Work series and a study of poetry by Victorian scientists.

MARION CAMPBELL's three novels are: Lines of Flight, (Fremantle Arts Centre Press,1985), Not Being Miriam (F.A.C.P.,1988) and Prowler (F.A.C.P., 1999). Not Being Miriam won the 1989 WA Literary Week Award for Fiction. Her novels have been shortlisted for the New South Wales Premier's Prize, the Victorian Premier's Prize (twice), and the Canada Australia Prize (twice). She has also written two extended works for performance: Dr Memory in the Dream Home and Ariadne's Understudies. She teaches writing in the Department of English with Cultural Studies at the University of Melbourne.

PAUL CARTER is a Melbourne-based writer and artist, whose current public art projects include Tracks (North Terrace, Adelaide) and Nearamnew (Federation Square, Melbourne). His new book, Repressed Spaces: the Poetics of Agoraphobia will be published by Reaktion Books (London) later this year.
 Loculi was originally written for Memento Mori, an exhibition of paintings by Pip Stokes (Span Galleries, Melbourne, 2001), where it also formed part of an audio-visual work with Gregory Burgess.

JUDY DUREY is a visual artist working in Installation, and a PhD candidate in the School of Arts at Murdoch University. Her work interrogates the affective and emotional fields held within silence to investigate the complexities of (re)stor(y)ing identity and personal narrative.

ROBYN FERRELL teaches philosophy at Macquarie University in Sydney. She is the author of many essays and scholarly articles, several books of philosophy and a novel.

KATE HISLOP is a lecturer in architecture in the Faculty of Architecture, Landscape & Visual Arts at the University of Western Australia, where she teaches in the subjects of design, Australian architectural history and criticism, and professional practice. She has published reviews and articles in numerous Australian architectural journals and maintains a small architectural practice. She is currently writing a PhD in architectural history, exploring global as well as local issues, and in particular the role of artifice, in shaping the architectural development of Perth in the nineteenth century.

KATE LAMONT is an operating partner in the Lamont family's food and wine businesses in Western Australia and has experience in the food and wine industries spanning two decades. She studied Wine Science and Viticulture at Wagga Agricultural College, and has published two books on food, cooking and the pleasures of life.

CARMEN LAWRENCE's parliamentary career began in State politics in 1986 and she made history by becoming Premier of Western Australia and Australia's first woman Premier. Dr Lawrence entered Federal politics in 1994, and she was appointed Minister for Human Services and Health and Minister Assisting the Prime Minister for the Status of Women. Dr Lawrence is currently the Shadow Minister for Reconciliation, Aboriginal & Torres Strait Islander Affairs; the Arts, and Status of Women. Prior to politics, she was a research psychologist.

MELISSA LUCASHENKO is a Murri woman from Brisbane who writes about urban Aboriginal life. She currently lives in Northern NSW with her partner and two children. Her most recent book is Hard Yards (University of Queensland Press).

SUSAN MIDALIA has a Ph.D. in English Literature from the University of Western Australia. She has taught in various tertiary institutions in Perth, Western Australia and currently works as a secondary school teacher and as a freelance editor. She has published in academic journals on contemporary Australian women's fiction. This is her first non-academic publication; she hopes there will be more.

ROSSLYN PROSSER lives and works in Adelaide. On a recent trip to Queensland her memory was stimulated by the smell of tropical air and the sight of mango trees.

MOIRA RAYNER has a national reputation as a lawyer and in social policy development. From 1986-1990 she was Commissioner/Chairman of the Western Australian Law Reform Commission and from 1990-1994 Commissioner for Equal Opportunity, Victoria. In 2000 she left Australia to establish the Office of Children's Rights Commissioner for London, where she has been very successful in modelling effective children's participation in management of the Office itself and in government decision-making as well as drafting the first Children's Strategy for the Greater London Authority. Moira has also held a number of contemporaneous part-time appointments including Chair, Council of the Financial Services Complaints Resolution Scheme; Commissioner, Human Rights and Equal Opportunity Commission; and a columnist for The Age. She has written a number of successful books, including The Women's Power Handbook, with Joan Kirner (first woman Premier of Victoria); Resilient Children and Young People, with Meg Montague; Rooting Democracy: Growing the Society We Want, with Jenny Lee and she is completing The A-Z of Children's Rights for Amnesty UK. Her next book is Joan Kirner's biography. Her current position is acting Commissioner for Equal Opportunity in Western Australia.

TANYA RING was born in 1974 and lives in Perth. Graduated in Architecture and currently works as an architect in a small-scale design firm. Feedback welcome: tring74@go.com.

ANGELA ROCKEL lives in Tasmania. She recently completed a PhD on the role of creativity in subjective change.

MARIA ROBINSON Ethan's Angel is the story of my journey through marriage and divorce, my longing for a child and my experience with reproductive technology as a single woman. This story is dedicated to the memory of my cat Ethan, who was my best friend throughout most of my journey. Maria Robinson is a pseudonym I have chosen to use. I am currently pursuing the option of overseas adoption. I hope that my story will be of some help to others experiencing similar issues.

NOEL TOVEY is a dancer, choreographer and was the artistic director for the Indigenous welcoming ceremony of the 2000 Sydney Olympics. Noel began his life in the depths of poverty and despair but went on to become successful as a choreographer and dancer. He is currently writing his autobiography, Little Black Bastard, from which he has excerpted these writings.

ANNETTE TREVITT grew up in small country towns in northern NSW. She lived in Sydney, before moving to Melbourne to study Animation. She has had a number of short stories published including one that she made into a short animated film for SBS TV.

BETH YAHP lives in Paris.

SUSAN VARGA was born in Hungary but came to Australia as a child. After pursuing various aborted careers, she settled to full-time writing in 1990. Heddy and Me, her first book, won the 1994 Fellowship of Australian Writers' Christina Stead Award for biography and was shortlisted for three other major awards. Susan's first novel, Happy Families, was published in 1999. She is currently working on a book on exile.

TERRI-ANN WHITE writes fiction and lives in Perth where she works at the University of Western Australia. Her last publication was a novel, Finding Theodore and Brina.

The Paper
a magazine about poetry and poetics

Issue 1 *A Miscellany of New Prospects on the Garden & the Pastoral*
A5   36pp   £2.50 / US$5.00

Issue 2 *An Album of Songs, Lyrics & Diverse Musics*
inc limited edition supplement by Christine Kennedy
Hiving The Sol – The Feminine Monarchie Revisited
A5   48pp   £2.50 / US$5.00

Issue 3/4 *Additional Apparitions: Poetry, Performance & Site Specificity*
inc limited edition chapbook by Geraldine Monk
Insubstantial Thoughts on the Transubstantiation of the Text
A5   200pp   £9.00 / US$20.00

Issue 5 *Elegies, Epithalamia, Etc – Occasions of Poetry*
inc limited edition full colour supplement by Christine Kennedy
Lamella Needles: A Bride's Manual for the Management of Married Desire
A5   64pp   £5.00 / US$10.00

Issue 6 *Movement / Motion*
out April 2003

Two issue subscription for issues 5 and 6: £8.00 [UK only]

Cheques and money orders payable to 'D G Kennedy'
29 Vickers Road   Firth Park   Sheffield S5 6UY   UK
email: dgk@kennedyd.fsworld.co.uk

Contributors to **The Paper** *include*: Steve Benson   Caroline Bergvall   Ken Bolton   Ric Caddel   cris cheek   Thomas A Clark   Martin Corless-Smith   Alan Halsey   Carla Harryman   Lisa Jarnot   Nathaniel Mackey   Peter Middleton   Drew Milne   Geraldine Monk   Jennifer Moxley   Peter Riley

Poetry First Editions

Catalogue available of collector's items of 20th Century poetry.

And/or join our mailing list for regular catalogues of second-hand modern poetry and selected new small-press publications in the modernist tendency and after.

Peter Riley (Books), 27 Sturton Street, Cambridge CB1 2QG.
01223 576422.   priley@dircon.co.uk

www.saltpublishing.com

salt

NEW AUSTRALIAN WRITING

Attempts at Being
Alison Croggon
1-876857-42-0
216 x 140 mm 188pp

£9.95
AUS$21.95
US$13.95

"Often shifting and allusive, her poems can convey the 'strangeness of dreams'... The 'stubborn voice' is restless, impatient, exploratory – attuned to bedrock reality. She can slip in and out of styles as readily as an amphibian slips from land to water."
Australian Book Review

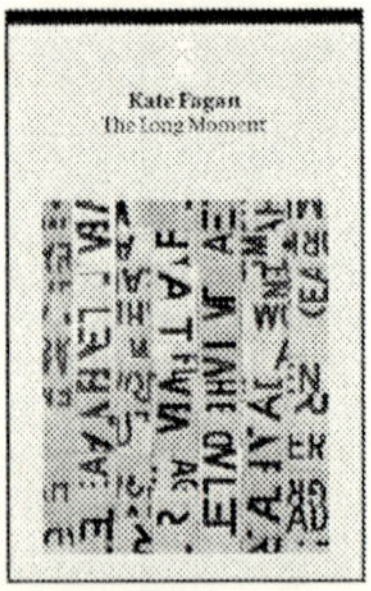

The Long Moment
Kate Fagan
1-876857-39-0
216 x 140 mm 108pp

£8.95
AUS$19.95
US$12.95

"A gorgeous and brilliant book, a work of complex sensuousness and deep intelligence. Its four major sequences are each formally distinct, but the works are all related to one another in being addressed to the material world...."
Lyn Hejinian

Screens Jets Heaven
Jill Jones
1-876857-22-6
216 x 140 mm 152pp

£8.95
AUS$19.95
US$12.95

"Jill Jones' poems are remarkable for their perceptions and insights, at once gentle yet resistant, accessible yet strict; the language assured in its effects and selection of detail. Her use of the meditative lyric is both masterful and compelling."
Judith Beveridge

Versary
Kate Lilley
1-876857-15-3
216 x 140 mm 108pp

£8.95
AUS$19.95
US$12.95

"What Kate Lilley gives us is the richness and vigour of the English Renaissance in the service of a complex set of postmodern concerns; scholarship as a handmaiden to art; and literature galvanised by passion."
John Tranter

PO Box 937, Great Wilbraham, Cambridge PDO, CB1 5JX United Kingdom

www.saltpublishing.com

salt

NEW BRITISH WRITING

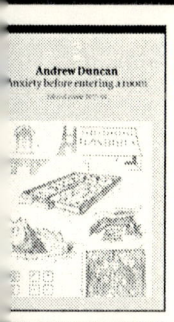

Anxiety Before Entering a Room
Selected Poems 1976-99
Andrew Duncan
1-876857-03-X
216 x 140 mm 136pp
£7.95

In a province, someone anglophobe and technophile is attempting to write documentary poetry about the situation at work, where the basic power relations never slip out of mind: an unending cascade of concrete and puzzling problems, of human conjunctures.

Empires and Holy Lands
Poems 1976-2000
Michael Hulse
1-876857-46-3
216 x 140 mm 148pp
£8.95

Hulse's readiness to take a subject head-on, matching imaginative scope with emotional directness, is very successful. He has the advantage of combining a dramatic imagination with the ability to think.
Sean O'Brien, London Magazine

The President of Earth
New and Selected Poems
David Kennedy
1-876857-10-2
216 x 140 mm 124pp
£8.95

"Kennedy's poetry is full of quirky argumentation and aleatory charm: 'A Walking Lunch', 'What Pefkos Said' and 'Horse Chestnut' are all fine and more than fine poems."
Metre

The Damage
New and Selected Poems
Drew Milne
1-876857-11-0
216 x 140 mm 124pp
£7.95

"Beckoning disjunctions and witty deformations shine their torch on tawdry contemporary realia, but lyrical moments and Scottish echoes fill the interstices with pleasing difference."
Edwin Morgan

PO Box 937, Great Wilbraham, Cambridge PDO, CB1 5JX United Kingdom

SALT

www.saltpublishing.com

salt

NEW AMERICAN WRITING

Aleatory Allegories
Susan M. Schultz
1-876857-01-3
216 x 140 mm 120pp

£7.95
AUS$19.95
US$12.95

"If *Allegory* gets pegged as a premoden trope and chance is the hallmark of post-modernism, then Schultz is interested in their collision as it plays out in the moral, natural and spiritual worlds of Hawaii."
Publishers Weekly

World: Poems 1991-2001
Maxine Chernoff
1-876857-30-7
216 x 140 mm 120pp

£7.95
AUS$19.95
US$12.95

"Maxine Chernoff explores a linguistic world of cuts and connections, of continual action. Her world is one of wonder, and enormous beauty."
Douglas Messerli

Source Codes
Susan Wheeler
1-876857-06-4
216 x 140 mm 120pp
22 halftone illustrations

£7.95
AUS$19.95
US$12.95

"Wheeler's 'sources' in this third book seem equally drawn from the allusive grand style of the Bishop/Lowell/Berryman line. Taking overblown advantage of these poets' colloquially pessimistic strains, Wheeler's talent for crushing rhymes exposes total disaffection." **Publishers Weekly**

Rehearsal in Black
Paul Hoover
1-876857-31-5
216 x 140 mm 112pp

£7.95
AUS$19.95
US$12.95

On Paul Hoover's *Viridian*: "There is a cool precision in these poems. Central to all of them (regardless of language's irrefutable limitations) is his keen intelligence and laconic wit."
Mary Jo Bang

PO Box 937, Great Wilbraham, Cambridge PDO, CB1 5JX United Kingdom

www.saltpublishing.com

Salt

A major collected poems

John James
Collected Poems

Collected Poems
John James
1-876857-40-4
Salt Modern Poets
216 x 140mm 388pp

**£15.95
AUS$43.95
US$22.95**

**Publication date:
September 2002**

"Impossibly romantic and optimistic, miraculously avoiding gloom and didacticism to achieve a continuously surprising and euphoric surface – related to – classic simplicity of line."
Andrew Duncan

JAMES was born in 1939 in Cardiff and
cated by the De La Salle Brothers at Saint
d's College there. He left in 1957 to read
osophy and English Literature at the
ersity of Bristol and later undertook
graduate studies in American Literature at
University of Keele. He was a founder of *The
scitator* in Bristol in 1963 and Arts Council
tive Writing Fellow, University of Sussex,
–79. He is Head of Communication Studies
nglia Polytechnic University, Cambridge.

PO Box 937, Great Wilbraham, Cambridge PDO, CB1 5JX United Kingdom

Printed in the United Kingdom
by Lightning Source UK Ltd.
9530400001B